Money

Money

A Story of Humanity

David McWilliams

**SIMON &
SCHUSTER**

London · New York · Sydney · Toronto · New Delhi

First published in Great Britain by Simon & Schuster UK Ltd, 2024

Copyright © David McWilliams, 2024

The right of David McWilliams to be identified as the author of this work has been asserted in accordance with the Copyright, Designs and Patents Act, 1988.

3 5 7 9 10 8 6 4

Simon & Schuster UK Ltd
1st Floor
222 Gray's Inn Road
London WC1X 8HB

Simon & Schuster: Celebrating 100 Years of Publishing in 2024

www.simonandschuster.co.uk
www.simonandschuster.com.au
www.simonandschuster.co.in

Simon & Schuster Australia, Sydney
Simon & Schuster India, New Delhi

The author and publishers have made all reasonable efforts to contact copyright-holders for permission, and apologise for any omissions or errors in the form of credits given. Corrections may be made to future printings.

Maps © Martin Lubikowski

A CIP catalogue record for this book is available from the British Library

Hardback ISBN: 978-1-4711-9543-3
Trade Paperback ISBN: 978-1-4711-9544-0
eBook ISBN: 978-1-4711-9545-7

Typeset in Perpetua Std by Palimpsest Book Production Ltd,
Falkirk, Stirlingshire

Printed and Bound in the UK
using 100% Renewable Electricity at CPI Group (UK) Ltd

MIX
Paper | Supporting responsible forestry
FSC® C171272

To Sian, for everything

CONTENTS

Maps   ix
Foreword by Michael Lewis   xiii
Introduction   1

Part 1: Ancient Money

1   Money in the Beginning   15
2   By the Rivers of Babylon   23
3   From Contracts to Coins   33
4   Money and the Greek Mind   44
5   The Empire of Credit   57

Part 2: Medieval Money

6   Twilight of the Feudal Economy   81
7   Saracen Magic   96
8   Darkness into Light   113
9   God's Printer   135

Part 3: Revolutionary Money

10 Invisible Money   159
11 The Father of Monetary Economics   177

12 The Bishop of Money   192
13 Money and the American Republic   209

Part 4: Modern Money
14 Empiricism and the Evolutionary   229
      Economy
15 Money on Trial   245
16 Yellow Brick Road   263
17 Modernist Money   279
18 Into the Abyss   294

Part 5: Money Unbound
19 Who Controls Money?   317
20 The Psychology of Money   337
21 The Evolution of Money   351

Acknowledgements   367
Endnotes   371
A Note on Further Reading   382
Picture Credits   388
Index   389

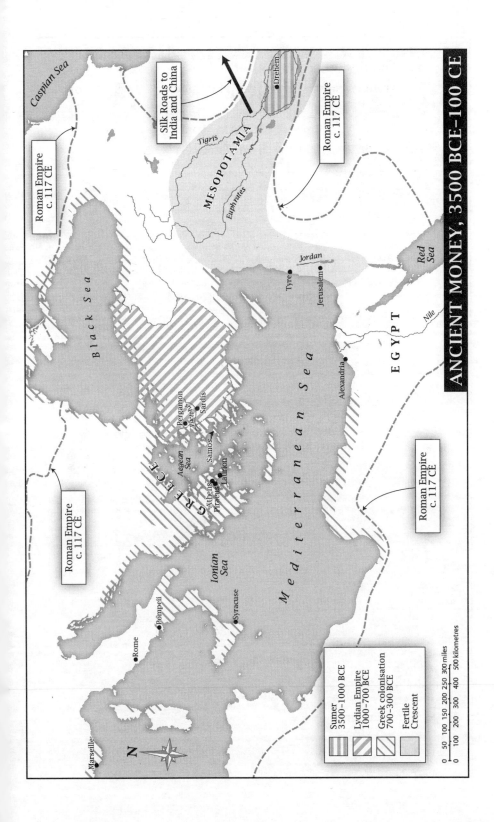

ANCIENT MONEY, 3500 BCE–100 CE

Caspian Sea

Roman Empire
c. 117 CE

Silk Roads to
India and China

Drehem

Tigris

MESOPOTAMIA

Euphrates

Roman Empire
c. 117 CE

Black Sea

Jordan

Red
Sea

Tyre

Jerusalem

EGYPT

Nile

Alexandria

Pergamon
Priene
Sardis

Aegean
Sea

Samos

GREECE

Athens
Piraeus
Laurion

Roman Empire
c. 117 CE

Ionian
Sea

Mediterranean Sea

Pompeii

Syracuse

Rome

Marseille

N

Sumer
3500–1000 BCE

Lydian Empire
1000–700 BCE

Greek colonisation
700–300 BCE

Fertile
Crescent

Roman Empire
c. 117 CE

0   50 100 150 200 250 300 miles
0   100 200 300 400 500 kilometres

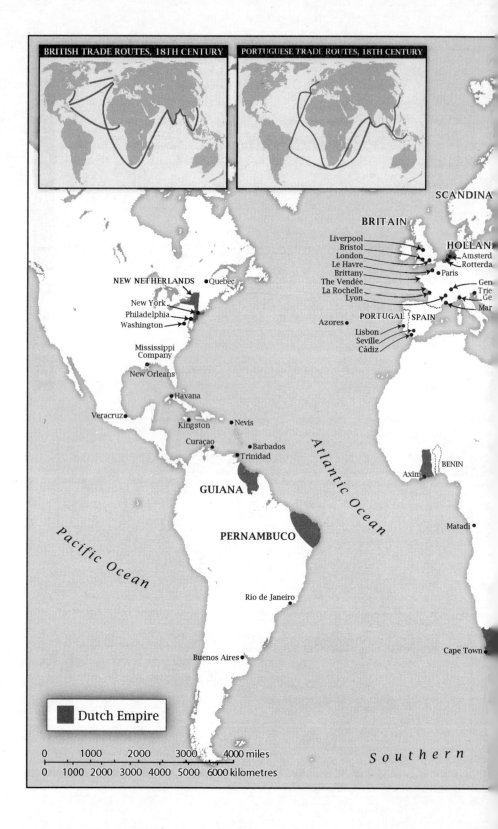

BRITISH TRADE ROUTES, 18TH CENTURY

PORTUGUESE TRADE ROUTES, 18TH CENTURY

SCANDINA

BRITAIN

Liverpool
Bristol
London
Le Havre
Brittany
The Vendée
La Rochelle
Lyon

HOLLAN
Amsterd
Rotterda
Paris
Gen
Trie
Ge
Mar

NEW NETHERLANDS • Quebec

New York
Philadelphia
Washington

Azores •

PORTUGAL SPAIN

Lisbon
Seville
Cádiz

Mississippi
Company

New Orleans

Havana

Veracruz •

Kingston

Nevis

Curaçao

Barbados
Trinidad

BENIN

Axim

GUIANA

Matadi •

PERNAMBUCO

Atlantic Ocean

Pacific Ocean

Rio de Janeiro

Cape Town •

Buenos Aires •

Dutch Empire

| 0 | 1000 | 2000 | 3000 | 4000 miles |
| 0 | 1000 | 2000 | 3000 | 4000 | 5000 | 6000 kilometres |

Southern

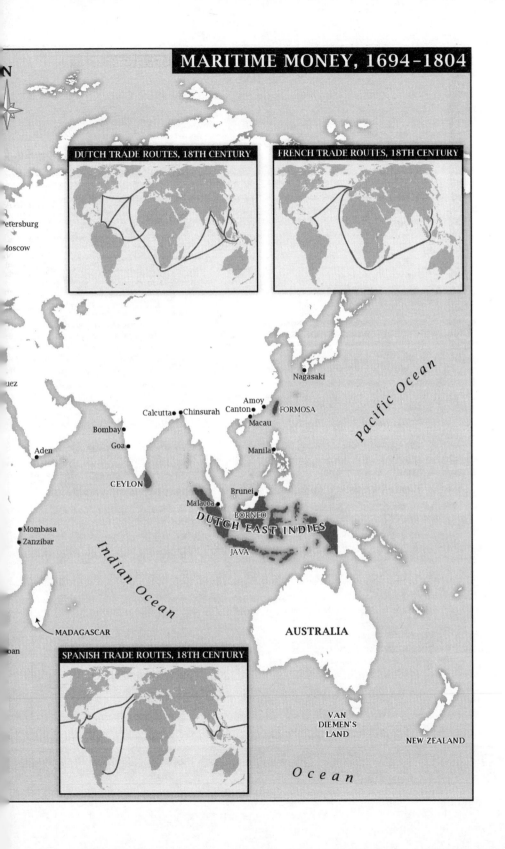

MARITIME MONEY, 1694–1804

DUTCH TRADE ROUTES, 18TH CENTURY

FRENCH TRADE ROUTES, 18TH CENTURY

SPANISH TRADE ROUTES, 18TH CENTURY

N

Petersburg

Moscow

Suez

Aden

Bombay

Goa

CEYLON

Calcutta

Chinsurah

Canton

Amoy

Macau

FORMOSA

Nagasaki

Pacific Ocean

Manila

Brunei

Malacca

BORNEO

DUTCH EAST INDIES

JAVA

Mombasa

Zanzibar

Indian Ocean

MADAGASCAR

oan

AUSTRALIA

VAN
DIEMEN'S
LAND

NEW ZEALAND

Ocean

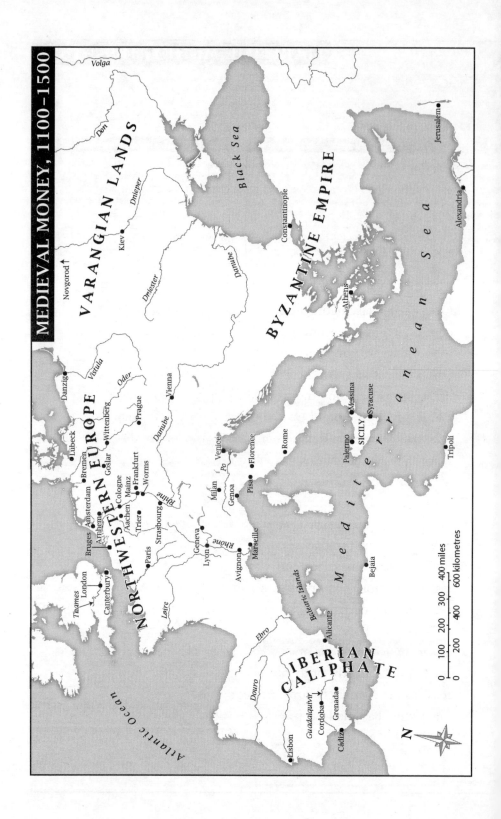

MEDIEVAL MONEY, 1100–1500

Volga

Don

Dnieper

Kiev

Novgorod

VARANGIAN LANDS

Dniester

Danube

Black Sea

Constantinople

BYZANTINE EMPIRE

Athens

Jerusalem

Alexandria

Mediterranean Sea

Tripoli

Messina
Syracuse
Palermo
SICILY

Rome

Florence
Pisa
Genoa
Venice
Po
Milan

Vienna

Danube

Prague
Wittenberg
Goslar
Frankfurt
Worms
Mainz
Cologne
Aachen
Trier
Strasbourg
Rhine

Danzig
Vistula
Oder
Lübeck
Bremen
Amsterdam
Arnhem
Bruges

NORTHWESTERN EUROPE

Geneva
Lyon
Avignon
Rhône
Marseille

Paris

London
Canterbury
Thames

Loire

Atlantic Ocean

Balearic Islands

Bejaia

Alicante

Ebro

IBERIAN
CALIPHATE

Douro

Guadalquivir
Cordoba
Grenada
Lisbon
Cádiz

N

0   100   200   300   400 miles
0   200   400   600 kilometres

FOREWORD

One of the fascinating things about this book is the way it connects money to important historical events that you may never have imagined having anything to do with it. Even if you knew that various Roman emperors bankrolled their lifestyles by debasing their currencies, you likely never appreciated just how bound up the collapse of the Roman Empire was with currency debasement. And who knew that Charles Darwin lost a fortune speculating in railway stocks, and that his theory of evolution sprang in part from his interest in economics? David McWilliams has written not just a history of innovations in money and finance. He's created a persuasive new argument for that history's importance.

The gist of his argument is this: where money – and financial innovation – is present, all sorts of valuable stuff occurs that doesn't occur where money – and financial innovation – is absent. Foreign trade is an obvious example, but there are many less obvious ones. The history of financial innovation maps pretty neatly onto the history of art, for instance – at least as art history is conventionally understood. Every traveller who has made a pilgrimage to the shrines of Western civilisation – ancient Greece, Renaissance Florence, seventeenth-century Holland – has, into the bargain, without knowing it, toured the history of financial innovation. Every great art boom appears to have been triggered by the invention of some version of the credit default swap.

McWilliams' sketches of financial innovators are another source of delight here. There seems to be some fixed rule that the men – and it seems to invariably have been men – who engage in financial innovation are precisely those you hope your daughter never meets. Johannes Gutenberg, Pope Pius II, John Law – McWilliams' narrative is a relay race run by cheaters who pass the baton to scoundrels who then hand it off to swindlers. The money team has a unique talent for earning other people's trust to do new things with their money.

Trust naturally becomes a central theme in these pages. The various inventions in money and finance – coins, balance sheets, double-entry accounting, reserve currencies, paper money, central banks, mortgages and so on – are each an expression of a species of trust that appears to have the ability to survive no matter how badly it is abused. At the same moment that the Dutch created their famous tulip bubble, for example, they also invented the perpetual bond – a loan that is never repaid. 'Can you imagine,' asks McWilliams, 'how much trust in money there must be in a society for people to finance a loan that they know is never actually going to be repaid and yet consider this to be a prudent form of saving?' It's as if we've all tacitly agreed that financial trust, even if it will often be betrayed, is too valuable to abandon.

Cryptocurrencies are obviously the latest twist to this tale. Born of mistrust of governments and banks, they have ended up replicating the same sort of need for trust, and violating that trust in all the usual ways. McWilliams sees what's happening right now in the history of money as a war for the right to be trusted. 'A major battle in the years to come,' he writes, 'will be between private money issued by private entities and public money issued by the organs of the state in the name of the citizen.' Whatever the future holds, McWilliams is worth trusting on the subject. Someone needs to be.

Michael Lewis, May 2024

INTRODUCTION

Money falling from the sky

Imagine money falling from the sky. Would you slip a tenner into your pocket before you told anyone? Chances are, most of us would trouser a few notes rather than inform the authorities.

This was the reaction Hitler was banking on when he planned to drop millions of pounds all over Britain at the height of the Second World War. Hitler understood what happens when money loses value. He lived through the hyper-inflation of the Weimar Republic and was aware that money is a weapon like no other. Money can destabilise a country, a view he shared with his ideological enemy Vladimir Lenin, who observed that the easiest way to undermine a society is to 'debauch its currency'.

In an interview with the *Daily Chronicle* in London published on 23 April 1919, Lenin is reported to have said that he had a plan to annihilate the power of money in order to destroy what remained of the old Russian state following the October Revolution of 1917:

Hundreds of thousands of rouble notes are being issued daily by our treasury . . . with the deliberate intention of destroying the value of money . . . The simplest way to exterminate the very spirit of capitalism is therefore to flood the country with notes of a high face-value without financial guarantees of any sort. Already the hundred-rouble note is almost valueless in Russia. Soon even the simplest peasant will realise that it is only a scrap of paper . . . and the great illusion of the value and power of money, on which the capitalist state is based, will have been destroyed.[1]

Hitler and Lenin may have been on opposite sides ideologically but they both understood the phenomenal power of money: undermine money and you undermine the fabric of society. The plan for the Luftwaffe to drop millions of banknotes over Britain was top secret, only known by a few senior Nazis. While some honest subjects of the king might go to the authorities, Hitler worked on the basis that most British folk would stuff a few notes under the mattress. He would enlist the people Napoleon famously dismissed as a money-obsessed 'nation of shopkeepers' against themselves. By bringing this counterfeit money into circulation all over the country, inflation would rip through the system, particularly as so much of Britain's economic resources was directed at the war effort. Only a small amount of consumer goods and essentials were being traded, and therefore prices would be volatile. In such conditions of privation, the cascade of new money would drive British prices skywards, triggering panic. Hitler hoped that the previously quiet and obedient British would experience a fire in the theatre moment. They'd freak out and the ensuing chaos would upend their Blitz spirit, compromising the war effort.

In July 1942, Hitler's new weapon cranked into production. It was to be the greatest forgery the world had ever seen. A telegram was sent to the commandants of concentration camps calling for printers, engravers, artists, colourists, typesetters, paper experts and former bank officials. The operation also needed mathematicians and code breakers to decipher sterling's numbering sequence. A most desperate cohort of traumatised, emaciated men limped into Sachsenhausen from camps all over the Third Reich. These 142 souls were tasked with breaking the Bank of England.

The concentration camp forgers printed £132,610,945 of fake sterling notes, equal to about £7.5 billion in today's money.[2] Dropping these notes over Britain would require squadrons of German bombers that were available to Hitler when the plan was hatched in May 1942, but by the time the forged notes were ready in 1943, the war situation had changed.[3] Germany was losing on the battlefield, the Luftwaffe's resources were stretched in Russia and the war effort couldn't spare the planes to handle the mass air drop.

Unlike Hitler, who was not in control of the Bank of England, Lenin was able to activate the official Russian mint to achieve the chaos he desired. Both men had similar aims: they wanted, as Lenin said, to shatter 'the great illusion of the value and power of money'. Both dictators, two demonic observers of psychology, understood human frailty, crowd dynamics and the depths to which people can descend.

Money can be more powerful than religion, ideology or armies. Mess with money and you mess with far more than the price system, inflation and economics – you mess with people's heads. The story of Hitler's forgery illuminates the power of money.

Economists' blind spot

The global discussion about money has been hijacked by my tribe. Like high priests of a new religion, we economists took it upon ourselves to explain the mysteries of money to the people. My career as a monetary economist began in the Central Bank of Ireland, the very tabernacle where money is magicked up out of thin air. In a similar way to a Catholic priest turning the host into the body of Christ in Holy Communion, central bankers take worthless paper and turn it into money. As miracles go, it's an impressive one. We all believe in it, and therefore it must be real. But is it real? In fact, money is abstract and is only given value as long as the rest of us (or enough of the rest of us) believe in it. Money, like faith, is a product of the human imagination.

From the central bank I moved to investment banking, where that money magicked up by the central bank is super-charged into another form of money, an incendiary promise that we call credit. Between them, central banks and commercial banks run the world of money, controlling how much money is out there, who gets it and at what price. These institutions are key to the mechanical story of money and can explain how it is pumped around the economy. Economists can tell you what to do if there is too much of it or too little. But understanding the plumbing – how money flows around the economic system – does not capture the interesting part of the story. A plumber might understand how water flows through the pipes but may not be able to explain why water is essential for life. The most exciting aspect of money is what it does to us: how it changes us, what it enables us to do, and how it brings out our deepest urges – some good, some appalling. Despite being a fully paid-up member of the economist tribe for many years, I've concluded that most economists do not really understand money.

Economists take the fun out of money. A highly emotional substance, money can be transgressive, sexy, dangerous, mind-altering. Money is power, it is domination but it can also be liberation. Money buys independence. Money motivates us and releases human energy, and what we do with the energy once we have it is up to us. Some want to spread the possibilities of money around, others want to hoard it for themselves. Money doesn't impose on human morals; it amplifies them. If a person believes greed is good, they will behave accordingly with money. If they believe in equality and human rights, they may use money to achieve these objectives. The point is that we imagine money into being, money changes as we change, and money changes us.

Today, whether we like it or not, our entire world revolves around this strange, invented notion that Lenin described as the 'great illusion'. Introduced thousands of years ago, money is at the centre of modern culture – a universal language understood by rich investors living in high-tech Silicon Valley and struggling rickshaw drivers in Old Delhi. People living thousands of miles apart, who don't understand each other's language or customs, understand money and speak to each other through it. Money is a force that dictates the flow of people, goods and ideas around the globe. Our efforts and talents are assessed by it; so too is the future. As we will see, one of the earliest characteristics of money was putting today's price on tomorrow. What is the rate of interest other than the price of time, expressed by money? When you take out a thirty-year mortgage, although you don't necessarily stop to think about it, you are painting a picture of what your circumstances might be in thirty years' time. In fact, you are imagining your future through money.

Money defines the relationship between worker and employer, buyer and seller, merchant and producer. But not only that: it also defines the bond between the governed and the governor, the state and the citizen. Money unlocks pleasure, puts a price on desire, art and creativity. It motivates us to strive, achieve, invent and take risks. Money also brings out humanity's darker side, invoking greed, envy, hatred, violence and, of course, colonialism, which was so often driven by the prospect of vast financial gain. Money is complex because humans are complex.

A magic tool

Money is an ingenious technology that humans invented to help us negotiate an increasingly complex and interrelated world. Imagining money as a tool or a technology is not how we usually think about it. It's not that we don't think about money; we do, and probably more than we'd like to. We need money to live and, because of this urgency, we rarely have the luxury of thinking about money in any other way. If you don't have enough cash, you worry about how you might get more. If you have loads of it, you worry about making sure you don't lose it. Most of us would like a bit more money, and if we could figure out an easy way of getting it, we'd probably go for that option. Money buys freedom: the essential promise which makes it so attractive is that, armed with money, you can change your world by gaining more control over your life.

Given money's central role in our lives, we rarely think more conceptually about it. We don't stop to ask ourselves relatively simple questions such as: What is money? Where does it come from? Can it run out? Can we generate more of it? Maybe this absence of conceptual questioning is a measure of the true success of money. As long as it's flowing, making the world go round, we are happy for money to exist without going into the details of how it came to be.

In the past, when trying to explain how our ancestors developed, we have often focused on a source of energy or a *physical* technology that aided their progress – for example, the invention of the wheel, the discovery of coal or the arrival of the plough. But what about the *social* technologies that helped organise us in pursuit of common goals by enhancing co-operation? One of these tools was language, which humans had developed over tens of thousands of years to communicate with each other in a more sophisticated, precise and collaborative fashion. However, it was with the advent of agriculture a few thousand years ago that social co-operation really took off. No longer hanging out with just family and extended kin, humans started to live in much larger permanent settlements alongside strangers.

Each of us has heard the mantra that money is the root of all evil, yet money is also an instrument of peace. Rather than kill their neighbours for food and property, the newly sedentary farming societies learned to trade using money. Money provided an alternative to, as opposed to a reason for, war. When we can exchange with each other and with different tribes at negotiated prices, why bother fighting?

Trade allowed an element of more peaceful co-existence between peoples, even complete strangers from different regions and cultures. We didn't just exchange goods, but we traded and adopted ideas, norms and innovations. From the establishment of agriculture, humanity was set on a course of development that would eventually lead to towns, nations and empires with centralised power structures and social hierarchies. As hunter-gatherers we had been locked in a battle with Mother Nature, but as humans started to colonise the land, we generated food surpluses that could be taxed by the state. We came up with writing, geometry, astronomy, numbers, mathematics, philosophy, architecture and political theory – all the utensils we associate with something we call civilisation. The cogs of human civilisation turned with one technological advance after another: the domestication of animals; the cultivation and cross-cultivation of various plants; improved methods of food storage; the distribution and transport of goods via the sea. Money was one foundational technology, often overlooked, that underpinned and animated human flourishing.

The more complex our societies, the more engrained money became. Early civilisations that adopted money acquired a competitive advantage over others, leading to innovations that radically changed the story of modern humanity. We will see that money is a disruptive technology, and that new forms of money continuously up-end old systems in an ongoing monetary evolution that triggers economic, social and political evolution in a feedback loop.

Plutophytes

Over the past 5,000 years, money has profoundly altered humanity and our relationships with each other and with the rest of the planet. It is arguably *the* defining technology of *Homo sapiens*. We have co-evolved with money: we have shaped money, but money has also shaped us. Anthropologists often refer to humans as a 'pyrophyte' species, one that is shaped by fire.[4] The thread linking the observations in this book is

that in the course of the last five millennia we have become
– and apologies to the linguistic purists as I made this word
up – a *plutophyte* species, meaning a species that has adapted
to and been adapted by money. For 400,000 years, the technology that most influenced human development was fire; the
contention of this book is that the crucial technology shaping
humanity in the last 5,000 years has been money. We *were* a
pyrophyte species but we have gradually become a plutophyte
species. This book is about the relationship between a curious
ape and a wondrous technology.

Unlike other technologies, money is ephemeral. It resides
in our heads, representing value, but it is intrinsically valueless.
For money to work, a leap of mental abstraction is required.
Counterintuitively, money is valuable not when it is scarce
but when it is abundant. In this sense, money resembles another
wondrous human technology: language. Both money and
language are crowd phenomena. Like language, the more
people who use money, the more valuable it becomes. In the
same way as dialects are subsumed into larger, more useful
languages, various forms of money, originally conceived to
trade within small groups, are subsumed into larger, more
useful and more adaptable forms of money, the most prominent of which is now the United States dollar.

The central property of money – that of representing
universal value, understood and accepted by everyone – is
one of the foundation stones of organised societies today.
Money has proved to be one of the most seductive and
enduring ideas of the past five millennia. Over time, all other
ways of organising complex human societies – whether it be
land-based feudal systems, aristocratic hierarchies or communist nirvanas – have ultimately been replaced by societies that
are based around money.

From hunter-gatherer to data gatherer

You, dear reader, are about to embark on a romp with an economist who, it's fair to say, has grown a bit sceptical of his own tribe's ability to tell the story of money. We will look at many of the cultures that played a role in the development of money and observe how each one innovated with it. We will see that proficiency with money coincided with other innovative breakthroughs such as writing, numeracy, law, democracy and philosophy. This co-evolution prompts the question: was money the reason for other developments or did these other developments lead to the evolution of money? What was the chicken and what was the egg?

We will begin in Africa with the first archaeological evidence of counting, which may even have been rudimentary book-keeping – not something we tend to associate with the Stone Age. From there, we move to early money in the urban settlements of Mesopotamia around 3500 BCE. We will see that Greek civilisation, with its notions of logic, democracy and philosophy, was underpinned by commerce and coinage, and that the great Roman Empire was built not just on conquest but on credit. Money usage declined in Europe during the early Middle Ages, along with some other corner-stones of classical civilisation. Having less money in circulation hindered progress. But money's re-emergence in the eleventh century propelled western Europe towards Florentine advance-ment, ushering in the Renaissance and later the Reformation. We will observe money in the revolutionary age from the Dutch Republic of the sixteenth and early seventeenth cen-turies through to the eighteenth-century American and French revolutions. Money's darker side is revealed by European colonisation when the interests of money were pitted against human dignity – and, lamentably, money won. We will examine the link between money, liberal thought and intellectual progress in the nineteenth century, moving from Darwin's theories through to modernism and up to the present day.

We will see that each breakthrough in the application of money – such as the rate of interest, the introduction of coins, or the use of balance sheets – led to further innovations, one development acting as a launchpad for another. The stories in each chapter are necessarily selective, focusing on innovations in money that I believe help to explain the link between money and human progress, one following from the other and each nudging forward the story of civilisation. This is a book written in Dublin by a white, almost pink, Irishman. If it were written by somebody else, somewhere else, the stories would be different and equally valid. I hope you will find the stories I have chosen as lively and interesting to read as I found them to write.

Along the way we will meet Kushim, the first person whose name has survived in written form; Xenophon, the world's first economist; the emperors Nero and Vespasian; and Jesus himself. We will swerve into the worlds of Dante, Fibonacci, Gutenberg and Peter the Great, and spend time with Jonathan Swift, Charles Talleyrand and Alexander Hamilton, before dropping in on Charles Darwin, Roger Casement, James Joyce and Judy Garland. Ahead of a date with cryptocurrency, we get to know the world's greatest forger, join the chaos of the Fox News studios in New York the day Bear Stearns collapsed in 2008, and meet the people who now control global money.

In Greek mythology, Prometheus was punished by Zeus for giving humans fire, a technology so powerful that Zeus feared we would overwhelm the gods with it. The Greeks recognised that mastery of fire marked a profound shift in the relationship between humans and the rest of the planet. They imagined that humans were created from the four elements: earth, wind, fire and water. These forces shaped their universe. Around 5,000 years ago we invented another force, a fifth element: money. If fire was the Promethean force of the ancient world, money is the Promethean force of the modern world. The clever ape has shaped the world, for better or worse, in a way that I believe would have been impossible without money.

The story of money is the story of humanity itself.

PART 1:

ANCIENT MONEY

I

MONEY IN THE BEGINNING

A Stone Age blockchain?

In the Royal Belgian Institute of Natural Sciences in Brussels lies the Ishango Bone, which dates back to around 18,000 BCE. It was discovered on the banks of the Congo in 1950, roughly a century after European colonists first became excited about the commercial possibilities opened up by the then largely uncharted river. Running through Central Africa, the Congo River was and still is the life blood of the region. It has acted as a trading superhighway for millennia.

The Ishango Bone is a baboon's femur with a series of notches cut into it. Archaeologists are divided over the artefact's purpose, but it is speculated that each notch indicates an amount owed by someone to someone else and that together they signify a trade or a set of credits and debits. Indentations in the bone may have been indicators that the trades were paid and therefore cancelled or that they were outstanding.[1] If the Ishango Bone was indeed a commercial tallystick, its notches also represent the first known example of value, a highly sophisticated concept. Valuing is an exercise in abstract thinking, not least because what I value and the price I am willing to pay for something might be completely different to what you value and what you would be willing to pay for the same item.

To get over this, could our African ancestors have developed a rudimentary form of trade for which they needed accounting? As the human story begins in Africa, it should not surprise us if the story of money begins there too. Amid the conjecture, what we *do* know is that these Africans were counting. The Ishango Bone is an extremely early recording technology, and if these ancestors were counting in order to trade, it was human beings who were likely to have been the base currency. Slavery was money's original sin.

In the standard account of the history of our species, humans roamed, settled and roamed again, before settling down around 5000 BCE in small communities that would come to be largely organised around money. But the Ishango Bone theory of early commerce suggests that our African ancestors may have been thinking about money much earlier than that. The people who notched the Ishango Bone were hunter-gatherers on the cusp of a new world. Central to their old Stone Age society was the technology that scared Zeus: fire.

Eve's kitchen

Archaeologists, anthropologists, biologists and ancient historians have emphasised how much of our domestication as a species was dependent on fire. James C. Scott, the American anthropologist, goes further, calling us a fire-adjusted or 'pyrophyte' species.[2] Our bodies changed as we adjusted to fire, our environment was changed by fire, and the animals we hunted and lived with were also altered by fire. Although still nomadic, the range of our hunting and gathering became tighter as we used fire to ensure that more and more nutrients were available with ever less effort.[3]

Humans have been using fire for over 400,000 years. Fire allowed us to settle in various camps throughout the seasons. We might have an image of the hunter-gatherer roaming aimlessly, foraging randomly, with little control over their environment, entirely at the whim of nature. It's more reasonable to think of the hunter-gatherers as having an organisational system – you could call it an early economy. Not an economy with currencies, taxes and the like, but an economy in the sense of a social structure, with hierarchies that the tribe understood.

In the economy of the nomads, most of the earth was covered in thick, almost impenetrable forest. By rearranging this landscape, they could make daily life easier. Those hunter-gatherers observed that natural wildfires cleared huge swathes of forest, revealing the hiding places and nests of animals they could eat. They'd have noticed how, after the burning, vegetation changed quickly with fast-growing grasses replacing the dense woodland.[4]

The evolutionary impact of fire is hard to overstate. Fire meant we could cook. Food is energy, and increasing the variety of food you can eat means more energy. Before fire, humans had subsisted on raw animal and vegetable matter. Fire gave us a diet that was much easier to digest: cooking does much of the chewing and digestion for us, delivering more calories with less effort. Cooking also took on a social dimension as eating around the hearth anchored the tribe. We can visualise our ancestors gathering around the fire, cooking, chewing, chatting, warming themselves, flirting, exchanging gossip, gazing at the stars, imagining the universe and telling stories.

It's not hard to envision the people who made the cave paintings 17,000 years ago at Lascaux, in modern-day France – which depict horses, deer and other local wild animals – conceiving the images together round the fireside. Fire was a time-saving technology: it opened up space to involve ourselves in abstract notions such as painting, self-expression, imagination and art.

Population explosion

Around 12,000 to 9000 BCE, farming emerged in the Fertile Crescent, Central America and China.[5] There is no evidence that these peoples learned from each other; each civilisation must have figured out farming in response to some greater elementary force. That greater force was global warming.

During the Ice Age, not only was the planet much colder, with ice sheets covering much of what we call the northern hemisphere today, but, crucially, it was much drier. In Ireland, we often associate the cold with the wet but if it is really cold, there is far less evaporation, fewer clouds and less rain. Our world in the Ice Age was cold and dry, meaning it was difficult for plants to grow. In this type of climate, farming isn't an option: it's too risky to depend on any one piece of land to produce the energy you need.

As the temperature rose and the ice caps melted, we experienced a sudden profusion of life. The world got warmer and wetter, and people started to live around places where they could make food grow most intensively. This didn't happen overnight; it probably took thousands of years, with hunter-gatherers foraging and hunting, while doing a little side-hustle in farming. Part-time farming was likely the norm for millennia, until we got better at it. Remember, the name of the game is energy. How much energy can we derive from farming, how intensively can we cultivate this energy and how stable can we make this source of energy? Bit by bit, grains became a more stable source of energy.

Humans living in tiny villages, with hunter-gatherers still roaming around, looked for crops that would give nutritional value as well as being simple to grow, quick to harvest and easy to store. Grains did the trick. Grains grew easily, offered high yields, were cultivated quickly and could be harvested within months of being sown. Evolution had also been kind to them: they were self-pollinating. These attributes of grain were essential in persuading nomadic hunters to settle down. Given the increased fertility of the warmer planet in general, the emergence of farming, and the domestication of animals for easy protein, we would have expected the human population to have grown rapidly. But this did not happen.

The first few thousand years of settling down were an epidemiological holocaust for humanity. When we began to swap roaming for farming, animal diseases such as flu, measles, smallpox, typhus and plagues of all sorts ripped through the first farmers. Pathogens jumped from recently domesticated animals to hapless humans, whose immune system had never encountered these microscopic invaders. In the first few thousand years of domestication, from around 10,000 BCE to around 5000 BCE, the cow and the pig constituted as much of a threat to us as we did to them.

Demographers of the ancient world put the planet's human population at around 4 million in 10,000 BCE. Five thousand years later, that population had only increased to 5 million, the growth slowed by devastating pandemics. The nomadic immune system, which the farmer inherited, was unprepared. It took many generations of evolution to build immunity.

By around 5000 BCE, evolution was doing its thing – passing on survival codes, allowing the immune system to identify invaders and the population to become more resistant to an increasing number of recognised pathogens. Around then, the human population appears to have taken off. By the time Jesus was kicking the moneylenders out of the temple, the population was roughly 100 million people, a twentyfold increase in only 5,000 years.

Coping mechanisms

As we settled, our communities became larger and more complicated, yet some of our hunter-gatherer traits stayed with us. One such trait is what anthropologists call social capacity. British anthropologist Robin Dunbar, when trying to understand why various primates had differently sized brains, wondered whether the size of the primate's social group correlated with its brain size.[6] It turns out brain size *does* correlate with group size: the neocortex, the part of our brain that deals with complex thinking and reasoning, grows in primates relative to the number of fellow primates they are likely to live with. Brains evolve to handle the number of social contacts we are going to have. Humans, foraging for the vast majority of our existence in small bands of nomads, have brains that evolved to deal with small groups. The arrival of agriculture and domesticity meant that, quite suddenly in evolutionary terms, over only a few thousand years, we were living in much larger communities. The human brain needed tools – or technologies – to make sense of this new complexity.

We tend to think of technology in terms of physical technology, like a hammer or a car, but there are also social technologies. Social technologies help humans work more efficiently in large groups, and include language, law and religion. These social tools, which emerged with urbanisation, co-evolved, organising collective human energy around common goals governed by clear sets of rules. Money is also a social technology, a coping mechanism that humans invented to deal with this abrupt shift in the way we lived.

For the hunter-gatherers, nature's challenges of food and shelter were the problems of small groups. The problems of domestication, on the other hand, were the problems of large groups, or what we might call organisational challenges. Health, wealth, distribution, dealing with strangers, trading with outsiders and coping with many people living cheek by jowl – these are complicated conundrums.

Once fuelled by grain, we were on a road that begins to look familiar to the modern observer. It isn't an accident that human civilisations occurred within the latitudes suited to growing cereals, from the Fertile Crescent to the central Chinese plains to Meso-America. As the world's population expanded from 5 million to 100 million in the last five millennia BCE, those places where populations grew most spectacularly required social technologies to cope. These are the places we see the first evidence of money, along with its close companions: writing and organised religion.

Grain had a number of characteristics that changed humans and human organisation profoundly. It could be grown, harvested and then stored, thus generating a surplus of energy that could be doled out over time. We reap what we sow. Crucially, with a grain surplus, the community could construct a system of value based around an easy-to-understand unit of measurement – a quantity of grain. A specific amount of grain corresponded to something else such as a day's work for a labourer, establishing a relationship between the price of food and the price of everything else.

Early money was grain-based; grain gave money a universal value. In Sumer (in present-day south-central Iraq), for instance, one shekel was equivalent to a bushel of barley.[7] The shekel could be counted and traded easily. The granary, one of the most important institutions in any ancient city, regulated the supply of grain and thereby the supply of money, much like a modern-day central bank. The more grain, the better the harvest, the more money in circulation. With a base money tied to, and given intrinsic value by, a commodity like grain, debits and credits, assets and debts – the rudiments of balance sheets – could easily be assessed. The grain economies created surpluses that could then be taxed by the state, siphoning off a cut for the rulers and their bureaucrats. The greater the grain surplus, the more productive a society's agriculture, and the more complex the society. A society that can more than feed itself from its agricultural output becomes more sophisticated. It can sustain priests, soldiers, traders, merchants and scribes as well as the aristocracy, royal family and various other hangers-on.

Grain-based money propelled humankind from a world determined by the natural technology of fire towards one driven by a human technology, money. The Promethean baton was being passed. This would not happen overnight, but the direction of travel was mapped out.

BY THE RIVERS OF BABYLON

Sleepless nights

More than 5,000 years ago, in Mesopotamia – the place, according to the Greeks, where Zeus and Prometheus created humans – a man called Kushim took delivery of a batch of barley, most probably to make beer.[1] He borrowed it for a specific timeframe: the contract specified that Kushim had two and a half years to pay back the loan. At an annual interest rate of 33.33 per cent, which was normal in Sumerian times, Kushim was on the hook.[2] Two and a half years gave him time to brew the beer, sell it, generate revenue and settle his costs, pay back his loan and start again. But obviously things could go wrong. It's not difficult for us to appreciate Kushim's financial anxieties. Could he get the beer made in time? Would he be paid? What rate of penal interest might apply if he failed? Given that it wasn't unusual in ancient times for the borrower himself, or his children, to be collateral, it's fair to say the stakes were high.

We can picture Kushim, late at night, praying for a bumper harvest. He has just borrowed barley. To pay it back, he needs to get his hands on more barley at a decent price. The last thing he needs is a poor harvest, which would push the price of barley upwards. On the other hand, when there's a bumper crop, the price of barley falls and Kushim is quids in. The rate of interest is the crucial price here, because this is what coaxes the lender to lend Kushim the barley. It is also the price at which Kushim, the borrower, is happy to do business, and he will have factored the rate of interest into his calculation of price, cost and profit. The fluctuation of the future price of barley is the risk factor.

Imagining Kushim's sleepless nights and his financial troubles makes him feel like one of us. The fact that he was being charged interest also implies that money had, by this time, evolved to such an extent that – even though it was something that stood for something else – it had become so valuable as to have its own price, completely divorced from anything real. With debt came the notion of the value of time, and with this came the concept of the price of money: the rate of interest.

This concept, commonplace to us now, was a transformative application of money.

The price of money

The rate of interest turned money into a commodity itself, which could be traded, lent and borrowed with its own price. The development of the rate of interest was an enormous leap forward because it allowed us to connect our present economic reality to some imagined future scenario. If the interest rate is too low, a lender won't lend to the future, and the commercial journey of investment in tomorrow stops. But if the rate is too high, a realistic borrower won't back themselves, and investment will fall. Without investment in tomorrow, there's no innovation and little progress. The rate of interest allowed people sufficient comfort to lend and sufficient incentive to invest with the borrowed money, so income flowed back and forth between borrowers and lenders. The rate of interest isn't merely a price; it is also a code, a mini-encyclopaedia of information about the person we are lending to, the chances of success, the risk in the region, the competition in the market, the technological infrastructure, and a whole host of other variables.

To see how borrowing and lending changes a person's world-view, consider what the rate of interest does to people's perception of time. Imagine you are lending to somebody at an interest rate of 10 per cent per year for five years. This rate tells us that the money lent has a cost that reflects the risk of you not being repaid and the opportunity cost of not spending that money yourself. The longer the term of the loan, the higher the chance you won't be paid back because it is further into the future – which by definition is unknow-able – and the longer you will have to wait before spending the money yourself. In order to make this worthwhile for the lender, money has to have a price – a cost to the borrower and income to the lender. This price factors in the value of time. To put it another way, a bird in the hand is worth two in the bush.

The rate of interest was revolutionary: for the first time, a borrower could use income from the future in order to spend in the present. This innovation was essential to getting income flowing and preventing money from being hoarded by those who had it, making it available to those who wanted it, like our hero Kushim. Imagine being able to get your head around the value of time, in a society still coming to terms with understanding natural phenomena like why the sun rises and sets. What the Sumerians lacked in practical understanding of the natural world they made up for with their comprehension and use of abstract thinking. Hostage to the vagaries of harvest and the rhythm of the natural world, plagued by hunger and disease, Sumerians involved themselves in a high level of mental abstraction about the value of time in an environment where concepts such as risk, reward and probability were everyday concerns. In terms of money, our ancestors were surprisingly modern. For example, Sumerians deployed not just simple interest but compound interest, whereby the amount of money owed grows exponentially over time.[3] Is it any wonder Kushim was worried?

Weights, writing and money

Kushim's barley racket is interesting enough in itself. But Kushim has another distinction: his is the first recorded name in human history. The first person whose name we know and whose life we can speculate about was not some powerful king or a wise man with a direct line to the gods. He was a run-of-the-mill hustler, our friend Kushim. In a document written in cuneiform, which pre-dates the great Sumerian *Epic of Gilgamesh* by many hundreds of years, Kushim is recorded as running his own home-brew outfit at some point between 3400 and 3000 BCE.

It might not be the most romantic origin story, but one of our most ingenious technologies, writing, came about because of another groundbreaking technology: money. Money was the first thing we wrote about. And by writing about money, we were also writing about weights.

For much of economic history, money was all about weights. People traded all sorts of stuff with each other – barley, oil, cattle, beer – and the amount owed was expressed in a weight.

In Mesopotamia, the shekel was established as early as 3000 BCE, and it pertained to a bushel of grain.[4] Depending on conditions such as the harvest, the amount of grain in a shekel varied. The value of the shekel – which means 'weigh' in old Hebrew – fluctuated.

Gold, silver and copper were weighed and expressed in shekels to settle trades at the end of a certain period of time, say a month or a year. Archaeologists have concluded that typically the precious metals themselves were not exchanged; rather there were large slabs of bullion, which were stored almost like a reserve of wealth.[5] Instead of exchanging the bullion, people who owed and who were owed amounts notched their debts and credits on a slate, an evolution of the Ishango Bone. These debts would be settled periodically with an asset transfer such as slaves or cereal. Day to day, Mesopotamian commerce was based on a shekel's worth of barley, used to clear small trades and debts between merchants within the city. This means that the shekel was *liquid*. Unlike something that was *illiquid*, such as property, its value was easy to unlock and transfer.

It was extremely simple to clear trades because everyone understood the rules, and there was rarely a sudden lack of barley because the granaries stored surplus. If local merchants were dealing with foreigners, they would accept a block of silver in return for goods. As there were no silver mines in the region and there is very little evidence of mining in the area, the trading cities of the Sumerian civilisation must have traded their surplus agriculture with foreigners miles away from their homeland in return for silver. How else would they have got their hands on it?

The Ishnuna Code of Law, the oldest known written body of law, thought to be from around the eighteenth century BCE, was found in Baghdad in the area of Tell Harmal in 1945.[6] These laws describe values expressed as shekels of silver:

> The price of one gur of barley is one shekel of silver.
> The price of 3 qas of pure oil is one shekel of silver.
> The price of one sut and 5 qas of sesame oil is one shekel of silver.
> The price of 6 suts of wool is one shekel of silver.
> The price of 2 gurs of salt is one shekel of silver.
> The price of one hal seed is one shekel of silver.[7]

Tightly controlled by the state, weights were a significant priority in early civilisations. The sanctity of weights was regarded as paramount to the efficient operation of the ancient economy. As the Old Testament states, 'A false balance is an abomination to the Lord; a just weight is his delight'.[8] What might sound casual – for example, the Greek currency from ancient times up to the adoption of the euro was the *drachma*, meaning a 'handful' – was in fact to be taken seriously. The drachma's origin, like the shekel's, underscores the clear link between weights and money that flowed through antiquity.

The history of civilisation sometimes gets bogged down in the big dramas. The battles, heroes and myths dominate. But there's another story. The story of the humdrum, the everyday – the dull, bureaucratic, repetitive reality of how places were run. On a day-to-day functioning basis, states demand co-ordination. And co-ordination demands lists. Lists of population, land, ownership, productivity, animals, yields, stores of grains. Centralised states function on taxation, and taxation only works if the taxman knows who to tax, where to find them, and how much to demand. He needs receipts, delivery times, volumes and comparisons. A state without statistics isn't a state. The list, therefore, is a foundational instrument of centralised rule.

By the time we hear about Kushim, an entire legal system had built up around property rights. Farming without property rights is tricky, and money allows those property rights to be made liquid and be given a value. Sumerian law was largely commercial, underscoring how central property rights, legal disputes and the legal profession were in society. Cuneiform, early writing, emerged to keep tabs on commerce.

Writing, laws and money emerged in response to urbanisation and political complexity. Of all these technologies, money was arguably the most beguiling and most useful because it made so many other things possible.

Money and numbers

In these ancient Mesopotamian cities, as commerce increased, people needed to know who owed how much and to whom. Ledgers were essential. Someone had to take notes, to ensure the city could follow the debt carousel. The more Sumerians traded, the more fluent they had to be in basic calculations; a trader who can't add up won't last long.

Initially, people counted with their fingers, which largely explains the five and ten structure as our base numerals. Many ancient cultures counted using both fingers and toes, with twenty as the foundation. Consider the French word for eighty: *quatres-vingt*. While English speakers call that number eighty – eight tens – the French call the same number four twenties. Obviously, some tribes knocking around France well before Caesar rocked up must have used base twenty, deploying all of their digits to calculate. Despite countless invasions and new cultures overlaying old ones, the French still use base twenty in their language.

The Sumerians developed the number sixty as their base. This choice was a technological innovation because money and trade demanded a number that was divisible by a huge variety of smaller numbers (and 60 is divisible by 30, 20, 15, 12, 10, 6, 5, 4, 3 and 2). For Sumerians, sixty was a magic number. Today, an echo of the ancient Sumerians is seen in the fact we have sixty seconds in a minute and sixty minutes in an hour. The trading bazaar required pragmatism over elegance: if you didn't grasp basic calculations in a monetised society, the chances of getting ripped off soared. The introduction of money forced people to think numerically.

With debts circulating in society came financial breakthroughs. In Mesopotamia, if I owed something to you and someone else owed me, I could step away and the contract could be restated between you, my creditor, and the next person along, my debtor. As far back as 3000 BCE, a type of promissory note was born, almost like a twentieth-century cheque.

The first spreadsheet

We tend to assume that cash flow models are a new innovation and in our world, every year, smart young people clutching degrees from the best universities are enrolled by banks to come up with financial reports assessing whether a company is under- or overvalued. Their data-driven financial forecasts, based on revenues and costs, form the basis for loan decisions. The first MBAs were offered to students in the 1920s, but the rate of interest in the ancient world spawned financial innovations at a time when people still believed in the gods, sacrificed animals for the harvest and examined the innards of chickens to forecast the weather. The traders of Sumer possessed a degree of financial sophistication that is hugely impressive.

Uncovering what could be described as the world's first ever spreadsheet, archaeologists found an inscribed tablet from the Mesopotamian city of Drehem dating from around 2100 BCE.[9] The rows and columns reveal a stunning early example of financial software. The tablet contains projections and forecasts about an investment in a livestock business. Like today's investment models, it contains assumptions about births and deaths of animals, allied to projections about fertility, foodstuffs and other inputs, leading to a specific profit and loss model for the business at the prevailing rate of interest.[10] This technology allowed investors to plug in various scenarios, with ratios and formulae, delivering a number at the far side of the model.

The Drehem tablet is a multi-year 'model' for a cattle-rearing business, with growth projections based on the cows' milk yields. In terms of financial planning and spreadsheet analytics, it is not a million miles from the sort of business plan that start-up companies trying to raise capital today might use. This ancient cuneiform model has various high growth and low growth scenarios based on things like animal mortality. If not quite an 'earnings per share' model, it's not far off. The implication of this spreadsheet is that more than 2,000 years before Jesus, the Sumerians were thinking about finance, interest, money and commerce in a way that could value businesses into the future, assessing what sort of yields and profits might be made, and how these yields and profits impacted not just the bottom line but the overall value of the business.

Sumerian civilisation came up with writing, accountancy, an intricate legal system and a sophisticated financial architecture, all anchored by the rate of interest. At its core, the rate of interest put a value on time. This was a breathtaking level of abstract thinking leading to a market for capital, financed by borrowers and lenders. The rate of interest took something inert, like silver, and animated it. Under the Sumerians, money came alive, releasing human energy, best encapsulated by Kushim's risk taking. With interest, money becomes dynamic: silver as money is worth more than silver as jewellery because, when lent out, it can earn interest, and interest is income. With the Sumerians, money was actually making more money.

Sophisticated as they were, the Sumerians – and their successors in the region, the Babylonians – had created commercial and organisational systems based on contracts. Money was still in people's heads, but soon it would be in our pockets and once money got into our pockets, commerce would explode, powered by a formidable monetary innovation: coins.

3

FROM CONTRACTS TO COINS

Was Midas framed?

Midas was a poor but unusually generous king of a parched land called Phrygia, through which flowed the River Pactolus. A great man for taking in strangers, Midas, despite his strait-ened circumstances, opened his door to visitors. One stranger who ended up at his table was Silenus, the foster father of Dionysus, the god of good times, late nights and general debauchery. As was his way, Midas laid out the red carpet for the stranger, offering him all that he had from his meagre supplies. Impressed by this spontaneous generosity, Silenus, himself fond of a jar, recounted to Dionysus the story of this poor yet charitable king. In recognition of his no-questions-asked hospitality, Dionysus granted Midas one wish.[1]

Ancient Midas suffered from a modern affliction: status anxiety. He held the title of king but he had no money. The contrast between his royal notions and his diminished coffers meant he saw himself as a source of ridicule and pity. Money could change this. Midas asked that everything he touched might be turned to gold. These days the name Midas is synonymous with short-sightedness, greed and avarice, but, on reflection, Midas was just a down-on-his-luck, decent skin who needed a break. Unfortunately, he had not thought through his economic experiment. He touched an apple; it turned to gold, rendering it valuable but useless, ornamental yet impractical. His beloved daughter ran up to hug her kind father and she too turned to gold. Realising his folly, the distraught Midas beseeched Dionysus to free him from this curse.

A jovial god of forgiving disposition, Dionysus took pity on Midas, remembering his earlier humility and generosity, and told him to bathe in the nearby Pactolus. (The river has long since dried up, but it's believed that this took place in central Anatolia, close to Mount Tmolus.[2]) According to legend, as an overjoyed Midas bathed, ridding himself of gold, the river turned a glittering, yellowish colour, flowing with precious metal, thereby allowing Midas to become wealthy without the inconvenience of everything he touched turning to gold. The successors to Midas' land, the Lydians, were blessed with a gold supply that the legend put down to the munificence of Dionysus.

The story the Greeks were trying to explain with this myth was how an empire had risen that had used gold coins as currency and created a vast trading network from Persia to the Aegean. The River Pactolus really did shine like gold but not because King Midas bathed in it. The Pactolus carried an alloy called electrum, known as white gold. (The word electric stems from the ancient Greek *elector*, meaning he who shines.[3]) Gold was mostly valued by Babylonians as ornamentation. But the Lydians did something new. They smelted gold and created a brand-new economic system based on coins.[4] The virtual money of the Sumerians, underpinned by contracts, laws, debts and a variable rate of interest, was about to transform into physical money, in the guise of gold, silver and copper coins. Metallic coins, linked to a scarce base metal, would gradually alter our perception of money. This was the moment when gold transmuted from ornamentation to money, leading to a widely accepted system of money in which a piece of metal, useless before it is minted, would be transformed into something so much more.

Coinage is quite the abstraction. Accepting coinage requires humans to accept a new faith where tokens 'represent' value. In the tabernacle of the human mind, the coin works as a short cut, denoting the value of an immense array of real commodities and experiences in one universally understood tiny bit of portable metal. That piece of metal, once turned into a coin and validated by a stamp, acquires a value more than the intrinsic value of the metal itself. This abstraction enabled people to operate in a far more complex world than had been possible before the invention of coins.

This chapter is about that transformation. It's about symbolic money. From accountancy and an era of debts settled every so often, we are going to move into a system that uses coins for day-to-day trading. During this time, society progresses from grain in a warehouse to coins in your pocket. With coins, commerce, money and transactions shift from being centred on one-off clearing events to becoming a part of everyday life.

The Lydians, a civilisation living in what is now Turkey between 1000 and 600 BCE, invented coins.[5] It was a technology so useful that coinage spread quickly throughout the eastern Mediterranean, helping to create an interwoven trading system that would become the Greek Empire.

Top-down versus bottom-up

Although we have many variations, there are two main ways of running the economic show. One is 'top-down', where the Big Man at the summit commands the economy to behave in a certain way, and controls the process from start to finish, according to an all-encompassing plan. Ancient economies tended towards the 'top-down' approach. Power in great civilisations, like Sumer, flowed from an elite class of rulers and warriors, advised by a druid or priest caste. At the bottom, the peasants worked the land, paying rents and tithes upwards. Trade was mandated to a small number of anointed and licensed wholesalers, best thought of as a commercial caste – like Kushim, who we met in the last chapter, in Mesopotamia.

In contrast, the bottom-up economy is organic. It's an evolutionary system of trial and error, where the market, based on prices, preferences and scarcity, organises the economy and society. Prices and profits, rather than plans and priests, determine whether something is working. People involve themselves in the bottom-up economy *willingly*, rather than at the point of a sword. In terms of an organising technology, a widely accepted system of money and coinage makes the bottom-up economy possible.

The top-down economic system was most probably based on reciprocity – barter and redistribution.[6] Reciprocity, exchanging goods or labour for other goods or labour, was based on tradition and customs, not on price. It hinged on reputation. We can imagine this working in small groups, but as groups grow, this doesn't work so well. Consider trying to barter with thousands of people. The introduction of gold coins nudged the Lydian economy, very slowly, towards a bottom-up system organised around money, ultimately bequeathing some people a modicum of power and sovereignty, albeit within a ruling hereditary hierarchy. Given that a single coin in the hand of a prince has the same value as a single coin in the hand of a commoner, coins went some small way towards loosening the grip of the ruling class. This idea of universal value, where a coin has the same value whoever spends it, is an important social development. Prior to coins, if you were born poor, you died poor. The advent of coinage marked the beginning of a move towards social mobility for a tiny minority. If you could acquire coins, you could acquire status.[7]

The embryonic Lydian market economy connected more people more efficiently and in a much less rigid fashion than the bureaucratic economies that preceded it, allowing a small empire to out-trade, out-think and outwit its much larger neighbours. From around 700 BCE and culminating with the reign of its king Croesus, which began around 560 BCE, the Lydian Empire flourished, introducing and continuing to innovate with coins: standardising them, creating a centralised mint run by the state, and introducing smaller denominations that brought ever more people into the web, thereby stimulating commerce.

The Greek historian Herodotus, writing in around 600 BCE, tells us that these Lydians are 'the first people we know of to use gold and silver coins and . . . the first retail tradesmen'.[8] By calling them retail tradesmen, the haughty Herodotus notes that these were commercial people, and he meant this as a put-down in the same way that Napoleon dismissed the English as a nation of shopkeepers. But the world has been built by shopkeepers. Retailers have their own energy – a monetary rather than a military dynamism. Commerce gifted the Lydians immense power. A hive of commercial activity, their vibrant capital Sardis anchored a trading empire that extended throughout much of modern-day western Turkey.

Herodotus describes these profit-oriented, free-wheeling artisans as having the same customs as his own civilised Greeks, except that they did not 'prostitute their female children'.[9] Commerce and coinage appear to have elevated the status of Lydian women, who could trade alongside their male counterparts. In a world where women were rarely more than chattels, Lydian women had the right to refuse a husband and select their own. Without overstating the case (remember these were societies characterised by mass slavery), these early signs of minor female emancipation emblematise the liberating power of money.

Money's magic

Before the Lydian Empire, the amount of money available in any kingdom was a result of the foundational crops and conquest. With their revolutionary coins, the Lydians broke the link between nature's seasonal cycles and money, creating an autonomous supply of gold tokens. Breaking the link between money and some agricultural energy-based anchor like grain may have raised some philosophical questions for the Lydians. For example, what actually is money? Can there be useful and wasteful money? Is profit legitimate? Can there be too much money? Whether the Lydians were asking these questions, we just don't know, but they are questions we still struggle with today and, as we will see, they definitely plagued the great Greek philosophers, inheritors of this wonderful Lydian innovation.

Once adopted, because of its obvious advantage, coinage proliferated all around the eastern Mediterranean. More coins begot more trade, and more trade meant the circulation and velocity of money – how quickly it changed hands – increased. Coins made money work harder. With all this money flying around, the bazaar flourished. Markets for a huge array of goods, foreign and local, ushered in an enormous leap in the economic and organisational structure of society. The market was the critical organisational mechanism that allocated resources around society, registering scarcity via prices, which moved with the ebb and flow of supply and demand. The Lydians were gradually creating an economic system that was beginning to look like something we would recognise today.

Not only did the Lydians have electrum to mint their coins, they also had access to the Silk Road through the capital, Sardis, which opened them up to trading opportunities extending east to west, linking the Aegean and the Mediterranean with the Euphrates, Persia and beyond to India and China.[10] A north–south axis also linked them to the Eurasian Steppe via the Black Sea, opening up further routes of exchange. A commercial buckle in the ancient world's busiest trading beltway, Sardis sucked in traders and goods from all over the globe. Along the way, taverns hosted travelling salesmen, speaking a multitude of languages, and buying and selling everyday items such as beer, grain, oil, wine and pottery as well as more valuable goods like pearls, perfumes, ceramics, cloth, ivory and marble. Coins were the great leveller. They made the stranger less strange, allowing people to make connections at a large scale, through a readily accepted medium.

Standardised money

Before the introduction of Lydian gold coins, trade was cumbersome and slow. Gold pieces had to be verified by weights and moneychangers. Imagine how much time this took – the palaver of scales, weights and the like. Obviously, between traders there was a complicated system of debits and credits. Millennia before, the Sumerians had introduced interest, putting a price on money and a value on time. The Lydians inherited this system, but they went one better. At first, coins were issued by the king, but before long they were also minted by individual goldsmiths and traders who fashioned their own coins based on weights and purity. As coins came into Sardis from far and wide, Lydian goldsmiths melted them down and restamped them, leading to competing currencies. Different currencies caused friction as traders didn't immediately know what each coin was worth.

What if this system could be standardised? Under the reign of King Gyges (680–645 BCE),[11] the Lydians introduced a state monopoly over the issuing of coins. In a further stroke of genius, they put the stamp of the king – a lion's head – on each coin. By making money and the state synonymous, the Lydians were conceiving a model of money that lasted for millennia. The Greeks took it up. So too the Romans, and almost every other state and empire since has relied on this Lydian innovation: the official, state-issued coin. Coinage was a source of enormous centralised power, as it is to this day. Before standardisation, coins were like various languages: some people understood what they meant but others didn't. With standardisation, the official coin became the official language of commerce. With one currency came less friction, fewer barriers to trade and a far more integrated market, offering a wider variety of choice.

King Croesus (c. 560–c. 546 BCE) oversaw the expansion of the Lydian state from a small mercantile community, hemmed in by the Persians to the east and the Aegean to the west, into the first empire based partly on wealth and commerce rather than exclusively on war and conquest.[12] A state monopoly on money created two distinct players in the new monetary economy: there was the 'issuer' of money – the state – and the 'users' of money – the people. You and I are users of money, not issuers. You might love to be an issuer, and believe me, my children think that I am one, but we are not. We are users. Users try to save, accumulate and, most critically, budget. We can run out of money. We regularly do. We work to get it, exchanging hours of our time for money.

The issuer doesn't need to do this. The power of issuing legal money is vested in the state. Within the borders of the state, we are obliged to use the currency that is issued by that state. We can't use the dollar in a euro country and vice versa. We might try to counterfeit money but we'll probably end up in prison. The state, on the other hand, can issue as much as it wants, an enormous power, arguably the most significant any state has beyond the ability to declare war.

Lydian gold bolstered the state, and the state, by converting the precious metal into money, bolstered the value of gold. With time, the Lydians recognised that it would be useful to divide their coins into smaller and smaller ingots so that they could trade more and more goods with more and more people.[13] Smaller denominations – equivalent to a day's work or a small portion of a harvest – helped the Lydians establish a bottom-up, free-trading, market-based economy, partly driven by smaller retailers: the kinds of shopkeepers and tradesmen pooh-poohed by big men like Napoleon and Herodotus. This shift from the dependency of farming life to the relative commercial independence of the retailer must have radically changed how these people saw the world.

The law of one price

Along with business connections, money also enhanced the Lydian gene pool. Unlike top-down economies of the past, people didn't always have to marry within the tribe. Coin-based dowries allowed strangers to marry each other, have families with members of other tribes and bring more people into contact with each other. Money bled into every area of society: religions accepted money as gifts, art and culture were valued with money, and disputes were settled with money. A person found guilty of a theft no longer had to be stoned to death for retribution. They could simply pay a fine.

In a society that understood money, all sorts of day-to-day things could be expressed in terms of one common denominator. The great organisational power of money, which economists call 'the law of one price', rendered the complex simple, making Lydian life and its economy much easier to understand. As everything could be valued against everything else, Lydians could make informed choices between a loaf of bread, a jar of olive oil, a glass of wine, sex with a prostitute, a wool tunic, and paying taxes, because all these could be compared with how much they cost vis-à-vis a day's work, using the clear arbiter of coinage.

The promise of status, gifted by money, is one of life's habitual motivators. But to acquire status required a new way of thinking and a new skill. You needed to understand money. Rather than telling a story about how the gods had empowered you to lead, you needed to be able to count. Numeracy nudges us towards rationality because numbers demystify the world. A world mediated by money constitutes a great leap forward, a personal, social and intellectual revolution that spawned an entirely new way of organising society, based on money. Coins and basic numeracy mark the very beginnings of a shift that would take centuries, from the celestial to the rational. But if the Lydians kicked off this process, their neighbours the Greeks, masters of logic, took to it with a gusto that had never been seen before.

4

MONEY AND THE GREEK MIND

From *mythos* to *logos*

Born 12 miles from Athens into a family of minor Athenian aristocrats during the years of the Peloponnesian War, Xenophon (c. 430–c. 354 BCE) was described by Diogenes as 'a man of great modesty and as handsome as can be imagined'.[1] Unlike richer philosophers, his family's income relied on the success of farming rather than the wealth from extensive land or slave ownership. Having to earn his monthly crust was probably influential in his thinking. A budget tends to focus the mind, but so too does the responsibility of leading men in battle.

As a young man, Xenophon, like other Greeks seeking adventure, enrolled as a mercenary in the war effort of Cyrus the Younger, in his quest to dethrone his older brother, the Persian king Artaxerxes II. It didn't turn out too well for Cyrus, who was killed in battle, while his mercenary military generals, the Spartan Clearchus and the Athenian Proxenus, were executed. This left the army stranded, hundreds of miles east of Athens, leaderless and facing winter in a foreign land. Entrusted with leadership of the 10,000-strong army, a brilliant young Xenophon managed to lead his men to safety, through what is now Armenia, to the Black Sea coast. This story is documented in Xenophon's *Anabasis* (as quoted by James Joyce in the opening chapter of *Ulysses*). Due to its relatively straightforward prose and meticulous detailing of the terrain encountered, *Anabasis* was, for many centuries, a primary text in the instruction of ancient Greek. Alexander the Great used *Anabasis* as a field guide for his own conquest of Persia.

If *Anabasis* reveals Xenophon the geographer, his other work, *Oeconomicus*, written with the same attention to detail, unveils Xenophon the economist. *Oeconomicus* is the first economics book ever written. Our word economics comes from this word, deriving from the ancient Greek words for 'home' (*oikos*) and 'to manage' (*nemein*), and literally translated as 'household management'.

Xenophon was writing after coinage and money had been adopted in Greece. If we compare his writing (around 500 BCE) to something from a pre-coinage society, like Homer's myths of the ancient Greek heroes (written around 700 BCE), we can discern a shift in Greek thinking in the intervening two centuries.[2] Each writer describes quite different societies, with different concerns and philosophies, norms and morals. Something had changed in Greek society. Earlier legends were about heroes and villains performing fantastical acts; Xenophon's writing was based more in reality. He described people expressing doubt, looking for proof, and doing ordinary, practical things. In Homer's time, the gods answered all the big questions, but from around 500 BCE onwards, the ancient Greeks had begun to develop more sophisticated thought processes. They had moved in quite a short space of time from reliance on 'soft thinking', using myths and notions of the divine to guide their understanding of the world, to 'hard thinking', in which individual logic and reasoning challenge religion and myth.[3] This was a shift from what the Greeks termed *mythos* to what they called *logos*. Mythos relied on narrative; logos, on the other hand, entailed logical and rational analysis – the basis of economics. What altered the Greek mind between Homer's time and Xenophon's time? And could money and coinage have had something to do with this shift?

Silver owls

The Greeks built an immense empire, based in Athens and loosely connected by trade, a common culture and a common currency, the Greek tetradrachm. Unlike the earlier Persian Empire, which had been agriculture-based, relying on grain surpluses, the Athenians, even at the height of Greek culture, couldn't feed themselves.[4] They depended on imported grain. As they rarely sought to conquer vast tracts of agricultural land, the Greeks had to come up with a way to coax others to grow crops for them. Up until Greek civilisation, we don't see large population increases that were not also sustained by huge agricultural surpluses. Even those fledgling retailers, the Lydians, held a large fertile land mass. Yet between 480 and 450 BCE the population of Athens rose by around 80 per cent, from approximately 30,000 to 54,000.[5] How did they do it?

Herein lies the genius of Greek finance. A sprawling empire managed to innovate so efficiently in coins and money and develop an effective enough legal system that trading outposts could be set up hundreds of miles apart. This empire was entirely dependent on foreigners to willingly feed Athens. By the fifth century BCE, Athens was importing three quarters of its staples.[6] The Greeks were expanding their empire one trade route at a time.

Athenians didn't have much land, but they had the sea, the port and lots of silver. In Laurion, just south of Athens, lay one of the richest silver deposits in the ancient world. Just as gold coins transformed Lydian society, silver coins transformed Greece. From the late sixth century BCE, the Greeks went into mining overdrive, minting their famous silver coin with an owl on one side and the goddess Athena on the other. The owl has an olive sprig in its mouth, symbolising one of the most important crops in Athens, olive oil. Called the tetra-drachm, the silver coin corresponded to four drachmas, the most basic unit of measurement in Athens. It was the most widely minted coin in the ancient world, lasting over 700 years in constant usage. Over that period, it is thought more than 120 million coins were minted.[7]

Given this level of production, at any one time there might be millions of drachmas in circulation. With one drachma being roughly equal to a day's labour,[8] this gives a sense of the dynamism of the monetised Greek economy. Coins flooded out of Athens at the port of Piraeus and goods flowed in from all over the Aegean littoral and beyond, generating economic activity throughout the empire and sustaining the many trading outposts linked by their owl currency. Commodities, luxuries, slaves, sex were all given a price and a denomination. With the drachma, farmers, artisans and merchants had a stable medium of exchange.

In earlier exchange-driven societies, trade was dependent on a web of relationships defined by hierarchy, tradition, sharing and reciprocity. However, abundant coins allowed the Greeks to move further along the journey forged by the Lydians. Coins simplified things. Profit could be calculated by an individual without the need to get tied up in knots worrying about reci-procity and repeat transactions. Money was, transaction by transaction, giving people slightly more autonomy. This was a double-edged sword. The stability of society had been upturned by coins; old traditions were replaced by new rules.

The Greeks were facing a problem: with some people becoming more autonomous, how do we know who is boss? Who can we trust? How should we live together? Greeks began to come up with an entirely new way of thinking about our rights and responsibilities in this modern coin-based society, which was expanding rapidly. If society is based on a rigid caste system, it's easy to rule. Terror is a dominant tool of control and institutions and religions tend to be based around fear and strictures. In a society mediated by money, where social status is somewhat mobile, rationality gains prominence over emotion and hard thinking challenges rule following.[9]

As the Greek economy continued to become more monetised, the Greek mind became ever more sophisticated, leading to many of the philosophical breakthroughs that remain with us to this day. A financially literate citizen thinks very differently to a financially illiterate one. For instance, Xenophon was grappling with the abstract notion of value, distinguishing between goods that have what we would now call 'use value', and those that purely have 'exchange value'. The illustrative example used in one story is the flute. A person who cannot play the flute doesn't have any use for it. However, because it can be exchanged for money or other goods, it has exchange value. And it wasn't just in these abstract matters that *Oeconomicus* was breaking new ground. While hardly a feminist by modern standards, Xenophon also argued that 'wives and husbands should be co-workers in the household'[10] and 'the wife who is a full partner in household management contributes as much to the welfare of the estate as does her husband'.[11]

Running through *Oeconomicus* is a general concern about

day-to-day issues, centred on how to organise society and households – in other words, modern economics. At the heart of
Xenophon's interests are the dynamic and philosophical foundations of money and how to create prosperous and
co-operative societies using money. He writes about how to
organise the system, how best to maximise resources, how to
keep accounts, how to value things, how to compare costs and
profits. These are complicated issues, but the average person in
urban Greek society was, by Xenophon's time, becoming more
financially competent.

Xenophon was influenced in his investigations by the philosopher Protagoras of Samos, born in 490 BCE, who had famously
declared that 'Of all things the measure is Man'.[12] He was
saying that, if all we know for certain is what we see before
us, then we must figure things out for ourselves rather than
outsourcing reasoning to the gods – in other words, trust our
own intellect and intelligence. Alongside Plato, Xenophon
studied under the tutelage of Socrates, who pioneered a method
for logical thinking. Questioning everything, these thinkers
began to challenge the philosophical foundations that underpinned their old economic and political systems, allowing them
to begin creating new ones. This curious and intellectually
adventurous society was responsible for birthing historians such
as Herodotus, who documented the Persian Wars, the physician
Hippocrates of Kos and the philosopher Aristotle.

Most notably, the shift in the zeitgeist led to the creation
of a new system of governance, based on the sovereign individual, whose creator, the Athenian statesman Cleisthenes,
would term it *demokratia* or 'rule by the people'.[13] It is important to note that this idea of democracy applied to only a
small portion of the society – after all, roughly one in four
people in Athens were slaves and half the population were

women. Rather than imagine Athens as some kind of free-market democracy, it is probably more accurate to think of Athens as a place like the American South before the Civil War, where democracy did not apply to *all* the people. But those who were able to embrace democracy involved themselves in a range of other intellectually revolutionary ideas.

Why was there such a flowering in philosophy, economics, medicine, democracy and ultimately the thoroughly modern idea of the engaged citizen and the republic? The co-evolution of Greek thought and the widespread dissemination of money, particularly in the form of silver coins, is too closely correlated to be dismissed as mere coincidence. Money gives rise to an element of individual control and personal responsibility. The Greeks, like the Lydians before them, would have seen that a baker with two drachmas has equal purchasing power in the market to a princess with two drachmas. Such relative equality, where hierarchy is flattened by trade, must have been socially revolutionary.

The *polis*, participation and politics

The Greek Empire was not only a commercial but an urban entity, made up of many dozens of free, self-governing city-states – a completely novel decentralised experiment in governance. To organise this new type of society, a new idea emerged: the *polis*. By the sixth century BCE, after the reign of Solon – the great reforming Greek king – the polis was firmly established as the foundation of all Greek civilisation. The polis was the civic, social, economic, military and political cornerstone of ancient Greece and the rules of the polis outlined citizens' rights and obligations.[14]

Anchoring the polis was participation. The active citizen

was a free individual in commerce, politics and thought. Commerce was mediated by a court system, politics was underpinned by democracy, and independent thought was constantly being fired up by philosophical enquiry. Broadly speaking, the economy was governed by the market, itself mediated by money. Greek civilisation was an urban concept, and the complexity of urban life was made easier to navigate by the organisational aspects of money.

Of course, the Greeks, as all city slickers do, looked down their aquiline noses at others. The poet Phocylides of Miletus, comparing the Greek city-states with other ancient cities, boasted that 'a polis on a barren rock, small, but settled in an orderly fashion, is greater than senseless Nineveh' (Nineveh was the enormous capital city of the Assyrian Empire).[15] Greek cities, clinging to the coast, were hives of commercial activity around the Mediterranean, Aegean and Black Sea, described by Plato as 'frogs looking into a pond'.[16]

The heart of each Greek city, whether it was Athens, Pergamon or Marseille, was the *agora*: the marketplace. A vibrant hive of trade, performance, flirtation, infidelity, ideas, sedition, drinking and eating, all organised around and by money. This was the place you went to shop, learn, chat, and breathe in the smells, hear the sounds and feel the pulse of the city. Coin-based currencies made various markets in the agora work more efficiently, and smaller denominations of coins enabled more and more people to participate via smaller transactions: you could buy a cup of wine with a very small coin.

Markets were not just hard-nosed places, though. It wasn't only commerce that flowed through them. The agora became a hub for poets and philosophers. The poet Eubulus gives us a flavour of the 34-acre Athenian agora: 'You will find everything sold together in the same place at Athens; figs, witnesses to summonses, bunches of grapes, turnips, pears, apples, givers of evidence, roses, medlars, porridge, honeycombs, chickpeas, lawsuits, first milk, allotments, machines, irises, lambs, water-clocks, laws and indictments'.[17] Street activity was the throbbing heart of Greek cities. Not for them wide boulevards for processions, religious ceremonies and military parades; the centre of the Greek city was a warren of streets, full of people hustling. Socrates used to hang out in the Keramikos area of Athens, then a rough part of the city – the sort of place where things happen. Young Socrates gossiped, and possibly more, with the prostitutes, gamblers and drinkers of the taverns. He listened to their stories, took stock of their opinions and travails while sucking up the experiences of the immigrants, opportunists and dreamers before he graduated to the agora, where he questioned people about their views, bringing about the Socratic method in the process.[18]

The Greek mind didn't only concern itself with trade, logic and philosophy; it spawned great innovations in mechanics. The classical Greeks were practical as well as romantic. Their vibrant economy, taking and refining ideas from across the trading world, came up with industrial innovations such as the piston, gears, screws, the watermill, and the pulley and crane for unloading ships in their port of Piraeus. As commercial citizens, Greeks had an interest in keeping taxes low. It's hard to be mercantile if the king is taxing you to high heaven, and to operate in a market, you needed to hang onto as much of your own produce to flog as possible.

King Solon, who ruled towards the end of the seventh century BCE, viewed high tax rates as a form of 'enslavement'. He did tax his citizens, but he did this by creating a fiscal sinking fund, almost like a state reserve, into which the people would pay their taxes and out of which the Greeks financed defence and other collective projects. By the fifth century BCE, the tax rate in Athens remained under 8 per cent. Compare this to Egypt, where peasants paid up to 50 per cent of their cereal crops and one sixth of their vineyard production in taxes, and craftsmen contributed between a quarter and a third of their produce, which meant the bulk of the surplus ended up in the hands of the pharaoh.[19] Not so for the Greeks. Low taxation meant they had more to sell, getting their hands on those little silver discs with owls on them. In this sense, the new monetary system was more democratic.

The money multiplier

Coins were initially minted to pay for soldiers. Before modern welfare states, the vast majority of government spending went to the army and the major beneficiaries were soldiers and those who produced weapons – an ancient form of the military-industrial complex. Numismatic evidence points to a proliferation of coins circulating during periods of war. For example, there is a surge in new coinage around the time of Alexander the Great's conquests and the Roman Punic Wars[20] and peak production of the Athenian mint coincided with the Peloponnesian War. Soldiers, armed with coins, became the ambassadors of commerce. Together with mercenaries, soldiers brought coins back from war and exchanged them for goods, adding to the local money supply and creating demand for products.

Coins brought disparate places and peoples together, connecting competing states and regions; this trade expanded economic horizons and created wealth. Coins also became embedded in religious and cultural rites, such as in the popular ritual of offering a coin when consulting the oracle at Pharae – even ancient fortune tellers needed to be paid. By tying coins to religion as offerings to the gods, superstition ironically spread the use of coins well beyond the reach of commerce.

The production of coins mirrors the economic and cultural growth of Greek civilisation. Although Athens itself went into decline around 200 BCE, the Mediterranean world it spawned remained Greek. The language of commerce was Greek and, as a result, Greek became a little bit like English today, a default second language. From around 300 BCE until the time of Christ, the world experienced a three-century period of sustained economic expansion. If we add the other great coin producers, the Romans, to this mix, we have a 500-year expansion from 300 BCE to 200 CE, where the age of coins coincides with sustained economic dynamism, never seen continuously before.[21]

The link between the sophisticated, intellectually curious and culturally expressive Greco-Roman Golden Age and the rise of money is hard to put down to mere chance. The development of this bottom-up technology allowed the market to challenge the old top-down economy, driving commerce and leading to higher living standards across swathes of the ancient world. (Archaeological and scientific evidence, from rising levels of lead and copper pollution in the atmosphere and the number of shipwrecks evidencing trade, to the increasing average size of houses and human skeletal remains, points to a coincidence of economic expansion with monetisation.[22]) When a society begins to change, the things that it believes in, such as religion, are also altered.

Money and a new religion

Why did Christianity, with its radical message of 'the first will be last and the last will be first', emerge when and where it did? Previous religions had elevated the super-human capabilities of the strong, but Christianity exalted the weak.

In contrast to the pre-monetary world of rigid caste systems, the attraction of silver coins was the possibility, however remote, of upward social mobility. If you were a smart individual who worked hard, with luck, you could conceivably advance in social status. This implied that the opposite was also true: if you were a loser in this new monetary economy, rather than a winner, was that not also based to some degree on merit? Such a possibility prompted new philosophical and existential dilemmas. The pre-money way of organising society was exclusively a caste system: you were poor because you were born poor, the gods had decided it was your fate, and it was not your fault. Arguably, there was an element of comfort in that.

Greek was not only the language of commerce, but also the language of ideas in this multi-ethnic region of the eastern Mediterranean. As these people embraced a new value system based around money, some started to embrace a counter-philosophy. A new religion was emerging, spreading in the marketplaces of cities and towns, the very places where money was also being used. This new religion was completely at odds with the ethics of the old gods: it dignified poverty and preached about forgiveness, generosity and humility. Think about the expressions 'the meek will inherit the Earth' and 'it is easier for a camel to go through the eye of a needle than for a rich man to enter the kingdom of God'. In this new commercial world, is it surprising that the promise of salvation in the next life for those who lose out in the monetary economy starts to capture imaginations?

By putting inequality at the centre of its message, Christianity was placing its ideas in the social context of the time. This religion, conceived when the market economy was spreading throughout the region, is often, even today, seen as the counterbalance to the pitfalls of money. Christianity's promise was truly radical. It emerged after 200 years of economic growth, materialism and a profusion of commerce and money. It set itself up against money in what would become one of the greatest narratives of the Western world – and one of its most enduring images is the betrayal of Christ by Judas for thirty pieces of silver. Could Christianity have emerged, in part, as a reaction to the disruptive impact of the coin?

5

THE EMPIRE OF CREDIT

High society

In the decades following the death of radical preacher Jesus Christ, his Greek-speaking disciples spanned out among the cities of the region, planting new ideas about morality and money, humility and selflessness. But in 79 CE the people of Pompeii hadn't got that memo about meekness, abstinence and self-sacrifice. Or if they had heard it while knocking around the communal sauna, it wasn't catching on.

Much like upscale Manhattan decamping to the Hamptons, every summer swanky Romans escaped the sweltering heat of the city by heading to the coast. As is the case today, the Bay of Naples, Amalfi and Sorrento were the choice spots, home-from-home for senators, generals, movers and shakers, celebrity chefs, hairdressers, manicurists and the odd emperor. In terms of people watching, there was no finer place, with parties and festivals, booze and good food, concubines and young patricians posing in the sun. Teeming with taverns, midsummer Pompeii hummed, heavy with gossip, rumour and innuendo. For members of Rome's high society, the month of August was party month, spring break, Mardi Gras and

Halloween rolled into one high-summer crescendo. Typically, the Mediterranean weather breaks in mid-August when the intense heat of late July and early August gives way to torrential rain, dampening the soil, rendering the final weeks of August steamy and sweaty. Perfect for debauchery. Today, the Italians still call this holiday season *Ferragosto* – the party of Augustus – after the emperor himself.

Luckily for us, among the upper crust in the summer of 79 AD, kicking back on the seafront, was Pliny the Younger, the premier columnist of his day, through whose eyes many of our impressions of Roman life have been made concrete. On the morning of 24 August, hungover after a late night, the reclining patricians gulped down fresh water flavoured with lemons and oranges, devoured dates and figs, stretched out, yawning, going over the night before and anticipating the one to come. As they recovered, heads pounding and tongues wagging, their world was suddenly and devastatingly ripped asunder as the great Vesuvius erupted. Terrified, they ran in all directions. The sky turned black with acrid, sulphuric smoke. Coughing and gasping, they watched in horror from their upmarket villas dotted around the bay as the bustling market cities of Pompeii and Herculaneum disappeared, entombed in a molten sarcophagus.

Days later, when the filthy smoke lifted, an extraordinary vista opened before them. All was calm. The still quietness of the snow-like blanket of dust must have been deeply unsettling after the violence of the blast that blew the top off Mount Vesuvius, projecting molten rock and lava from the earth's core into the bright Neapolitan sky. Eclipsed, the sun no longer shone and flaky, warm dust fell gently from the darkened heavens. Were the gods tampering with the evidence, hushing up the crime of the century, pretending it had all been a bad dream? The snow-dust fell softly on Pompeii and Herculaneum and, as it must have felt to those who witnessed it, all over the universe.

Both cities, trading entrepots, were encased by a thick layer of volcanic ash. In time, the world moved on and forgot these places. Potash fertiliser, made from the ash of burned hardwood trees, created ideal growing conditions. Over time verdant fields and pastures sprawled around the bay, hiding an extraordinary secret. In 1860, as they were digging around the base of the now dormant volcano, a team of archaeologists led by Giuseppe Fiorelli uncovered an entire microcosm of economic activity submerged under this ash duvet.[1] With each careful scrape of the hardened lava, Fiorelli and his team were introduced to their ancestors. Luxurious villas, pompous statues, gladiatorial stadiums, exquisite mosaics, bread mills, brothels, baths, theatres, gymnasiums, even bowls with left-over soup – a buried city full of vibrancy and economic vitality sprang to life before the archaeologists. Pompeii offers us a direct insight into the economic and social life of the Romans: where they ate, how they communicated, how they spent their money, who they spent it with, where they travelled and how they voted.

The remains of this lively port city show us the fruits of an economic empire that placed money at the centre of daily life. Mosaics in the entrance halls of ancient Pompeii residences exclaim '*lucrum gaudium*' ('Profit is a delight') and '*salve lucrum*' ('Hail, profit!').[2] The art of hustling, making something out of nothing, ran in Roman blood. This commercial trading city had far outgrown the limitations of its local economy. Pompeii was a miniature version of Rome in the sense that, like Athens before it, Rome could not feed itself and relied on commerce to persuade others to grow wheat for it.

For a region with a relatively bare hinterland, with little to offer in terms of agricultural produce, apart from viticulture and floral yields, the prosperity of Pompeii was a result of its embrace of trade. Archaeological evidence shows just how far the Pompeiians were willing to go in search of commercial opportunity. A golden necklace, with roughly shaped emeralds only available in Egypt, was found on one of the skeletons in the 1860 excavation. There were two skeletons of African origin as well as an Indian ivory statuette. Pliny the Younger's uncle, Pliny the Elder, had warned about India becoming a hoarder of Roman gold some decades earlier.[3] Ostentatious Romans, obsessed with the finest Indian jewels, silks and muslins, ran a massive deficit with India that was plugged by gold. For Pliny, such extravagance signalled the licentious path down which Rome was travelling. He was not impressed. From what was uncovered in Pompeii, including large quantities of coins from the western Mediterranean towns of Ebusus and Massalia, it was clear the locals were trading with the world, buying, selling, hustling and bargaining.[4]

Com Merx

The citizens of Pompeii worshipped profit, as represented by their favoured deity. Dotted across the town, on beautifully ornate mosaics and frescoes, is a recurring image of a winged man carrying a bag of coins. The god Mercury was depicted on nineteen of the twenty-nine painted commercial façades that have been revealed.[5] An impressive shrine dedicated to Mercury adorned the central food market, watching over the arena of commercial exchange. The Pompeiians held him in high regard not because of his lightning bolt-throwing prowess, or some other Olympian trait; they prayed and offered sacrifices to him because he was the god of commerce – a negotiator, salesman, charmer, a trusted partner as well as a trickster, moneylender and deal maker. Mercury is also quicksilver, the only metal that can remain liquid at room temperature, shapeshifting, ever-changing, never solid or fixed, always open to new positions. Mercury and his principal tool, money, evade obstacles by trading, negotiating and compromising.

Romans, after all, are the people who gave us the expression 'Baths, wine, and sex ruin our bodies, but they are the essence of life'.[6] You need money for all that good stuff. Quick-thinking Mercury, armed with his own cunning and smarts as well as his technology, money, dominated Pompeii's markets and bazaars. The ordinary citizen understood the transformative power of commerce. In fact, our word commerce can be translated literally from the Roman phrase '*com Merx*' or 'with Mercury', and with Merx the Romans would transform themselves and transform their empire.

The Romans were financiers who turbocharged their empire by innovating with credit – money in the form of a promise. As credit, capital flowed from the regions to the centre, from where it was recycled in various financial guises. The Romans had banks and bankers – otherwise known as *mensari* or moneychangers – companies, insurance contracts, shareholder capitalism, speculation and a legal system to underpin contracts. They had long-term loans and debt for equity financing, private corporations and a myriad of other financial instruments. Underpinning this financial architecture was credit. Credit requires a deep understanding of the mercurial nature of money, which, like the Romans' god Mercury, could be both deal maker and trickster — always on the move, never stationary, rarely leaving a trace.

Pecunia non olet

From one side of his coins, looking remarkably like Elton John, Vespasian could be any other middle-aged Roman bigwig. On the other side is the forlorn symbol of the recently conquered Judea. She is sitting captive, hands tied behind her back under a palm tree. After years of skirmishes and problems subduing this province, Vespasian — at this point a Roman general — had had enough of the Jews, who'd been annoying the Romans in Galilee, rebelling and failing to pay tribute. Around 70 CE, he had attacked Jerusalem, deploying his best troops, the legionnaires, whom he paid monthly with coins backed by that most prized commodity: salt. The modern word salary comes from this idea of being paid in salt or paid with a coin linked to salt, as too does the expression 'worth his salt'. Vespasian meant business.

Following his victory in Judea, which leveraged him into the position of emperor, Vespasian promptly had new coins minted with a clear message to other restless regions: if you fancy a row, you will end up like the uppity Judeans captured on the coin, allowed to live under palm trees in their own homeland but as slaves, not a free people. Under the Romans, coins were not just currency; they were propaganda reminding millions of subjects who was boss.

The empire now stretched from Syria to York, Cologne to Tyre. People moved and traded with each other, using Roman law, technology and money, trading spices, silks and jewels from the east, slaves and wool from the west, furs from the north and salt and gold from the south, all bought and paid for with Roman coins. Rome, following the Greek lead, became one of the most monetised empires the world had ever seen, due in part to its free-spending banker-legionnaires, gelling the vast territory together, unifying disparate cultures, religions and languages under one imperial currency. Recent DNA testing on the skeletons of four early Londoners from the Vespasian period reveals two with North African heritage, one Mediterranean and only one native Briton.

When Vespasian wasn't throwing his weight around, he was throwing up buildings. Understanding the symbolism of big public structures – how they could both keep the locals in the backstreets happy and signal to any foreigner the power of Rome – Vespasian built prodigiously. The Eternal City would be the centre of the world, home to the biggest theatres, thickest city walls, widest streets, most dynamic forum, most luxurious baths, finest chariot racecourse and of course, the holy of holies – in the Colosseum itself, which Vespasian started – the best fun and games. No other metropolis could eclipse Rome.

Rome's rapid expansion needed money. This is where Vespasian, as tax strategist, came into his own. The treasury was always short of cash. Running out could be fatal for the emperor, so good tax planning might well prolong his rule. Vespasian was the first of his dynasty, aware that with one false move he was a goner. Grasping an essential in modern economic management, the importance of a broad tax base, he understood the argument that you shouldn't put all your eggs in one basket, and pursued the sensible approach of a little bit of tax on a lot of things, rather than a lot of tax on a few things. He threw the tax net wide.

When they weren't cheering Christians being eaten alive by lions, Romans had other odd habits, including cleaning their teeth and togas with urine. Urine contains ammonia and, as anyone who fancies reading the ingredients of a twenty-first-century Toilet Duck will see, one of the main agents in toilet bowl cleaning is ammonium nitrate. Ammonia removes stains, leaving surfaces a brilliant white. As any Roman house-wife knew, a dash of urine-scented ammonium scrubs up that toga we spilled wine on last night. Romans also brushed their teeth with a pee- and water-based paste. You might think that infatuation with brilliant white teeth is limited to denizens of failing US companies (the weaker the share price, the whiter the teeth), but Roman toffs also tried to mask the ageing process with bleached fangs.

Such was the value of ammonia that Rome's gigantic public loos were home to a rather indelicate artisan, the urine collector. The Romans built public toilets from their earliest days. Their understanding of hydraulics is of course evident in their aqueducts, engineered to sanitise their cities with flowing fresh water, but also in their communal lavatories. Vespasian, the tax-base broadening champion, saw an oppor-tunity to tax urine and levied a charge per bottle of pee, meaning not only were there pee collectors, but there were specialist taxmen who collected tax from the urine collectors. Who says every problem doesn't create its own solution?

Vespasian was an outsider, a soldier who took advantage of the chaos at the end of the Claudine dynasty. His dynasty, the Flavians, were not patrician. How could they be when he was a mere soldier? Possibly his dexterity with money and taxation stemmed precisely from the fact that he was not an aristocrat. He appreciated more than the stuffy patricians how money buys influence and power, particularly if you were not born to it. But not everyone was enamoured with Vespasian's tactics. Happy to spend his father's money but sniffy about its prov-enance, Titus, Vespasian's entitled son who would inherit the job on the old emperor's death, fancied himself as a bit of an aesthete.

Taxing urine offended his sensibilities. Titus was speaking for other aristocrats who shared his distaste, contending that raising tax from urine was beneath Rome. How could they use money from such a source? Was nothing off bounds when it came to *com Merx*? To this day, aristocrats' disdain for commerce is a badge of honour. No one pretends to dislike money more than the truly posh. Particularly when they don't have enough of it. The windbag Cicero in his *De Officiis* comments that 'Trade, if it is on a small scale, should be considered demeaning . . . there is no kind of gainful employment that is better, more fruitful, more pleasant, and more worthy of a free man than agriculture.'[7]

Beneath the snobbery is fear: fear of usurpation. Money is an incendiary energy and one of its most revolutionary attributes is its ability to propel social advancement. Entitled people understand this and are afraid of it. Private clubs, old-school ties and other exclusionary networks are deployed precisely to pull up the class drawbridge against richer parvenus. The Roman old guard, threatened by new money from adventurous legionnaires and provincials on the make, needed to erect barriers of refinement, such as manners, culture and other discriminations, to protect the hereditarily wealthy from the newly rich. When it came to the vulgar reach of commerce, urine was taking the piss.

Vespasian, the soldier emperor, observed the aristocrats' contempt, relished it and retorted with equal disdain, facing down filial snobbery with the observation, '*Pecunia non olet*'. 'Money does not smell'. Vespasian understood this; he embraced money's fleeting quality, its lack of trace. Money is ephemeral and the Romans loved it. It was this embrace of the abstraction of money, its fluidity and transferability, that allowed for the creation of one of Rome's greatest innovations. Trying to break free from the tyranny of coins, limited by the availability of gold and silver, the highly creative Romans fine-tuned one of money's most powerful characteristics: credit. Although the Romans did not invent credit (as we saw, the Sumerians were borrowing and lending), Roman innovation brought credit to another level.

Turning conquest into credit

As more and more provinces fell to Rome and the Roman legions, more taxes could be levied on new subjects. Slavery drove down the cost of crop production, while driving up the return to the Roman expropriators of land and capital. Such surpluses were income that acted as the fount of Roman credit. All credit requires income to pay back the principal; for the Romans that income came out of their subjects' pockets. Consider a wealthy province like Syria – home to traders, merchants and artisans of the highest calibre, vibrant cities and fertile agriculture – becoming subject to Roman taxation. The right to raise taxes in wealthy Syria, an incredibly lucrative asset, was a prize of conquest, auctioned off to a private corporation in the Roman Forum. The aristocratic owners of this corporation, called *publicani*, then leveraged these assets by selling shares to smaller Roman investors, not unlike a privatisation in modern times, thereby linking the wealth of the citizens to the prowess of the army and the interests of the aristocracy. As long as there was an income stream from the regions, a web of credit was made available to various classes of Romans, so that many had a stake in the imperial project. Investors were paying for shares to buy a stream of income into perpetuity, a stream that could be increased by the Roman corporation with little or no say from the taxed subjects. We have numerous accounts of regions being bled by these rapacious tax collectors at the behest of the companies' Roman shareholders.

Shares in these companies were widely held, and they were manipulated by speculation and rumour about the fortunes of the army in the regions, pushing valuations up and down when shares were traded in the Forum. Rome was a privatised empire and even as early as the second century BCE, the writer Polybius observed that almost every stratum of Roman society was involved in the credit and shareholding game in one way or another.

> All over Italy, an immense number of contracts far too numerous to specify are awarded by the censors for the construction and repair of public buildings and for the collection of revenues from navigable rivers. Harbours, gardens, mines, lands, in a word every transaction that comes under the controls of the Roman government is farmed out to contractors. All these activities are carried out by the people, and there is scarcely a soul one might say who does not have the interest in these contracts and the profits that are derived from them.[8]

Investment societies and clubs were set up where investors pooled their resources to buy shares, allowing ownership to permeate to even the lower end of the equestrian classes and beyond. The plebeian class was kept on side with bread and circuses – subsidised or free wheat and free entertainment in the Colosseum – paid for by loot from the regions, while the upper and merchant classes were given a 'carried interest' in the empire by an ongoing stream of income emanating directly from the unfortunate taxpayers of the regions. In this way, the expansionary imperial project paid for the basic welfare state that the Romans created for the lowers, while the uppers, with ample credit, were kept in clover. Of course, it wasn't just the provinces that fed the Roman money machine: roughly one in three people in Rome were slaves and their exploited labour enriched Rome too.

The credit system created a Roman drone, or 'rentier', class, that got to where they were not only by playing the credit game, but – crucially – through political connections. A modern image that might help bring the interplay between Roman finance and politics to life is Russia today and the intrigue around the Kremlin, with oligarchs falling in and out of favour. Securing the monopoly permit to extract or extort value from someone else or out of the ground, as is the case in Russia, was the name of the Roman imperial game.

As government contracts and forced levying of taxes was a significant route to wealth for the citizens of Rome, the scope for corruption, baksheesh and bribery was enormous – and enormously seductive. In such a frenzied environment, licensed companies were set up to finance public works, such as toll roads or viaducts, which all yielded levies and fees to the owners. While these feats of great engineering were lucrative to an extent, the thick monetary gravy was in tax collecting, made all the more attractive by the support of loyal legionnaires, bored, far away from home and ready to fight for their salary. Is it any wonder, with such a financial incentive structure, that Roman legions pushed on and on, extending the boundaries of empire further from the Eternal City? Money and credit drove empire.

During the years of imperial expansion, the underlying system of licence-based capitalism, easy credit, mass participation and backhanders enmeshed politics and money like never before. When seen from the perspective of today, finance in ancient Rome appears remarkably contemporary. We tend to think about credit crises as modern phenomena, but the credit cycle was as unforgiving then as it is now. The extensive use of credit made Roman politics and society susceptible to the vagaries of this new and erratic internal enemy, the credit cycle, with its chief protagonist: the speculator.

The world's first credit crisis

In 31 CE, the emperor Tiberius, head of the Claudian dynasty, was enjoying semi-retirement in Capri. The emperor was a consolidator, preferring diplomacy to war. With a well-run treasury and a peaceful empire, money flowed into Rome and interest rates fell. Peace breeds confidence: people forget the bad times, and credit markets typically remain healthy with few visible clouds on the horizon. All financial crises follow a period of very low interest rates.

Tiberius' seclusion was shattered by news of an alleged coup led by a young pretender named Sejanus, backed by a large number of senators and aristocrats – with so much money at stake, being on the right side of a coup could be highly lucrative. But the Claudian family didn't get to the top without learning a few tricks. Gathering intelligence, the shrewd and ruthless Tiberius indulged the ambitious consul, smoking him out. Once the emperor and his spies had assessed which of his former allies might side with the younger man, Tiberius made his move. Sejanus was killed and his gang of traitorous senators and patricians was rounded up. Just to let everyone know who was boss, Tiberius had the plotters' bloodied heads stuck on spikes protruding from the Tiber.

Out for their evening walk on the banks of the river, in a city convulsed by commotion and revolt, the citizens were left in no doubt what could happen if you backed the wrong horse in the Forum.

Shaken by the sheer number of senators prepared to betray him, Tiberius moved against them in the place it hurt them most: their pockets. The empire of credit was in the middle of a property boom, the treasury was full, and low interest rates had pushed up land prices. The credit-based Roman economy was thriving. And nowhere were these riches being accumulated more lavishly than in the Senate. According to the historian Tacitus, the vast majority of the senators had, by 33 CE, become moneylenders, using their contacts to access capital in the city at low interest rates before lending money out all across Italy and into the provinces at draconian rates, trousering hefty margins.

Seeing that the treasonous senatorial class were up to their gills in debt and land speculation, Tiberius stipulated that senators must keep a certain percentage of their total income in their Italian lands, forcing them to sell speculative land in the provinces to raise cash. Land being dumped on the market at such short notice triggered land prices to fall, but the debts that the senators had incurred to buy the land remained the same. Their balance sheets imploded. All the while, banks which had until recently been making loans started to call them in. The available money supply contracted suddenly, as rich Romans with gold and silver hoarded these precious metals.

The Tiberian credit crunch may have been 2,000 years ago, but human behaviour when it comes to money hasn't changed much over the centuries. We saw similar dynamics play out during the Great Depression. After the 1929 stock market crash, the bubble burst and in the resulting panic the price of land and other assets fell. People anxiously hoarded gold, realising that it was a precious store of value. However, the more they stockpiled, the more the price of gold rose, and the more liquidity drained from the system. The same thing happened in Tiberius' Rome almost two millennia earlier. A liquidity crisis quickly morphed into a bankruptcy crisis, heightening anxiety and fear. All of Rome wanted gold and silver, but it was being hoarded. Liquidity, the ephemeral supply of credit that is based on confidence and is necessary to lubricate the financial engine, had vanished. Rome faced a crisis.

Lender of last resort

When things turn sour, and prices start to fall, debtors must sell good assets to pay for debts on bad assets. Indebted Romans had to sell prime real estate in Rome, Capri or Naples to pay for their reckless investments in, for example, Syria or Egypt. The collapse in land values in the provinces caused prestige land values in Italy to fall too. As with the subprime crisis in 2008, the market in 33 CE Rome was prone to this sort of contagion because it was so tightly interrelated: new credit had been lent out for speculation against collateral that was typically a villa in Rome or the surrounding area. Tied to each other like men tied to a rope, the weight of each ruined balance sheet dragged the next one over the cliff. Banks in the great commercial cities of Tyre and Alexandria failed. The credit crunch destroyed both the reputation and the wealth of senators.

Tiberius, after much deliberation, realised he had gone too far and that things were getting out of control. Always aware of the mood of the city, he twigged that in trying to teach the conspirators a lesson and show the senators who was boss, he had imperilled the entire Roman web of credit, proving that the forces unleashed by money in a credit cycle are bigger than any politician or ruler. We will see this time and again as the story of money unfolds.

Tiberius changed tack. What is the solution to too little money? More money, and lots of it. According to Tacitus, the emperor bailed out the banks by injecting 100 million sesterces into the credit markets. In return, the emperor took collateral in the form of land worth *double* the amount of the loan. The market recalibrated. Tiberius became the 'lender of last resort' – the ancient world's central banker. He wrote the playbook for Ben Bernanke, the chairman of the US Federal Reserve during the 2008 crash, by introducing quantitative easing, Roman-style. Unlike the Fed, which in 2008 operated a 'no strings attached' bailout,[9] Tiberius used his control of the mint to demand collateral worth twice the value of any loans he lent out. Rarely can liquidity have been more expensive. Yet the senators couldn't refuse. Not playing ball on the emperor's terms would have bankrupted them, so they stumped up their land at a deep discount to avoid the debtors' prison and the shame of financial ruin. Tiberius' intervention was a master-class in what a central bank and treasury could – and should – do in a credit crunch.

Money in late Rome

The 33 CE crisis and the management of the credit cycle by Tiberius reveals how money and power, via the magic mechanism of credit, are intricately linked. The credit cycle both gives and takes away. The shift from coins to credit enabled Rome to expand its empire but it also made it financially fragile.

With credit, booms and busts are more frequent and are tied to group psychology and the pendulum of greed and fear. The credit cycle profoundly affects the economic and political cycle. The energy released by credit pushes up the price of everything, affecting the national mood, leading to spending, risk taking and all sorts of economic activity triggered by the availability of credit. Upswings can lead to costly mistakes, but the effervescence and optimism released by credit also push the economy, and, in the Roman case, the empire, forward. This forward propulsion is money in action. Without money, in its more volatile costume as credit, economic expansion, however uneven it may be, goes into reverse. And this is what happened later.

Rome had created an empire of credit to sustain a vast intercontinental commercial enterprise. However, irrespective of how integrated and dexterous the credit and legal infrastructure was, the foundation of the Roman monetary system was still coins – gold and silver. Rome's primary source of silver was the abundant mines of Iberia, but the more the Romans traded, the more silver they required; and so, despite their rapacious appetite for expansion and their plunder of the treasuries of conquered peoples, over centuries the supply of gold and silver fell short of demand. This shouldn't surprise us. There's a physical limit to how much gold and silver is out there, but an expanding economy with proliferating trade networks and a consuming upper class wants to grow and acquire new things, and the demand for coins will ultimately outstrip supply. You can't create gold out of nothing, although for centuries alchemists tried.

Credit can fill that gap, but credit functions best when people have underlying faith in basic money, the value of the coins in their pocket. Ultimately, credit leads to corresponding debts and those debts must be paid; they were paid in coins and property that was valued and denominated by the foundational currency. In the same way as debt these days – no matter how convoluted the structure might be – is expressed and settled in a currency like dollars, Roman debts were similarly expressed and settled in denarii. Tamper with the basic value of the currency and you destroy trust in the system. At the time of Tiberius, Roman coins were linked 100 per cent to silver. Over the centuries this was to change. Acquisitive Rome was faced with a dilemma: how could it keep expanding the empire's economy with a fixed supply of silver while at the same time maintaining the value of its coins?

When a nation's money supply is insufficient to meet the needs of the economy, it has three options. The first is to maintain the fixed money supply – that is, not issuing any new coins – but this means if there is an increase in trade or production leading to a rise in goods in circulation, the price of everything, including wages, must fall. If there are debts in the economy, the fall in wages will mean that the existing debts are impossible to pay back. People will be working more and more to pay off the same debt, and obviously this leads to defaults. This process in economics is called debt deflation. In the 1930s, America experienced debt deflation, leading to mass default, and a recession spiralled into a depression.

The second option for a country with a silver or gold deficit is to acquire more precious metal, either by trade, borrowing or plunder. The Romans traded and borrowed but ultimately such a militaristic society was always going to rely on plunder. Even so, eventually the Romans ran out of places with silver and gold mines to conquer.

The third approach is subterfuge. A country can try to pull the wool over people's eyes and revert to trickery by debasing the currency. You can get away with this for a while, but people see through it and, ultimately, the debased currency leads to hyperinflation. This is the approach the Romans took.

Debasement means the mint tampers with the metal component of the coins, adding less precious silver or gold in favour of more abundant and less valuable metals like copper. Not long after the reign of Tiberius, the emperor Nero couldn't resist debasing the currency. He calculated that he could deceive the general population, siphoning off precious gold to mint into extra coins for himself. And we will see that, despite his libertine reputation, in matters of debasement Nero was only in the halfpenny place compared to what came after him.

Debasement blues

By the time we get to 260 CE, when the emperor Gallienus ruled the roost, Rome's silver coins had 60 per cent less silver than when Tiberius was top dog. As it took 200 years to debase the coin by 60 per cent, that gradual debasement was acceptable because the economy had expanded by far more than 60 per cent over the same period. However, what happened to Roman money in the next eight years was abnormal.

Rome in the third century CE faced several existential crises that threatened the imperial order, manifesting themselves both externally and internally. Centuries of being the world's only superpower gave Romans the impression of an unassailable realm, but cracks were emerging in the system that Augustus, Tiberius' predecessor and the founding emperor, had established. Under this system, as long as the tax base was maintained, the army fed, paid and looked after, and the frontiers secured and stable, the empire could remain more or less prosperous, unified and coherent. However, in the third century CE, with the emergence of the Sasanian Empire in the east, Rome was faced for the first time with a muscular power that could be said to be its equal. At around the same time, in the west, on the Germanic borders, the Roman army was experiencing shock defeats. With less secure borders and the possibility that the empire might, for the first time in 400 years, be retreating, the tax base began to shrink. As it became harder to enforce taxes abroad, taxation at home, on those who were easy to tax, shot up. All the while, Gallienus continued to spend lavishly and paid for this largesse by constantly debasing the currency, reinforcing the sense of an empire unmoored. Did the debasement of Roman money lead to the empire's weakness or did imperial weakness lead to the debasement of Roman money?

Gallienus managed to cut the silver content to only 4 per cent over his eight short years on the throne. He was minting increasingly worthless coins hand over fist. Such debasement of the currency suggests a breakdown of the legendarily efficient Roman taxation system. It is not necessary to debase the currency if taxes are flowing into the state's coffers. It is only when taxes stop flowing, when the state runs out of money, that a country needs to debase its currency to avoid economic stagnation. The very acceleration of the debasement under Gallienus evidences governmental chaos and supports the fact that Rome was losing its power in the regions.

In desperation, Gallienus introduced a new coin to replace the already debased but centuries-old denarius. This new coin, called the antoninianus, was supposed to be worth two denarii but in truth contained far less silver, and the resulting hyper-inflation caused panic among ordinary Romans. Who could they trust? In the end, Roman coins had so little metal and were so fragile that the imprint of the emperor could only

be minted on one side. In 284 CE, amid monetary pandemonium, a new emperor came to power.

Conditions of complete institutional breakdown, where
trust in the central power of Rome had evaporated, enabled
a man like Diocletian – a soldier from Dalmatia – to emerge
as emperor. When the economy is stable, succession tends to
be a fairly steady process from one ruler to the next. When
the world is in a state of flux, everything is up for grabs.
During the anarchy of hyperinflation, Diocletian, a hard man,
made his move. A kind of Roman Harry Truman, he spent
twenty years trying to sort out Roman money, ill-advisedly
resorting to a variety of price caps and interest rate ceilings.
His efforts may have brought consumer prices down, but the
consequence of caps and ceilings at a time when inflation was
still high, and the memory of hyperinflation fresh, undermined
the fragile working of the credit system.

Every credit system is based on lenders having the incentive
to lend and borrowers the incentive to borrow, *willingly*, at a
rate of interest that rewards one but does not punish the other
too much. Scholars of the period note that around the time
of Diocletian, we see the disappearance of references to the
deposit banking system that was once the bedrock of Roman
money.[10] Could Diocletian's efforts to reimpose monetary
order after Gallienus' delinquency have made things worse?
Consider his 12 per cent cap on legal interest rates, introduced
to stop predatory lending. If the rate of inflation remained
above 12 per cent, which it did, what incentive was there to
lend? Lending dried up, which might explain the disappearance
of references to bank deposits in Roman historical sources
after 300 CE. It's not difficult to see how the credit system
failed to recover from such a period of hyperinflation. By the
twilight years of the empire, Roman merchants were invoicing

each other in commodities rather than money, which is precisely what happens when people are terrified of inflation.

There can be little doubt that destroying the state with inflation was not the intention of the Roman leaders of the third century CE. But could it have been the result of their actions? The fall of Rome is a subject that has attracted immense interest and there is little agreement about why the western Roman Empire disintegrated. Not too long ago, an exhaustive survey of the various explanations found that 210 different causes had been proposed by historians from antiquity to the present.[11] This isn't an argument we're going to settle here. However, it is worth considering the notion that money and credit sustained the Roman Empire, leading to amazing feats of financial innovation that for hundreds of years greatly enhanced the coherence and reach of Rome. The destruction of Roman money and the beginning of the destruction of the western empire happened at around the same time. Is this a coincidence?

Just as the expansion of empire took time, the disintegration happened gradually, but could the degeneration have been triggered by hyperinflation and the destruction of the credit system? Did money kill the Roman Empire? We'll never know, but of the 210 different reasons cited by historians, the death of Roman money is surely up there.

PART 2:

MEDIEVAL MONEY

6

TWILIGHT OF THE FEUDAL ECONOMY

Dark Ages

Imagine it's sometime between 900 and 1000 CE and you are a farmer somewhere in northwestern Europe. You can't say where, precisely, because you have never seen a map and have little knowledge of the world outside your hamlet. All that you know is tied up with farming. A local baron owns your land, and he professes fealty to a king. Nobody you know can read, write or count beyond their fingers and toes. You're left to your own devices. Unfortunately, you don't have any devices. This, as we'll see, is a problem.

Being a farmer in northwestern Europe in the early years of the tenth century is hard. You eke out a living trying to grow enough food to feed yourself, while giving anything extra to the baron. You've never heard of a command and control economy, but you're living in one. We could call it the bully and plunder economy. In feudal societies, the top dogs bullied and plundered those below. We are a long way – over thirteen centuries – from the Greek notion of the civic-minded citizen in his representative republic. In this part of Europe, civilisation had gone backwards. Life might be better if you lived somewhere with more sun and less rain, but you can't leave. Your home is surrounded by an impenetrable and terrifying woodland. In fact, the fairy stories you tell your children feature the horror of the dark forest. Everything you own you must plough back into the earth to survive. The bare patch of land that you have cleared, a back-mangling job, is always flooding. Winter is coming and, because of the crop failure, it looks like another year of boiling tree bark and begging for charity or dying of hunger.

There is small succour at the end of the week, when you and your family traipse 10 miles to the nearest parish. There, a man in special robes and a pointy hat speaks in parables in a language you don't understand. But you've been told the basic gist of it: suffering in life is OK, because when you die, you'll go to heaven. Oh, and by the way, for the privilege of getting you into heaven, these people in the chapel ask for a tithe to ensure safe passage. Your least grimy, least blighted crops must go to the priest. And for that you should be grateful.

It was called the Dark Ages for a reason.

No money, no progress

In terms of economic development, Europe in what we now call the early Middle Ages can be divided into four areas. The southeastern, or Byzantine, quadrant was the most developed, and money continued to be minted and used extensively there. The runner-up was the southwestern, or Iberian, quadrant, the frontier with the developed Islamic world. In third place was the northeastern, or Varangian, quadrant – essentially Baltic Vikings connected to the south by the Volga and Dnieper rivers – which linked the Byzantine economy with the commodity- and furs-rich region that is modern-day Russia and Ukraine. The laggard was the northwestern quadrant, the region of Europe that today is home to Germany, southern Sweden, Denmark, the Low Countries, northern France, Britain and Ireland.

In the early Middle Ages, coins were minted only sporadically across northwestern Europe despite abundant silver deposits in Bohemia.[1] Silver and copper coins had disappeared around the end of the sixth century,[2] while gold coins circulated to an ever-decreasing extent. As we know from our study of the Lydians, small denominations of coins and urban life go together, as without small coins of copper or silver, small-time, artisan-based trade – what we might call commerce – is impeded. And, not surprisingly, urban life in the region went into reverse in this era.

Unlike the Romans, who minted so many coins that they ran out of metal, the northwestern Europeans of this period reverted, in the main, to a type of barter economy where the monastery sat at the centre of the local economy and tithes were paid in crops and animals. All but the most basic artisanal products disappeared and the monastery acted as both the centre of theology and the centre of commerce, such as it was. With the lack of commerce, the world shrank. The great trading routes of the Romans, linking London to Marseille, dwindled. And without the propulsive force of money, coins and credit, critical know-how was lost. People stopped making certain things. For example, some everyday developments used by the Romans fell from use, such as dyed cloth, concrete, glazed ceramics, aqueducts (for drinking water and sanitation), paved roads, frescoes, realistic sculptures and portraiture, papyrus paper, indoor flush toilets, complex bridges, screw presses, hydraulic cranes, segmented plate armour, cavalry saddles, greenhouses, lighthouses, most glassmaking and silver-work, use of opium and scopolamine as pain relievers, and vinegar as antiseptic, central heating, and surgical tools.[3]

Progress on a variety of fronts – political, economic, cultural and social – stalled. In the absence of widespread coinage, it's highly unlikely that there was any meaningful credit. Without credit, there's not much commerce, and without commerce, what motivation does anybody have to innovate, much less to acquire new skills? Communities became isolated; contact with people other than immediate neighbours dwindled. We tend to learn and progress by copying each other. The Golden Age of the Greco-Romans was a period of shameless imitation. The Greeks imitated the Lydians and Phoenicians, who borrowed from the Egyptians and Persians, and the Romans imitated the Greeks, and so on. This process was given life by trade networks that exchanged not just money and goods but ideas and expertise. Anthropologists call this constant acquisition of knowledge our 'collective intelligence', that deep well of tricks, customs and skills passed on and dissem-inated collectively from generation to generation, which we overwrite and update as we go. In the early Middle Ages this iterative process slowed down dramatically.

In the east, the region known as the Eastern Roman or Byzantine Empire, money and commerce continued to flourish, as we will see later, and so too did cultural, scientific and economic enquiry. Europe's Iberian quadrant progressed under the influence of the Andalusian Caliphate and its connections to the more commercial Islamic world, while the Varangian quadrant, linked to the wealthy Byzantine sphere, also moved forward gradually. In contrast, the north-westerners languished, surrounded by great forests. It would take northwestern Europe a while to catch up, but when it did, its progress would change the world.

Cathedrals

Around the eve of the new millennium, 1000 CE, we see a new Europe emerging. From the eleventh century, north-western Europe began to experience an economic, financial, social and political transformation.

The eleventh century is a blurry time. Before the printed word, documents were scarce. Where written records fail, architecture can help the curious observer.[4] European Gothic cathedrals are the pyramids of the Middle Ages, and they tell a story about what was happening to money at this time. Christian celebrations to mark the first millennium after the birth of Christ led to an explosion in religious fervour. Apparitions and mystical occurrences were all the rage. Over the next 200 years, near-contemporaries of our downtrodden farmer would build some of Europe's most famous cathedrals, from Canterbury to Notre-Dame. How did we go from mud and misery to this?

In terms of their bulk and majesty, these gigantic cathedrals underscore the immense power of the Church – an institution central to the feudal economy. Power rested with the Church and the lord, the twin axis of monk and master. Monks and monasteries were financed by tithes levied on the local peasants, and more sizable donations from the local knights, who in turn squeezed yet more rents from the poor tenant peasants. The knights kept the peasantry in check with force and the Church kept the knights in check with God; both monk and master divided the spoils, propping each other up in a marriage of mutual convenience. But the key thing here is that this feudal system was stable. The size of the economy stayed the same. The new mega-churches are evidence of a step change in the amount of cash the holy men were pulling in via tithes. The economy, which had been roughly fixed for a thousand years, in the space of a century or so grew. Or rather, it exploded. This propulsion was the result of a revolutionary technology that drove the economy and fuelled a new monetary system that transformed northwestern Europe into an economic power-house.

Send in the ploughs

At this time, all wealth still stemmed from the land. From around 1000 to 1350, it is estimated that forest cover in central and western Europe declined from 40.2 per cent to 18.6 per cent of land. Europe embarked on a giant clearance: forests were burned or cut down and the subsequent land ploughed and put under tillage. This transformation suggests the arrival of some game-changing agricultural technology.

With its moist, heavy clay and rainy weather, northern European soil was difficult to churn, which was necessary if it was to become arable. Unlike the Mediterranean south, where a key concern was too little water, in the north the problem was too much. The plough our farmer would have been using was adapted from a Roman design. The wooden 'scratch ploughs', as they were called, merely scratched the surface of the earth, creating shallow gullies. These tools are ideal for use in the Fertile Crescent where topsoil is dry and water scarce, but because northern European clay is heavy, these flimsy wooden ploughs splintered in the soggy ground. As a result, northern Europeans farmed in small parcels of land, leaving the rest of the territory to forest. Their soil might have been waterlogged but it contained bountiful nutrients and much potential. Enormous yields could be generated if only they could churn the fields with a deep, incisive plough.

There were two ways you could grow the economy during the early Middle Ages. Number one: get more people. Number two: get more land. In the last chapter, we saw that the Romans invaded northern Europe to acquire more land and expand their economy. But when the Romans left, their giant armies, organisational nous and money left with them. The subsequent European population was kept in check by periodic famine, high mortality rates and disease. If the population rose too quickly, living standards would fall, badly affecting diets and making the population more vulnerable to the next poor harvest, plague, famine or flood. This conundrum, where population growth slams into the limitations of the land, would later be called the 'Malthusian trap', and the result was that living standards, or income per head, hardly budged. We will meet Malthus in a while, but for now, let's take on board the idea that the population was hemmed in by the productivity of the land. No productivity, no population growth.

Because the amount of land was fixed, and because the number of people was capped by what they could grow, the revenue of this system remained static for centuries. There were too few people to make more food, and there wasn't enough food to make more people. Without surplus food, there's no urbanisation, and therefore towns rarely grow above village size and the vast majority of people live off and on the land. But if they could figure out a way of getting more out of the land, they'd break free from this trap. More food from the same amount of land, farmed by the same number of people, would drive up farm productivity.

Introduced, it is thought from Hungary, around 1000 CE,

the heavy metal plough changed everything. It liberated huge tracts of land for tillage and, because it was so heavy, the farmers only had to plough the field once. They were getting more out and putting less in. The plough meant more bountiful and predictable harvests, leading, for the first time since the Romans, to consistent economic growth. With the new plough, agricultural surpluses expanded, pushing down the price of food, facilitating population growth and the emergence of something novel: disposable income, however meagre.[5] And maybe something even more novel: free time. The modern economy was ever so gradually beginning to take shape. But the plough, critical as it was, wasn't enough on its own. That physical technology required a social technology to organise the increasing population and its commerce more efficiently. The social technology was money, which was making a reappearance in this region after its centuries-long decline.

The return of money

Germans love beer, the more local the better, and one such regional brew is gose, which has been made for over a thousand years in the small Lower Saxony town of Goslar, nestled in the Harz mountains. It is immortalised by the scatological couplet 'Die erst Gose geht meist in die Hose' ('that first Gose goes straight to your pants') – a heavy concentration of salt in the mix delivers a shock to the digestive system with compromising results. Salty gose was well established by the early eleventh century, popular up and down the trading routes of central Germany because it was drunk by the thousands of miners who flocked to Goslar at the turn of the second millennium to prospect for silver. The abundance of new

German silver from Goslar would kickstart money back into circulation in northwestern Europe and alter the development path of the region. With the plough in one hand and a bag of silver in the other, northwestern Europeans began their march to progress.

Enormous quantities of Goslar silver were minted. In Sweden alone, archaeologists have found over 70,000 German pfennigs and over 30,000 Anglo-Saxon pennies, almost all minted between 990 and 1050. Trace elements of various minor impurities indicate that the vast majority of these coins were minted at the Rammelsberg mountain above Goslar.[6] The Swedish find suggests that the German coins made their way to England and Sweden, where they were re-minted and then used for trade across the North Sea and into the Baltics. As trade, animated by new silver coins, took off, the region saw another development. During the eleventh century, in both Germany and England, there was a significant expansion of towns and commercial centres created by royal instruction. The plough had dramatically increased agricultural productivity, releasing farmers from the land, and the new commercial trading towns began to fill up. These new towns were given the right to host a market and also to mint coins by royal charter. At a stroke, our two technologies – the plough and re-emergent money – fused, creating a new urban world.[7]

German silver travelled both to the west as far as Ireland, where mints were set up in Dublin (then a Viking settlement), and to the east as far as Kiev. All over the region, the number of mints exploded, which, taken as a crude measure of the amount of coins in circulation, suggests a phenomenal increase in monetisation. In each town, original German coins circulated in parallel with local re-minted and restamped coins.

The turn of the millennium, so often dismissed as a dark, drab and violent time, signalled the start of a new monetary economy in northwestern Europe.

With money came other changes. In many kingdoms – Bohemia, Hungary, Poland, Kievan Rus', Norway and Denmark – the first minting of coins coincided with, or came just after, the official acceptance of Christianity. In order for these formerly pagan kingdoms to convert – think of the Vikings, who dropped Thor and Odin for Jesus – their courts would have to have been influenced by Christian priests, missionaries and advisors, who came from Christian societies to the east, such as Christian Byzantium. As we've seen, coins – unlike in most of Europe – had been continuously circulating in the Byzantine Empire and were a well-understood emblem of sovereignty there. The monetary historian Peter Spufford convincingly argues that the spread of Christianity and the spread of coins were not merely coincidental.[8] They were both centralising forces. The ideas of one god in Christianity, one monarch representing god on earth, and one officially minted coin (with the king's head on it) reinforcing the king's earthly dominion fitted together in a snug, interlinked triumvirate of power: worldly, heavenly and financial.

Leaving the land

While the king might have been consolidating his power at the top, society was shifting at the bottom. With more money in circulation and fewer farmers required to produce food, less time on the farm meant more time for exploration, and at a stretch, even art and learning. Leaving the farm, workers began to specialise in trades, settling in the new officially established cities. Migration was fuelled by talk of a better life in the city. Gossip and rumour played a critical part. It has ever been thus: as teenagers brought up in a depressed Ireland of the 1980s, our chat was peppered with stories of cousins or brothers who were doing very well for themselves 'over' in London. Each success story motivated the next person to take the boat. Moving away is often an act of personal transformation, and the sovereign act of backing yourself can be enormously liberating, potentially triggering all sorts of ideas and personal ambitions.

Trade expanded, mediated by the new silver money, and artisan cottage industries developed, establishing a rudimentary market economy. Specialised artisans supplied the now wealthier 'higher ups' with what they needed, generating value by transforming raw material like wood into a secondary good such as a chair. In the new towns and villages, an intricate economy began to evolve, where the income of the baker was dependent on the spending of the tailor. Everyone's income was based on everyone else's spending: as people spent, another person's income increased. The extra income you earned became discretionary income, which you could spend or save. In this part of the world, for the first time in a millennium, a small artisan might have had something called savings. As this interrelated economy evolved, so too did the requirement for both increased coins in circulation and banks – or at least safe places – for the energetic artisan to put his cash.

In time, demand for clothes, artefacts and various status goods – from fancy dinners to silks and spices, hides and furs – would emerge. These goods were imported from the Baltics, Russia and Crimea. With increased trade came networks, relationships and new ideas. Standards became important and the artisanal class developed common rules, pooling resources to buy raw materials and formulating regulations for their market, bonded by a communal interest in establishing a reputation. Appreciating that the whole is better than the sum of the parts and collaboration is the route to innovation, artisans set up guilds, sharing skills and financial heft, allowing the many to act as one. We see evidence of craft guilds by the late eleventh and early twelfth centuries.

This new economy required a place where farmers and artisans could sell their wares, and this, together with the towns created by royal instruction, led to a rapid expansion in the number of market towns, market squares and market days. Socially, the emergence of the artisan added another permanent layer to social stratification: a new urbanised character, more sovereign in income and thought, driven by profit and money.

Urbanisation

If you were an artisan in the Middle Ages, you lived in an urban environment, quite distinct from your ancestors, those peasants on the land who were beholden to some hereditary knight or baron. Absent since the days of Rome, the figure of the merchant re-emerges in the early Middle Ages. This social change is captured by the German expression '*Stadluft macht frei*' ('the city air makes you free'). Floating in the air of the city were radical ideas of freedom and individual sovereignty, encouraging for the dissenter and the outsider. Places where tradition, family and pedigree began to become less important, cities rewarded ability, networks and grit. A bourgeois artisan making their way in the world acted as a challenge to the old order and power base of inherited family fiefdoms bolstered by religious dogma. This countervailing force of money – and its broker, the merchant – would gradually upset the powerful stranglehold of Church and squire.

Towns facilitated a certain amount of anonymity. As populations were growing and people were on the move, newly arrived city-dwellers needed surnames to distinguish themselves. It was no longer enough to be John from Nottingham, because there were loads of Johns from Nottingham. Surnames, attached to careers, solved the problem. Trades perfected in the artisanal workshop were passed from master to apprentice, which often meant from father to son. In a sense, the trade defined the individual, or at least distinguished him, and, in England, we saw the emergence of popular surnames like Bowyer (the bloke who made the bows), Fletcher (the bloke who made the arrows, from the French/Norman word *flech* for arrow) and Stringer (the bloke who made the strings for the bows).

The surname Smith, the most common surname in English, became ubiquitous due to the demand for metalwork for ploughs. The economics of name proliferation are fairly straightforward. The local smith had a reliable stream of work and income and therefore the smith's children had a better diet and more survived to have yet more children of their own. This attracted yet more peasant apprentices who would go on to become smiths. The proliferation of the artisan smith with his forge, bellows and ironwork skills also led to the popularity of the surname Kovac (and variations of it) in many Slavic languages, Schmidt in German, Forges in French, Ferrera in Portuguese and Spanish, MacGowan in Irish and so on.

Getting more from less

Productivity is the elixir of economic growth. Higher productivity drives up output per head and drives down costs per head, allowing both wages and profits to rise. This meant that the incomes of the peasant rose, but so too did the value of land. The baron, king and Church got rich as the plough pushed up productivity, leading to something we hadn't seen before: mechanisation. In these new towns, as the artisans worked away, a host of new inventions emerged that would instil notions of productivity, time and cost into people's lives. Precision engineering led to the mechanical clock, and clocks changed the world. In the new towns, nothing underscored the shift that productivity wrought more than the communal clock. The clocktower became the centre of the market town, measuring our world against time. Productivity and the clock reinforced each other, as the mechanical clock made our sense of time more granular. The farmer's output could be gauged on the basis of how much grain was harvested over a period of hours and, of course, this was expressed in terms of that other precise technology, the new silver money.

As the barons and cardinals became richer, they became adventurous. What was the point of having the new wealth associated with productivity and money if you weren't going to use it? The Norman overlords of northwestern Europe began to get ideas about conquest and, blessed by the Church, they used their new wealth to finance military expeditions to Jerusalem. The Crusades would not have happened when they did had it not been for the agricultural surplus and wealth generated by the plough.

From the start of the eleventh century, after the introduction of the plough and the reintroduction of money via silver

German coins, northwestern Europe experienced an extraordinary transformation. Populations exploded and healthier, richer northern Europeans began to get itchy feet. Europe was now on the clock, and time was money. The Dark Ages were well and truly over.

7

SARACEN MAGIC

Mental arithmetic

In the summer of 1185, a young man stood on the very quay where the Black Death would, years later, slip silently into Europe. The Sicilian port of Messina was an important hub of Mediterranean trade. Buzzing with hustlers, slaves and farmers, the port and its taverns overflowed with Norman Crusaders on their way to the east. In the alleyways, money-changers exchanged different coins from right across the Mediterranean. On the dock, North African merchants hawked eastern spices and saffron heading west, and local wheat bound for Europe to the north shared the quay with leathers and fine ceramics on their way south. Ethnic differences, so fundamental at the time, melted away somewhat when it came to dealing in the international language of money.

As the Arab merchants bargained, our young man, Leonardo of Pisa, noted the prices, amounts and quality of the goods on offer. Far from his Pisan home, Leonardo meandered through the markets, breathing in the smell of pepper, cinnamon, cardamom, nutmeg, almonds, camphor, myrrh, sticky African resins, gum from Ethiopia and Egyptian mastic.

He listened intently as the Arab traders ran rings around even the most experienced merchants from Genoa, regarded as Europe's sharpest. The Arabs had one tool the Europeans lacked: they could count in their heads. Leonardo of Pisa could see that while mental arithmetic was beyond the ability of even Europe's most studious scholars and monks, the average Arab date seller could calculate weights, ratios and prices with lightning-quick accuracy. Precision with numbers gave the Arabs an edge. Where did they learn this magic?

The secret Saracen tool was mathematics. Anchoring this new way of thinking was the concept of zero, which allowed the Arabs to count in large numbers, to mentally conceive of balance sheets with positive and negative numbers, and to use an amazing tool, algebra, derived from the eighth-century Arab mathematician al-Khwarizmi.[1] These advantages put the Arabs on a different commercial footing to their European competitors. While European traders relied on the clumsy abacus, a technology unchanged since Roman times, the Arabs displayed extraordinary mental agility that allowed them to express an amount of dates, figs or raisins in terms of an amount of wheat, corn or nutmeg. They accepted various coins, from places like Alexandria and Cyprus, and gave change back in the local Sicilian currency, the follaro, without missing a beat. The Europeans were dealing with money. The Arabs were dealing with finance.

Sicily was the centre of a trading web that extended from Alexandria to Genoa, via Tripoli, Al' Cant (Alicante in Spain today) and Marseille. One such trading post was Bejaia, in what is now Algeria. The dark Gothic cathedrals of the Normans spurred a demand for candles. Beeswax was the premier industry in Bejaia, which gives us the root of the modern French word for candle, *bougie*. European merchants who visited Bejaia, attracted by the beeswax industry, came across Hindu-Arabic numerals.

Leonardo's father was a Pisan official based in Bejaia, and his upbringing exposed him to Arab educators, setting him apart from his contemporaries in Italy. While they were learning scripture and Virgil by heart, he, under Arab tutors, was learning an entirely new language and technology: algebra. While they were using deductive reasoning, he was deploying inductive analysis. Armed with this knowledge, Leonardo of Pisa, better known as Fibonacci, would change the face of European mathematics and set out a new template for sophisticated balance-sheet management and bookkeeping. Innovations like these would drive a new era of commercialism, wealth creation and, ultimately, the patronage of the arts that was the basis for the Renaissance. It might not be too far a stretch to say that without Leonardo da Pisa, there is no Leonardo da Vinci.

Not everybody was happy with this new development. William of Malmesbury, the monk and celebrated English historian of the twelfth century, referred to Arabic numerals as 'saracen magic'. This idea of magic stemmed from the ability of the Arabs to arrive at mathematical conclusions that seemed like sorcery. Who was whispering to them? How did they know how to calculate in their heads using huge numbers? Malmesbury feared the power of mathematics and its foreignness. In his view, Jerusalem had just been recaptured from the heathen by the courageous Crusaders for the glory of God. What good would it be to capture the seat for Christianity if the magic of Islam captured the minds of the merchants of Venice?

Zero

Embraced to revolutionary effect by the Arabs, the concept of zero had been rejected by Christians and the philosophies that Christianity was based on. Zero was the void and Greek philosophy refuted the void. Those who framed what became Western thought – Pythagoras, Aristotle, Plato and Ptolemy – all agreed that there could be no nothing. The Greeks thought they could define everything by provable ratios, patterns and geometric symmetry where everything has a relationship to everything else. The West avoided zero for centuries, with enormously negative consequences for science, commerce, accountancy and a host of other daily activities.

While Europe and Christianity turned their back on zero, the Hindu civilisation of India had no such qualms about voids and infinities. They were working with zero from as early as the third century CE. Unlike Christians, who hope their soul will end up in heaven, the objective for a Hindu is nothingness. Other than cremation in Varanasi, the only way to liberate the soul from the cycle of rebirth is to achieve the void by understanding the true nature of reality. When the soul leaves the body that dies, its destination in a new body is determined by the good or bad karma that has accrued through behaviour in life. Through endless rounds of rebirth, the soul learns, and when enough good karma has accrued, the soul is freed from the body into a purely spiritual existence, at one with the universe – in other words, infinity. Today, Indians laugh at the joke: What did the Indians give the world? Answer: Nothing. Meaning, in effect, everything. Perhaps the Hindu faith allowed Indian mathematicians to take to zero with gusto? Maybe it was part of their understanding of the vastness of the universe and humanity's inconsequential role in it?

At its mathematical essence, zero allows us to go from positive numbers to negative numbers. We pass through zero to get to the negative. If your mathematics is always based on counting things, as it was for the Greeks and Babylonians, it's hard to imagine going below or through zero into negative numbers. Negative numbers mean the absence of something. Even today, the concept of negative numbers is surprisingly difficult for children to wrap their heads around: ask any primary school teacher and they will concur that children find it confusing initially. For the Greeks and subsequent Christian thinkers – and our own children, for that matter – maths is real, not abstract. You teach a child that one and one is two by holding one apple in one hand, and another apple in your other hand. Putting them together you have two. Likewise for the ancient Christians: two cows were something they could get their heads around but negative two cows were not.

Money makes zero real

There is one place where the concept of zero, and less than zero, makes complete sense: when we are talking about money. Creditors *have* money (positive numbers) and debtors *owe* money (negative numbers). Another attribute of zero is that it can be used as a placeholder. Without zero, how do you represent large numbers, like 1,000,000, and how do you subtract, add, divide and multiply them? In practical terms, zero propelled the ancient world into the digital age, a world of modern numerals, big numbers, precision and empiricism, with enormous ramifications for money and commerce.

When the Arabs conquered the great Persian Empire in the seventh century, they learned the Hindu numerals, which the Persians had borrowed from further east, representing one, tens and hundreds. Arab mathematicians adopted this magical technology. The Arabs called zero *sifr* or *as-sifr*, derived from *shunya* in Sanskrit, meaning 'the void'. In modern French, *chiffre* means figure. In Hebrew, zero is *sifra*. As this contagious terminology jumped cultures and nationalities, the Arabic *sifr* became *zefirum* in the Latinised language of the Normans, and then *zefiro*, *zephyr* and *zefro*, eventually morphing into zero in modern English.[2]

Arabic scholars played around with the possibilities of zero, setting up schools in their great centres of learning, from Baghdad to Córdoba. These intellectual hubs doubled up as commercial hubs of an overlapping system of commerce and culture that proliferated across the Arab world, a vast free-trade zone where camel caravans trekked across the desert and ships linked the Mediterranean to the coastal cities of the Levant. Spices, silks, salt and slaves were exchanged for muslin and cotton from India via the Red Sea, shepherded by the traders of Muscat, whose dates and figs were also in huge demand. Goods were traded out of Egypt to Genoa and on to the great Carolingian cities of Avignon and Marseille, as people, ideas and money zigzagged the Mediterranean.

We know how zero and numerals jumped from the Indians to the Arabs, but how, during the Crusades, when the Arabs and the Christians were sworn enemies, did this Arabic technology get into the hands of Christians? The transmission mechanism was Norman Sicily.

Why Sicily?

The arrival of the plough, the enrichment of northern Europe and the explosion of its population had a surprising and unintended consequence: the Crusades. Without the surplus agricultural wealth associated with the plough, the Crusades couldn't have been financed and all the local squires would have remained knocking around the marshy wetland they called home. Against all odds, Sicily did not become embroiled in the destructive Crusades. Home to Byzantine Greeks, Latinised Norman Christians, Arab Muslims and Sephardic Jews, the island grew rich and sophisticated in the twelfth century, helped greatly by its refusal to go to war. What was going on in Sicily that was not going on elsewhere?

Its prime location, at the frontier between Europe and North Africa, made Sicily the epicentre of Mediterranean trade. With all sorts of people coming and going, the island had long been cosmopolitan, allowing religious and ethnic variety to flourish. Wave after wave came and settled. The Phoenicians were followed by the Greeks, and the island was a key battleground in the Punic Wars between the Romans and Carthaginians. Much later, by 535 CE, the Byzantines had taken it, only to be overcome by the North African Muslims around 900 CE.[3] This pattern of conflict, occupation and peace, arising from the island's geographic significance and resultant economic prosperity, led to an unusually multicultural society, and among the more unexpected visitors to Sicily were the Normans.

The success of Norman mercenaries in Sicily is one of the more eye-popping geo-strategic stories of the twelfth century. In 1160, a band of Norman tough guys who had been throwing their weight around Calabria were invited to Sicily by one of the two competing Arabic emirs on the island. For a fine purse, the Emir of Syracuse and Catania, Ibn Thumna, encouraged these Normans, under the leadership of a man named Roger, to attack Ibn al-Hawwàs, the Emir of Agrigento and Castrogiovanni.

Normans were vigilantes for hire across Europe at this time;

this favoured side-hustle kept them in wine, goblets, fair maidens and stirrups. In 1167, far to the north in Ireland, the aptly entitled Strongbow was 'invited in' by a local Gaelic chieftain who, in a spot of inter-clan bother, called on these French-speaking hard men to do a job for him. Strongbow's arrival constituted the first – but not last – invasion of Ireland from England. As hired muscle, Strongbow was probably expected to take his money and leave, but he and his Norman fighters decided to stay in Ireland. They never left.

The Normans in Sicily, as would be the case in Ireland, took a look around, understood the potential of the island, exploited the divided nature of the local rulers and decided to take command and colonise. The Normans in Sicily found themselves in an alien culture, with different languages, customs, clans and affinities. Rather than fight the diversity, they assimilated, managing to integrate and prosper. In Ireland, the French-speaking Normans fitted in so well that to this day they are described as becoming 'more Irish than the Irish themselves'. Everyday Irish language is peppered with Norman French words such as *airgead*, meaning money, from *argent*; *garsún*, meaning boy, from *garçon*; *seomra*, meaning room, from *chambre*; and *eaglais*, meaning church, from *église*. In Sicily, these former vigilantes navigated a new direction, eschewing violence abroad, making sure that when the eastern Mediterranean plunged itself into sectarian brutality, Sicily took a different path.

French sociologist Marcel Mauss once observed that in order to trade, humans first must put down the spear. This was true in Sicily, where the trading dynamic dampened conflicts between the main religious and ethnic tribes on the island. Indeed, cross-cultural trade was inherent to Sicily's economic value. Grand Count Roger I, and later the notably far-seeing Roger II, embraced not just trade but also the dissemination of knowledge, particularly mathematics and the adoption of zero, ultimately introducing Hindu-Arabic numerals. By making counting, multiplying and dividing far easier than the old cumbersome Roman numerals (just try adding XXVIII and MXIV in your head without translating it into our numerals first), Hindu-Arabic numerals signified that Sicily was a modern commercial state, in contrast to the states at war all around it.

Many centuries later, Kemal Atatürk would do something similar when, as president of the new Turkish Republic, he abandoned what he thought of as the backward Arabic script of the Ottomans and the Caliphate for the modern Latin script of the West to show the world the new secular – and thus modern – Turkey. For Atatürk, changing the alphabet consti-tuted a highly visible and practical break from the fracturing old Ottoman Empire. For Sicily's reforming Normans, the introduction of these numerals was an equally powerful signal. Arabic numerals constituted the future; the Roman world, with its unsophisticated numbering system, was ancient.

In Sicily, Christians and Muslims came together through business. Muslims constituted most of the merchant class, along with a small but vibrant Jewish community and some Greek Byzantine Christians. Most farmers were Muslim. A combination of well-irrigated pastures and volcanic soil rich in nutrients, along with hot summers and mild winters, made Sicily perfect for agriculture – a thousand years earlier, it had been known as the 'breadbasket of Rome'. Wheat was still its main export and merchants from all quarters of the Mediterranean also traded salt, coral, sulphur and iron there.

Few ethnic rows are made worse by mutual profit and, astutely, the Normans had a policy of allowing Muslim communities to operate with a significant level of autonomy. They also adopted many Muslim customs that were deemed economically efficient, such as the imposition of a tax based on the *jizya* model that had existed under Muslim rule, allowing for group-targeted taxation. Arabic, the language of commerce, rather than Norman French, the language of the court, remained the official language of the chancery (or the *diwan*). Traditionally, Normans in Europe named their towns after saints, but this Sicilian branch instead chose to call the island's main port Messina after Al-Medina, which itself is Arabic for city, and the names of its three other cities underscored their different cultural provenances: Marsala is *mars al-Allah*, the harbour of Allah; Syracuse is the Greek name for the marsh in Corinth that the island's first Greek colonists came from in 400 BCE; and Palermo comes from the Greek *panormos*, meaning sheltered harbour.

Normans, Arabs, Jews and Byzantines lived together in relative harmony. As Sicily's twelfth-century ruler Roger II put it, '*varietas populorum nostro regno subiectorum*' – 'variety is the spice of life'. While the rest of the world, from Britain to Egypt, was taking sides in the Crusades, killing, butchering and destroying, this exceptional multi-ethnic Sicilian soup of ideas, goods, money and people mixed and traded together. Tolerant Norman Sicily experienced a golden age of enquiry and innovation in architecture, medicine and science while speaking the universal language of money, markets and profit.

Plurality

In the late twelfth century, Sicily's maritime network of trading routes linked Persia with Normandy, Moroccan Berbers with

Constantinople Greeks, bishops with imams, and Orthodox priests with Kabbalist rabbis. Norman overlords, Arabic mathematicians, Byzantine merchants, Jewish astronomers and Lombardian bankers lived and traded together, swapping information, knowledge and techniques in a myriad of tongues: French, Latin, Arabic, Greek, Castilian and Ladino.

This inclusiveness is evident in the coins the Sicilians minted. A nation's coin is more than a unit of account; it is a symbol of what the nation believes in. Since the day that Alexander the Great decided to put his image on his coins, the signalling power of the coin has been understood by all rulers. Why do you think Cuban notes are emblazoned with a picture of Che Guevara? Or that the old Soviet ten-rouble note had a picture of Lenin next to the hammer and sickle?

The follaro, the standard minted silver coin of Norman Sicily, emblemised the island's synthesis of cultures. On one side, an Arabic inscription denoted the date of minting according to the Arabic calendar, while on the other side was inscribed the first and last letters of 'Christ' in the Latin alphabet.

In 1132, Roger II commissioned his magnificent Palatine Chapel in Palermo, putting the island's three great civilisations on display. Architecturally, Latin Normans, Greek Byzantines and the Muslim Arabs had evolved their individual styles, and rather than adhere to one, Roger incorporated all three in his citadel of power and faith.

Due to the Islamic ban on images of the Prophet and idolatry in any form, and having borrowed Persian knowledge of fine rugs, gardens, water fountains and sumptuous buildings, Arabic culture had cultivated an intricate, pattern-based style of decorative carving and design that became known as the Arabesque. If the Arabs prided themselves on the austere, understated but beautiful Arabesque style, the Greek Byzantines preferred full-on, in-your-face bling. Byzantine Orthodox churches were altars to ostentatious displays of opulence. Understanding both of these cultural biases, Roger constructed his Roman Christian cathedral in Palermo with a nod to both the Arabic and Byzantine Orthodox traditions in an architectural synthesis of all three. With exquisite wood carving in Saracen design, the ceiling is pure Arabesque, while the pillars are adorned with replicas of Byzantine golden mosaics. The use of Greek inscriptions in the chapel of St Peter is also indicative of the parity of symbols throughout the cathedral's design, with Roger saying to his Arab and Byzantine subjects that they have a place not only in Sicilian society but in its most holy place too.

Even the ceremonial robe that Roger would have worn for all official occasions signified that the three cultures were valued. The Norman overlord wore a mantle of gold embroidered silk set with pearls, enamel plaques, sapphires and a ruby. The cloth was made in the Byzantine Empire and embroidered by Muslim craftsmen in Sicily. The Arabic inscription running along the seam tells us it was made in Palermo in the year 528 of the Islamic Hijri calendar (1133 CE) and lists the blessings and virtues bestowed on the king. Imagine the Norman ruler, the head of a civilisation of religious knights, standing beside his Roman bishops celebrating Easter in his cathedral with its Muslim and Orthodox influences, wearing a piece of Middle Ages haute couture that emphasised the plurality of Sicilian society.

With all the island's wealth, its fine goods, and the benefits of both peace and co-operation, is it any wonder that Roger decided to give the Crusades a wide berth?

The world's first business bestseller

In 1202, having spent years learning the secrets of Saracen magic from the traders of Bejaia and witnessing algebra in commercial action on the docks of Messina, Leonardo of Pisa – the man who we know as Fibonacci – published the book that would transform commerce in Europe.[4] It was called *Liber Abaci*, the Book of Calculations, and in it Fibonacci set out algebraic principles that, essentially, enabled merchants to make money. He had the journalistic gift of making the strange seem commonplace and the tangential seem relevant. By posing real-life examples of conundrums faced by traders, Fibonacci brought maths to life. Had he written in the language of the academy, the book would have had limited relevance. But because he wrote it for the merchants, Fibonacci revealed the true genius of the great teacher: an ability to escape from the tyranny of his peer group. If he had tried to convince the scholarly monks, his work would have been picked apart by vindictive 'experts' and its credibility undermined. Taking the route of all great communicators, Fibonacci sidestepped the gatekeepers and went straight to those who would get the most value from this new technology: the merchants.

Liber Abaci became the go-to book for traders and an essential tool of international commerce. It could be regarded as the first bestselling business book. Revelatory as well as revolutionary, it explained how to calculate interest rates, how to circumvent the Church's usury laws, apportion profits, and assess revenues and costs. It gave merchants a roadmap to express their produce in terms of someone else's products, in fractions and in a common currency. The fact that the book devoted many pages to puzzles regarding interest rates, banks and usury made it quite provocative: the Church looked unfavourably on it as a challenge to its monopoly on the money-lending business. Condemning moneylenders to hell is a pretty good way of protecting your turf: damnation has the added upside of never being challenged in court. Of all those most threatened by the financialisation of European small business, the biggest, most successful and longest-surviving multinational the world had ever seen, the Church, with its corporate head-quarters in Rome, had a lot to be worried about.

One of Fibonacci's most consequential insights concerned the relationship between money and time. He teased out what economists call the time value of money, which is better understood as the financial equivalent of 'it's better to have an egg today than a chicken tomorrow'. This idea that money today is better than a promise of money tomorrow is what underpins all borrowing and lending. It's what we call the opportunity cost. If I lend to you, it means that you have the money and I can't use it, so there is a cost to me. The money I earn back from you after you pay me back must be adjusted for the opportunity that I have forgone. The way to calculate this is to divide all the money I get back from you by the prevailing interest rate. Why the interest rate? Because the interest rate is what I would have got by simply keeping my money on deposit. We all intuitively understand that now, but back then, giving money a value over time was revolutionary. It also allowed merchants and bankers to discriminate between various projects that they were being asked to finance. The Sumerians had introduced interest rates thousands of years previously, but Fibonacci made the time value of money more accessible by setting this theory out in algebraic terms that were easy to calculate. Fibonacci's clarity brought these ideas to both the merchant class and the banking class. And it led, inexorably, to their combination: the merchant banker.

The balance sheet

The Pucci Palace in Florence, dating back to the fourteenth century, has extraordinary rooftop views of Brunelleschi's cathedral dome. Whatever you say about the Florentine merchant princes, they were good at holding onto their brass. The palazzo's library contains vast archives with ledgers, documents and correspondence to and from merchants, agents and buyers across the world. The Florentine merchant was a committed letter writer and underpinning most of these letters was the ledger, containing the balance sheets of a whole host of businesses. The balance sheet was the main weapon of the new class of merchants, and it would never have come about were it not for Fibonacci's numerical evangelism.

Writing about 200 years after Fibonacci, the monk Luca Pacioli (who taught mathematics to both Leonardo da Vinci and Albrecht Dürer) described the 'Italian' approach to book-keeping. This double-entry bookkeeping revolved around having a set of accounts, drawn up by merchant bankers and their clerks, for households, companies and wealthy individuals, set out in debits and credits. Each debit had to have a corresponding credit on the balance sheet and at the end of whatever period they were measuring, these accounts had to balance. Once the accounts were settled and everyone was paid, the process could start again. Obviously, fastidious double-entry bookkeeping reduces the margin for error, even in complicated accounts, but more than that, once accounts become commonplace, ordinary people begin to think of the world in terms of accounts. Today, it is not unusual to hear national news broadcasts refer to the 'current account' of the country – never mind a company, a football club or a household. This way of looking at the world, which is unlike anything that went before, began with Fibonacci's introduction of 'saracen magic' to Europe.

Possibly *Liber Abaci*'s most profound ramification was as intellectual as it was practical: it nudged more and more people towards reasoned, quantitative enquiry. At the core of quantifiable mathematics is the notion of precision. The ledger is the foundation of reasoned conclusion. As they say: the numbers don't lie. The old world was one of conjecture, miracles and guesswork. Fibonacci's new world rested on objective, quantifiable value and empiricism – a novel and fundamental concept. The human mind's capacity to reason with precision is one of the great breakthroughs in our comprehension of the world around us. Mathematics is the technology that allows us to move from the vague to the meticulous, from nebulous guesswork to exact fact. Fibonacci changed how we learned, taught and calculated. The feudal economy was giving way to another age: the Age of Money.

God-fearing Florentines initially banned Arabic numerals, but suppression rarely works, particularly if a new technology is capturing people's imaginations. It is impossible to stop a powerful technology. Even more critically, it is impossible to stop a powerful technology that enables people to make money. By the end of the thirteenth century the Florentines realised their folly and, as commercial players, introduced zero to their world through special business schools. By 1350, Hindu-Arabic mathematics was so popular that over a thousand pupils within the walls of Florence were attending special 'reckoning schools'. These reckoning schools, the Harvard MBAs of the fourteenth century, were based on the transformative mathematics of Fibonacci. Just as MBAs worldwide have spawned a managerial caste – the foot soldiers of the corporate world – the reckoning schools produced their own commercial caste.

Notable pupils of these Florentine schools were Niccolò Machiavelli and Leonardo da Vinci. Even Dante Alighieri, great critic of the bankers' excess in Florence, sent his son to such a school to learn the dark arts of commerce.

Having numbers, balance sheets and mathematics was one thing, but to get the best use of these innovations, the Florentines developed a stable currency they could believe in, one that would give merchants confidence and security. A new sort of money was entering the world via Florence. And Dante, Florence's most famous son, saved a special place in his *Inferno* for those who abused it.

8

DARKNESS INTO LIGHT

Divine comedy

Beloved of Seamus Heaney, Samuel Beckett and James Joyce, *The Divine Comedy* is regarded by many as the finest work of European literature. Oscar Wilde asked for a copy of the *Inferno*, the first part of the *Comedy*, to ruminate on in his own personal inferno, Reading Gaol. Primo Levi, like many Italians, knew much of the *Comedy* by heart and in his memoir *If This Is a Man*, set in the living hell of Auschwitz, Levi recounts trying to recall its lines to prove that art and civilisation lived on even amid the Nazi attempt to snuff out both.

Born in 1265, Dante was a son of medieval Florence, a city quite different to the shining citadel that had emerged by the time he wrote his masterpiece.[1] Dante's *Divine Comedy* – written in political exile between, roughly, 1308 and 1321 – maps a progression from Gothic darkness to pre-Renaissance light. He had lived through breakneck economic growth, enormous political upheaval and disruptive social change. Dante's Florence was an experiment, a cocksure metropolis, a self-governing city-republic run by educated laymen and mercantile guilds, playing the two continental power bases, the Vatican and the Holy Roman Empire, against each other. In one corner was Rome, a strict vertical hierarchy run by clerics, under the pope. In the other, the Holy Roman Emperor, descendant of Charlemagne, ruler of vast territories from Italy to Germany. In the middle, between these two superpowers – one armed with guns, the other with God – lay the plucky little Republic of Florence, armed only with a promise. Risky business. While Florence could be crushed by the combined might of both powers, it had a trump card: it embodied an idea. That idea was the possibility of upward social mobility based on a new form of government, and this promise of individual transformation was seductive.

From 1250 to 1300, the population of Florence grew from around 20,000 to 100,000.[2] Giovanni Villani, the famous chronicler of the city, notes that by 1338, Florence hosted 600 notaries, 146 bakers, 100 apothecaries, 60 surgeons, 30 hospitals, 80 banking houses and firms of moneylenders and 10,000 children in elementary schools.[3] The Florentines would call their city, with its magnificent public spaces, art, architecture and palaces, the New Athens. The transformation of Florence from a small provincial town to the city of Boccaccio, and later Brunelleschi, Leonardo and Galileo – the cradle of the Renaissance and the fulcrum of extraordinary artistic, intellectual and political dynamism – was forged by a period of intense financial and civic innovation. A model state, a centre of commerce, learning, beauty and a form of democracy, Florence was a merchant city, among the first of its kind. Rather than being organised around titles, knights or feudal overlords ruling by divine right or aristocratic privilege, Florence was organised by money.

At the centre of this universe was the florin, their gold coin. While the Vatican had scripture and the emperor had legions, the New Athens had money. And with money, it would change the way European urban civilisation developed. It is difficult to overstate how different such a city-state was from the prevailing mode of feudal rule by aristocrats, the Church and warrior knights. In contrast to that form of medieval and overwhelmingly agrarian state, Florence evolved as a sort of bourgeois democracy, run by elected guilds of merchants and their financiers, the merchant bankers who travelled and traded around the globe from London to Cairo. The extent of their trade networks and the casual cosmopolitanism of the people is evidenced by the wide-ranging stories in Boccaccio's post-Black Death *Decameron*, whose characters, by the 1340s, were travelling from Beirut to Spain and Paris to Alexandria.

Italy in the fourteenth century was the trade nexus of Europe, the natural stop-off point between east and west, and Florence was fast becoming its commercial, financial and intellectual epicentre.

Western Europe was in the grip of an early stage of unprecedented globalisation, a great opening, with a merchant class emerging as its ascendant adventurers. Globalisation then, as today, was an urban phenomenon and the cities, rather than the countryside, flourished with trade. In economic terms, cities create 'value added'. Merchants bought wool from peasants, fashioned products and then sold on to the final consumer at a higher price – they added value. Early social reformers, this civic bourgeoisie built orphanages, hospitals, schools and sewerage systems. These social revolutionaries, who transformed Florence in the late thirteenth century, aimed to upset the old order – and money was their weapon.

The Florentine guilds

Although it may sound dull and unheroic, as well as being skilled artisans and entrepreneurs, Florentine merchants were adroit managers, understanding how to get the most out of their resources. By the late twelfth century, they were organising each trade in a guild – an entirely new way of running business. Florentine manufacturing operated as a collective, a mutually supportive community. Guilds facilitated strategic commercial thinking: merchants could pool resources, lend each other machinery, negotiate as a bloc, finance each other and reduce costs of inputs by bulk buying. They could also innovate together, operating on the 'two heads is better than one' principle.

Guilds were medieval start-up incubators, allowing artisans to experiment and share information. For example, in the late twelfth century, a Florentine artisan working with glass – most likely a glass blower – realised that the weird shapes of glass that his work was producing could be used to improve his ailing sight. For years, people had known that convex-shaped glass could magnify their sight. However, no one had invented the bridge component, using the human nose and two little metal arms as stabilisers, and enlisting the ears for balance. It seems so easy now, but someone had to come up with the idea and then tinker around with a prototype, making sure the glasses could stay on. With these rudimentary glasses, the Florentines created a hands-free technology that would dramatically increase an artisan's working life through better sight. This might seem like a small thing, but the kick to productivity by keeping just one master craftsman active well after his natural sight had deteriorated was consequential, while keeping hundreds of them at work was transformative.

Even small innovations, organised at scale via collaborative guilds, mattered enormously to the productivity of the city. The co-operative nature of the guilds amplified the impact of any invention. You could say that the guilds helped to turn invention into innovation – innovation being the commercial application of invention.[4]

Within a brief period of about fifty years, we see the establishment of the major institutions on which Florentine prosperity would rest. In 1190, the Seven Great Guilds, or *Arti Maggiori* – for judges and notaries, bankers and international traders, moneychangers, silk merchants, doctors and apothecaries, wool merchants, and dealers in furs – were established. Early members of the guild of doctors and apothecaries were the Medici family, Medici stemming from the Latin for medicine. By 1200, the League of Florentine Bankers emerged, who would link up with bankers in London; Lombard Street in the City of London is named after the medieval Italian bankers from Lombardy who lent to the less financially sophisticated English. In 1218, the first guild of pawn shop owners, forerunners to the great banking families, was set up. The pawnbroking method of taking in collateral for cash revolutionised Florentine banking in the fourteenth century. In 1233, we have the first merchant census that compelled every inhabitant to register their profession or occupation and affiliation to a guild. The guilds elected the *podestà* (the power) who would run the city.

A golden coin

In 1252, awash with gold flowing into the city's thriving textile industry, the Florentine merchants decided to innovate financially, pooling their resources to mint their own currency, the 25-carat gold florin. The florin's design, with John the

Baptist, the patron saint of the city, on one side and a lily, the emblem of Florence, on the other, signified that the city and religion were equally important. Financially, the florin became the symbol of Florentine power, mercantile might and reputation – a credible coin backed by the wealth of the republic, which Europe could trust. In time, as we will see, this credibility resulted in the florin becoming Europe's reserve currency.

The Florentines made a clear distinction between money they used every day within the city and money they used internationally or for long-distance trade. While the gold florin was for long-distance or wholesale trade, they also minted a silver *moneta di piccoli* for local retail trade, or small trade, as the name suggests. These were two completely different currency systems, with a fluctuating rate of exchange that was carefully managed in Florence, as with similar local systems in Genoa and Venice.

From around 1275 onwards, Florence boomed. Many of the architectural masterpieces modern visitors associate with the city were planned, if not completed, during a mesmerising period of commercial energy that lasted from the late thirteenth century until the arrival of the Black Death in 1348. In this period before the plague, work began on the churches of Santa Maria del Fiore (1296), Santa Croce (1294), Santa Carmine (1268) and Santa Maria Novella (1279), as well as Giotto's Campanile (1334) and the Palazzo Vecchio (1298), which today hosts many Renaissance paintings and sculptures, and from where Niccolò Machiavelli would preside as secretary of the republic.

Florence set out to defy Rome with its splendour, but Florentine architecture was democratic. Its buildings were built by civic-minded merchants for the people, and these city elders aimed to create beautiful public, rather than private, spaces. Unlike princely European dynasties or the cardinals of the Church, who hoarded their wealth, Florence's guilds and merchant princes spread their largesse, competing to make their city '*la più bella che si può*' – as beautiful as possible. The richest wool guild, for example, funded many projects, including Santa Maria del Fiore. This desire for a beautiful city meant avoiding private expressions of wealth, and laws were enacted to limit the height of towers. In other Tuscan cities, such as Siena and San Gimignano, rich families flaunted their wealth by building high towers within the city walls. The more democratic Florentines banned these, opting for the more uniform height of palaces, giving their streets a classic uniformity and a sense of central planning power. Even the wealthiest merchants lived 'over the shop'. Florence's urban planning reinforced its bourgeois aspirations: patronage and wealth went side by side, underpinned by confidence in the currency.

Adam's sin

In contrast to this newly emerging cityscape of ordered, demo-cratic beauty, the Florence of Dante's youth was a frenzied place – a warren of dark, dirty streets where people lived cheek by jowl. The cobbler, saddler, tailor, goldsmith and barber plied their trade on the street, which served as shop, factory and slaughterhouse. The place reeked of blood, live beasts, human excrement, fish and a foul stench from the tanneries. In the rivers and canals, dyers washed their cloth, except during the vine harvest when all fresh water was reserved for wine. The town crier roared news of births, deaths, weddings, adul-teries, bankruptcies and other news gleaned from returning merchants whose networks lay beyond Italy. Prostitutes and thieves were dragged naked through the streets and flogged, while heretics burned at the stake for crimes against God, and thieves sizzled for crimes against money.

The young Dante walking around these alleyways would have witnessed daily scenes of casual cruelty. Punishment was stitched into the fabric of society – sinners must suffer publicly, forgiveness was uncommon and slights and insults were met with justice, which sometimes included death. As a child, he would have smelled burning flesh and heard the agonised cries as these sentences were carried out. Such images stayed with Dante and would form the bedrock of the abominations meted out to the various sinners in his *Inferno*, which has given our culture its ideas of hell and the visualisation of its torments.

Dante reserved one of his most ghastly punishments for the crime of forgery. In Canto 30 of the *Inferno*, the counterfeiter Adamo is condemned to the eighth circle of hell, just one above Lucifer in the ninth. In this Canto, Dante and Virgil, his guide through the underworld, meet two falsifiers, one of whom is the unfortunate Maestro Adamo, a real-life counterfeiter who in Dante's youth had tried to debase the Florentine florin.

Adam – who was English – had studied in Brescia, a city in competition with Florence. He was persuaded by prosperous Brescian merchants to debase the florin, by replacing three carats of the usually pure gold coin with copper. The coin weighed almost the same, but it was a fake. Dante pairs Adam with another liar, Simon the Greek, the man who tricked the Trojans into believing the Trojan horse was an innocent gift. This betrayal led to the destruction of an entire civilisation. Why would Dante equate Adam, an everyday, opportunistic counterfeiter, with Simon, the man who betrayed Troy? It seems disproportionate, but only if we fail to appreciate the central role of the florin in underpinning the might of Florence.

One florin was worth about €125 (£107) in today's money, and to give you a sense of what that meant at the time, a slave girl or a mule could be bought for fifty florins – about €6,000 (£5,150).[5] We know that, as the Florentines expanded commercially throughout Europe, the florin became the trademark of the strength of the city as much as a medium of exchange. Pure gold, weighing 3.53 grams, it became the reserve currency of mercantile Europe, giving it the pre-eminent role in international finance, not unlike the US dollar today. Across the continent, goods were exchanged in florins, debts were settled in florins, loans were extended in florins and wealth was both measured and stored in florins. The Hungarian currency is still called the florin (or forint) and the Dutch guilder used to be called the same – in fact, the shorthand symbol for the guilder was an 'f'. Today, the Dutch overseas territory of Aruba uses the Aruba florin as its currency.

The florin quickly became the hardest currency in Europe. That means it was accepted widely as the unit of account from London and Bruges in the north to Alexandria and Tyre in the south. When the world accepts your currency readily it gives the currency that most elusive of qualities: liquidity. A simple definition of liquidity is the ease and time it takes to settle a trade in a currency. The more liquidity, the easier it is to trade. If, in the case of a coin, there is significant demand for the products underpinning the coin, the number of coins supplied will go up and, while their value will stay the same, their intrinsic usability and therefore practical value increases.

In Florence's case, the products underpinning the coin were textiles. By 1338, ten years before the Black Death arrived,

Villani estimated that of its 100,000 inhabitants, 30,000 were working in the dyeing and clothing trades, across 200 wool workshops.[6] English, Spanish and French wool was imported to be processed into luxury high-end textiles for re-export, and the profits were reinvested by the banking system.

Given its liquidity, everyone wanted to settle their account with the florin. The state that mints the coins that everyone wants has soft power. Soft power is the power of persuasion. In today's context, consider the power the US dollar gives the United States. Oil, copper, steel, uranium, rare earths, timber, cotton, silk, diamonds – all these commodities are priced internationally in dollars, and to buy them the purchaser must first buy dollars, which the US generates for free. The florin played the same role in the medieval economy, bestowing significant financial advantages to Florence, the issuer.

Being the reserve currency gives the issuer the outrageous privilege of some of the world's commodities and other products being priced in your currency, even though you don't mine them or produce them. Now think about what happens. Money from across Europe and beyond flowed into Florence, where it was re-minted. The demand was for the florin, the coin itself, which pushes up the price of the florin but pushes down the price of goods for the Florentines. They get bargains everywhere as their currency rises in value. Meanwhile, the rest of the world must provide more stuff to get its hands on the florins that it needs to settle its trades. For Florentine bankers, this is a bonanza because it means they can invest abroad cheaply: they snap up deals while at the same time benefitting from liquid capital markets at home. Florentines became the favoured buyers because they had the currency everyone wanted.[7]

For Dante, the counterfeiter was an atrocious criminal because by undermining the currency he was undermining the government, which had its basis in fiscal and financial probity. The counterfeiter wasn't just damaging the currency; he was threatening the very existence of the republic. A practical purpose of the florin was to promote trade by giving the user confidence that the currency was unblemished by forgery. Therefore, Adam's crime was a crime against Florentine credibility – not just internally, but externally too. Anyone who interfered with Florentine money was interfering with Florence's ascent.

The monetary mind

Money wasn't just altering the way the Florentines went about their business; it changed the way they thought about the world, putting them on a collision course with the old regime, in an echo of Fibonacci's financial heresy. Banking, and in particular merchant banking at scale, meant walking a fine line with the Church. The Church condemned the notion of making money out of money because it contradicted a central doctrine, perfected by Thomas Aquinas, known as the 'just price'. The just price meant that all money had to relate to something real or tangible like work or land. This is where the religious St Thomas Aquinas meets the atheist Karl Marx. They both rejected one of money's key attributes – abstraction – maybe because abstraction confuses the dogmatic mind. In a dance of ecclesiastical elegance designed to allow the Church to remain the only moneylender in town, the Vatican came up with a rhetorical conundrum: if the interest rate is the price of time, measured by the interest rate on lending for a week, a month, or even longer, who can value this? How can a mere mortal tell the value of time? Only the Lord can do this, obviously, as the Lord is the creator of time. Usury was therefore a crime against God because God invented time and only God, or his messengers on earth, the bishops, could put a price on it.

Being secular, the reckoning schools that had been set up to teach Fibonacci's mathematical innovations challenged ecclesiastical education, by replacing dogma with logic, superstition with numerals and guesswork with rigour. As merchant power expanded, a showdown between God and Mammon became increasingly likely. The business schools, while still very much reserved for the children of the well-off, changed the way people were educated. Education was no longer the preserve of the humanities, with monks leading the way. Bankers and merchants were now at the vanguard of a new type of numerical education, involving risk, probability, measurement and, ultimately, training people to value the future rather than simply unravel the past. We were beginning to witness a shift from deductive to inductive reasoning, escaping the shackles of what we already know and embracing notions of what we might yet discover. The numerical world, mediated by money, was inconsistent with the teachings of the Church, mediated by scripture. The merchant, a bit player at the time of Dante's birth, was ubiquitous by the time of his death in 1321. Money was propelling Europe out of the pre-Dantean darkness and into the Renaissance light.

The power of networks

There are few better accounts of the day-to-day pace and excitement of a merchant's life than *The Merchant of Prato* by Iris Origo, first published in 1957. Drawing on 150,000 letters and thousands more records from a self-made merchant, Francesco di Marco Datini, born in Tuscany around 1335, it offers an insight into the private and business life of a successful trader, revealing how sophisticated and integrated the global economy was by the late fourteenth century. On the Merchant of Prato's ledgers was inscribed the motto 'In the name of God and Profit'.

We meet Datini as an ambitious apprentice in the papal city of Avignon. Over the next thirty-five years, through a combination of rigour, risk assessment and daring – and armed with Fibonacci's mathematics – he built a global company with a trading network covering thousands of miles across land and ocean. His records include a diary of daily anxieties, along with love letters to his wife Margherita, who upbraids and consoles him, acting as his sounding board and confidante. The couple are childless but when the merchant, as we'd say in Dublin, 'went and got' one of the slaves (a Tartar called Lucia) pregnant, Margherita took the child in and raised her as her own daughter. With Datini on the road and Margherita, a Florentine noblewoman, holding the fort back in Prato, effectively overseeing the business at home, their many letters kept each other informed about what was going on. We see a couple dealing with the ups and downs of a long and not always straightforward marriage. Datini also describes his friendship with Ser Lapo, a notary, fine wine expert and bon viveur. Their chat about food and wine, the household, the clothing trade, and their thoughts on money, politics and religion are all in the mix, making the concerns of their daily life familiar even though they unfolded seven centuries ago.

The geographical range of Datini's business is extraordinary. He bought the finest wool from the English Cotswolds, while the brilliant dyes and fixers that made his product sparkle – vermilion, brazil, grana, saffron and alum – were procured from a trading network that covered the Black Sea, the North

African coast, the Balearics, Spain and Lebanon.[8] One piece of clothing might be the result of deals with English, French and Flemish abbots, and a network of contacts across Venice, Genoa, Barcelona and Mallorca. Datini followed the money, keeping an eye on every detail in this complex web. And this was just for the clothing end of his business.

Merchant power is not what you know but who you know; though in Datini's case, it was probably a combination of both. His clout stemmed not from an army or some hereditary title but from his network, evidenced by thousands of his letters.

Datini's archive reveals a network, a vast intercontinental system of contracts, relationships and obligations. Fibonacci's mathematics enabled this system as it was the common language of disparate merchants; Datini was one of many. Pacioli's technology, the balance sheet, and his double-entry bookkeeping were also employed, helping to benchmark each venture. The glue holding this dynamic network together was money. Without the common mediator of money, complex commercial networks do not make any sense. There is too much going on for each merchant to keep tabs on everything, so the merchants had to trust something to reduce all this activity to a comprehensible number. That something was money – profit and loss, cost and revenue, expressed in a common denominator.

A helpful way to think about network economics is to consider today's social media: a platform like Instagram depends on its millions of users, and the more people who use it, the stronger the network becomes. Money, because it is a social technology, has always encouraged and been encouraged by networks. Whether we are talking about the basic networks as first emerged with the Lydians and then the Greeks, or these more sophisticated Florentine networks, the essential properties of network economics remain the same. Structurally, networks are horizontal hierarchies rather than vertical ones. A vertical hierarchy is an old-fashioned top-down system, underpinned by obedience. The two regional power bases that threatened medieval Florence, the Vatican and the Holy Roman Empire, were classic vertical hierarchies.

The authority of warlords and priests stemmed from practice or convention in an organisational system structured by subservience, lines of command and a court of power operating around the 'Big Man', such as a pope or a king. However, if resources are spent on the sole objective of satisfying the Big Man and his cronies, they will be wasted. When everyone bows to the Big Man, falling out of favour is damaging at best or deadly at worst. Within vertical hierarchies, dissent is dangerous, but without dissent, where does innovation come from? If everyone conforms, how do we get better, how do we introduce new ways of doing things and, if we don't reward disruption, how do we progress? Vertical hierarchies can appear robust, but they are brittle.

In contrast, networks are constantly subject to strain and therefore they adapt. Horizontal hierarchies are more likely to foster intellectual and commercial enquiry, the conditions that make economic evolution possible. Networks benefit from the strength of weak ties.[9] If a network's ties are too strong – as with strict religions, intense localism, obdurate nationalism or families – these networks are restricted. Trading networks, mediated by money, are more flexible because money is the ultimate weak tie, bringing us together in a non-exclusive manner; money is used by everyone. And the more who use it, the stronger it is, yet the weaker the absolute ties. When seen as a network builder, the power of money becomes enormous.

Something was happening in Florence and other trading cities: the vertical hierarchies, governed from above, that had run societies for millennia were slowly beginning to be challenged by a new type of power structure, the horizontal network. The more dynamic the environment – say, a rapidly expanding urban economy – the more people will come into the network, creating more new products and new ideas and making the network stronger. Networks revolve around clusters where activity is intense and connections are easily made. These places bristle with economic energy. The city-states, like Florence, were commercial clusters, and the weak tie of money bound these clusters together. Florence's twelfth-century guilds were localised networks, but by the end of the fourteenth century, they were going global, driven by international finance.

In a pre-Renaissance world of kingdoms, new monetary networks threatened the status quo. Vertical networks are closed, based on borders and countries, but horizontal networks do not respect national boundaries, being both cosmopolitan and supra-national. The merchant class lived in city-states, and they weren't as interested in wars of territorial expansion. They understood that war is expensive, wasteful and balance-sheet depleting. And wars destroy networks. Best avoided. Money and the mercantile world offered an entirely new way of life to ambitious go-getting people, and merchants soon figured out how to broaden their opportunities, using a weapon more potent than the sword, more evocative than scripture. Merchant power was based on money and if this new caste could figure out a way of wresting control of money from the king and the mint, they'd be unstoppable. We were about to move from an era of money to an era of finance.

The Ishango Bone, found in the Congo Basin and dating from around 18,000 BCE, is the earliest evidence we have of human mathematics and, possibly, money. It has been speculated that the notches on this tiny bone indicate a balance sheet, which would make this the first recorded evidence of accountancy.

This inscribed tablet is from the Mesopotamian city of Drehem, and dates from around 2100 BCE. It is the first known example of financial software, containing forecasts about an investment in a livestock business.

With an owl on one side and the goddess Athena on the other, the Greek tetradrachm was the most widely minted coin in the ancient world, lasting over 700 years in constant usage. It unified the disparate Greek colonies that dotted the Mediterranean, the Aegean and the Black Sea.

Greek traders in the agora measuring and weighing goods. Putting money and commerce at the centre of the city, the Greek agora, a grand urban bazaar, served as the locus for not just commerce but ideas, discussion, gossip and entertainment.

Nineteen of the twenty-nine painted commercial façades that have so far been revealed in the ruins of Pompeii feature Mercury, the god of commerce. Here he is centre-stage in a fresco from the House of the Vettii.

Ordinary Pompeiians buying bread with their small change. Small coins amplified the power of money: the smaller the coin, the smaller the transaction and the more people brought together in the webs of the commercial world.

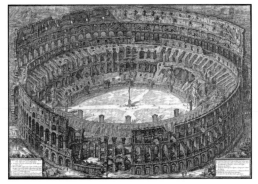

Vespasian's most enduring gift to Rome was the Colosseum — seen here in a 1776 drawing by Piranesi — which was paid for by loot from the regions. The emperor understood the power of money and how people, once they have it, forget where it came from as long as it has value.

In Goslar in Lower Saxony at the turn of the second millennium, money made its reappearance in northern Europe after centuries of decline. This sculpture on a medieval guildhall in Goslar's main square, showing a man defecating coins, underscores just how rich the town became as a result of its silver mines.

The medieval marketplace was home to a powerful new class: the merchants. Here money changers, bankers, traders and hustlers settled bills of exchange, lent out money and fuelled the expanding economy.

The follaro, the standard minted silver coin of Norman Sicily, evidences the island's synthesis of cultures. On one side, an Arabic inscription gives the date of minting according to the Arabic calendar, while on the other side is inscribed a Christian reference in Latin.

The roof of the Palatine Chapel in Palermo displays Sicily's three great civilisations – Latin Normans, Greek Byzantines and Muslim Arabs – living in harmony. In this Norman structure, the wood carving is of Saracen design, the ceiling is Arabesque and the pillars bear replicas of Byzantine golden mosaics.

Born in 1265, Dante Alighieri (depicted here by Botticelli) was a son of medieval Florence and his *Divine Comedy* maps a progression from Gothic darkness to pre-Renaissance light.

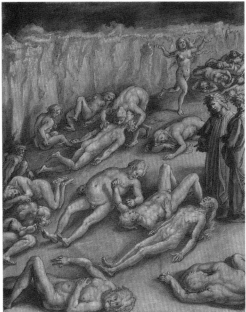

In this 1587 illustration by Stradanus, Maestro Adamo, the counterfeiter in Dante's *Inferno*, is shown writhing in pain with a distended belly caused by dropsy. For Dante, an attack on the florin was an attack on the integrity of Florence itself.

The Piazza della Signoria in Florence, overlooked by the Palazzo Vecchio. Unlike princely European dynasties or the cardinals of the Church, who hoarded their wealth, Florence's guilds and merchant princes competed to make the public spaces of their city '*la più bella che si può*' – as beautiful as possible.

Johannes Gutenberg's background as a goldsmith working with precious metals influenced his attention to detail. Once you saw a Gutenberg bible you would never forget it. It felt like the future and was completely different to the handwritten manuscripts that had preceded it.

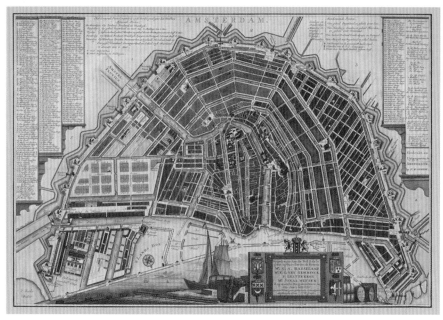

Amsterdam – shown here on a 1766 map – was a monetary metropolis, but it was characterised by public modesty despite the underlying wealth.

Rembrandt's *Christ Drives the Money-Changers from the Temple* (1626). The seventeenth-century Dutch mind was pushing the boundaries of art as well as money.

During the Song dynasty (980–1280 CE), paper became the primary instrument of state money in China. This note dates from 1375, during the subsequent Ming dynasty.

Money out of thin air

Notwithstanding the iconic status of the florin, there was an equally important financial development taking place in Florence: the emergence of banking. Banking at its most basic level is the business of depositing and lending money. The genesis of modern banking in Florence had three sources: pawnbroking, moneychanging and merchant banking. Florentine pawnbrokers lent money against the collateral of a wide range of goods. Moneychangers, meanwhile, hung out in fairs and markets, laying out boxes of coins on a bench – a *banco* in Italian (hence the origin of the word bank) – and, using scales to determine weights, they bought and sold coins. As traders flocked from all over Europe to the markets of Florence, a huge variety of foreign coins would be doing the rounds. From their accumulated profits, the moneychangers were able to become moneylenders.

Merchant banking emerged as a natural sequence to the 'putting out' system, the medieval term for lending to farmers to tide them over between sowing and harvesting. In the feudal age, as in Kushim's Mesopotamia, the economy was a seasonal affair, tied to nature's vicissitudes. Essentially, commerce was earth-based. We ate what came from the earth, we wore what came from the earth, we lived in what came from the earth, and for most people after food, clothing and shelter there wasn't much more. Due to seasonal time lags, Florentine merchants had developed many techniques for lending, not only to cover the sowing and harvesting shortfall but also lags for the processing of raw materials into goods. In this interval between seed and cereal, between wool and clothing, the harvester, the worker in the field, the spinner, the weaver and so on needed working capital.

The Florentine *Arte della Lana*, the wool weavers' guild, lent raw materials, such as raw wool, to other workers at a predetermined price which would be paid off when the worker returned the finished garment – an early form of invoice discounting. The new entrepreneurs lent raw materials and tools, the necessary capital to initiate production. It did not require any giant leap of the imagination to start lending money directly for investment purposes, charging a decent rate of interest or, to get around Church sanctions against interest, levying other fees and markups to make sure the lender turned a twist.

The money machine

Initially, when a merchant wished to transfer money to another merchant, they would physically take the coins from one deposit to the other if they were dealing with different banks and different vaults. It was a cumbersome, time-consuming process. Why not just issue a written document to the banker indicating that the depositor wished to transfer such an amount to another depositor? This was called a letter of credit. Hey presto, we have the origin of the cheque and the chequebook. If you trusted the bank to be good for the credit, then these pieces of paper were as good as money. A merchant who was owed money could ask his debtor to issue him a letter of credit, and he could then use that letter of credit to pay some of his own debt, thus bringing a third merchant into the network, who may have no connection with the original debtor. The important thing is that the reputable bank, usually a family bank, acted as a clearing house where all these letters of credit could be settled. In this way, the letter of credit expanded the network of trust.

A first cousin of the letter of credit was the bill of exchange, largely a Lombardian banking innovation (though possibly lifted from the Arabs before them). During Datini's lifetime, this instrument revolutionised international trade, linking Florence to Lyon, Bruges to Barcelona, merchant to producer, and supplier to banker. A bill of exchange, issued to a merchant by a European bank, was recognised abroad for a specified amount of money. As long as the bank was good for the money, a trader could use this bill of exchange to pay for produce. The bill of exchange became a sort of international tradeable currency, allowing the mercantile system to flourish exponentially: more bills of exchange, more goods, more trade, more money, more collateral, more bills of exchange. In time, the great trade fairs of Europe became as much about settling thousands of bills of exchange for trade that was going on all over the continent as they were about exchanging produce. Sitting at the top of the system was the merchant banker.

Bills of exchange are virtual money – money with no constraints but trust and faith. Trusted Florentine banks evolved, alongside those in Genoa, Naples, Milan and Venice, into the area of credit creation by moving to what economists now call fractional reserve banking. It is termed fractional reserve banking because the idea is that a banker only needs to keep a fraction of his reserves to cover the possibility that a depositor wants their money back. In this way the banker uses the rest of the money on deposit to create loans, and the growth of credit is exponential. This development in the evolution of money is like moving from the plough to the steam engine. Here's how it worked.

In normal times, you leave your deposits in the bank. The same was the case in the fourteenth century. This money is highly valuable to a banker and is at the core of fractional reserve banking. Merchant bankers realised that a large part of the money deposited with them was not frequently withdrawn. There was a very good reason for this: holders of gold and silver were an easy target for thieves. The slow withdrawal of deposits meant the merchant banker could lend some of this money to other borrowers. As long as the banker retained a reasonable reserve of cash to meet sudden withdrawals, he could benefit by lending the money at a high rate of interest.

As the merchant banker built up his reputation for trust and honesty, more deposits flowed his way. He was then able to further expand credit into the Florentine economy. In many cases the money that he was lending moved through the economy and ended up in the hands of other merchants who, in turn, deposited that money with the same bank. This led to a process of loans, eventually creating deposits, which in turn could be used to create further loans, which in turn created further deposits, and so on, transforming banks into money machines. That multiplier effect is the fount of all finance.

Crucially, finance broke the link between the royal mint and money. In the old days, only the mint could issue money. With the emergence of merchant banking, the banker had the power to create money. Finance, making money out of thin air, began to shift power in society from the king to the merchant, from the vertical network to the horizontal network and from the palace to the office.

Merchant banker, power broker

Datini, despite his devout faith, became a merchant banker, making money from money. Like other merchants, he got around the Church's ban on usury by charging other fees instead of interest, but the end result was the same – more cash being made from cash, in turn leading to more loans, contracts, debtors and creditors. These developments spawned a new class of clerks, notaries and lawyers. Commercial law developed in tandem, setting the rules for merchants, their agents, suppliers, customers and bankers.

Why stop at trade finance? If the letter of credit system was working, why not lend for consumption? Merchants had to live, after all. A new layer of letters of credit emerged, financing consumption for the growing merchant classes. Datini was a man who began his career in Avignon selling shields, swords and chainmail. Now, astride a global empire, his own bank financed the whole operation and that of many others.

By the time of his death in 1415, Europe was connected by a patchwork of trading routes, up and down rivers, over mountain ranges, north to south, east to west, and at the centre of these routes were the merchants. Not even the devastation of the Black Death in 1348 could dent the extraordinary monetary, social, intellectual and political development of Florence. Despite the Black Death, the florin, Florence's foundational currency, did not devalue. The city might have lost half of its inhabitants, but the attachment to the hard currency was absolute.

In the century after the plague, driven by the merchants and network economics, Florence radiated in the astonishing intellectual, artistic and commercial genius of Cosimo de' Medici, Leonardo da Vinci and Michelangelo. Cerebral brilliance was allied with artistic virtuosity and anchored by the economic muscularity of the merchant class, creating an entirely new model for political power. This alliance would lead to a questioning of everything that had gone before, and this would usher in first the Renaissance, followed by the Reformation and the Enlightenment. It is difficult to see how any of these great leaps forward could have occurred without the accompanying innovation in and power of money, credit and commerce driving the economy away from feudalism.

A new map of Europe was emerging, with productive Italy at the centre, and Florence one of the jewels in its crown, whose most celebrated resident would come to be known as Renaissance Man – a subtle, talented polymath, at home in a variety of languages and animated by art, philosophy, mathematics, finance and commerce. It was a long way from the small walled town of Dante's youth. But this didn't happen by accident. The catalyst that drove the merchants forward was money and, in particular, bank-created money, which broke the power of the mint as well as the tyranny of the coin. Bankers lent to each other on the basis of sound reputation, not base metal. Money created by private banks, which we now call finance, supercharged this process, with loans driving deposits, begetting more loans. Money was moving commerce from the physical to the abstract. Mere paper, backed by a bank's reputation, was as valuable as the florin itself backed by gold. We were moving into a different world and the geographical centre of that very different world would shift from the Italian peninsula to the Ultramontane regions beyond the Alps.

9

GOD'S PRINTER

The hustler

Johannes Gutenberg was a great man for an argument. Many of his fights ended up in court, leaving us with records of a talented chancer, regularly sailing too close to the wind. Gutenberg fell out with creditors, partners, former employees and fathers of potential brides. He fought over money, stock, promises, patents and women – or more accurately, his own casual intentions towards women. Gutenberg the bounder is not a tale we have heard much about, but certain clues suggest he was a scoundrel. A colourful paper-trail of suits and countersuits paints a vivid picture of a hustler-entrepreneur, living on the edge in fifteenth-century Europe.

Gutenberg found himself perennially in debt, with a dodgy credit rating and constant cash flow problem. An ambitious goldsmith, he needed money, but having defaulted on previous debts, his reputation was tarnished in the streets, taverns and alleyways of Mainz. The fact that he'd reneged on a Strasbourg marriage promise and was being pursued by the father of the bride suggests our man wasn't averse to burning a bridge or five. Conventional, Johannes Gutenberg was not. From a risk perspective, let's just say J.G. wasn't triple A, more a walking junk bond. But Gutenberg knew there was money in God, and if he could find a way to board the ecclesiastical gravy train, he'd be sorted.

While the Italian merchant bankers may have been creating their own money machine, up in the flat German hinterland, money was still very much in the hands of those with the pointy hats and incense. The closest young Gutenberg was getting to the golden tabernacle was hustling in the precarious end of the religious market – tacky merchandising. In the early 1430s, we find him drenched in the holy city of Aachen, trying to flog pilgrims 'blessed' mirrors. There's a certain type who to this day earn their crust selling merch at festivals and, as they will attest, the difference between a profitable day's trading in the open air and a commercial disaster can often be the weather. Tragically, for Johannes on the day of the 1432 festival, the heavens opened, the feast day was cancelled, leaving Gutenberg with unsold – and worse still, unsellable – stock, along with a stack of bills, not to mention outstanding loans.

Twenty-eight years old, out of work, and up to his gills in debt, Johannes was going backwards. He needed something better than flogging knock-off holy mirrors. He knew what retail felt like; next time he needed to go upmarket. Despite his shambolic finances, Gutenberg had a revolutionary idea. He was sitting on an invention that would disrupt the business of scribes, notaries and monks forever. In the immediate term, he figured his contraption would benefit the dominant financial institution of the day: the Church. He had no idea just how consequential his printing press would end up being. Right now, young Gutenberg needed finance to execute his plan to become chief printer of the Archbishop of Mainz.

Luckily for Gutenberg, commercial Germany of the fifteenth century was awash with annuities, brokers and moneylenders. Risk appetite had been heightened by financial innovations, and money was plentiful. Germany was a patchwork of kingdoms and trading cities, each minting their own coins. With many different currencies circulating and no official exchange rate, a gap opened up for arbitrage. The Church forbade usury, but at trade fairs canny merchants exploited the imprecise exchange rates to extract profit by charging for loans without the Church knowing. The fluctuating exchange rates drove trade all across Germany.

Borrowing from tomorrow

From 1337 to 1453, the Hundred Years' War between France and England diverted Mediterranean trade eastwards. France and England's difficulty was Germany's opportunity. Italian trade moved away from the Rhône, which flowed through war-torn France, towards the Rhine, moving up through peaceful Germany. In Italy, major geo-strategic shocks resulted in the peninsula losing its geographical advantage. The arrival of the Ottomans closed down the Silk Roads, compelling the European Christians to find another way to India, and rather than being a trade route, the Mediterranean became a cul-de-sac. Columbus opened up the Atlantic to the New World while de Gama reached the East via Africa, shifting Europe's maritime trading axis from the Mediterranean to the Atlantic.

Countries such as Portugal, Spain, Holland and, later, Britain, prospered in this world. Improved access to gold markets in West Africa and extra mining in the Balkans meant silver and gold were more plentiful in Europe; silver production in Saxony, Bohemia and Hungary is estimated to have increased fivefold in the middle decades of the fifteenth century. At the same time, new powers emerged in the Czech lands, Poland and Hungary, and from the Hanseatic Baltic to the agricultural Danube, central Europe's financial axis shifted away from the Mediterranean and towards the central land mass and the new German economy.

While these events altered Europe's economic geography, innovations in money transformed Europeans' sense of time. In the Middle Ages, most people had little need for any long-term finance. Concerned about famine, weather, crop failure, plague and God, they did not have the luxury of seeing beyond the harvest. For most, the concept of the long run didn't exist. But for the landowning local squire, the long run was real, and the future was something to invest in. Even today, one of the key differences between rich and poor is time horizons. Rich people's time horizons are longer. When you are not worried about paying bills today, you have the luxury of planning for tomorrow – say university or a career. You can wait for an investment to pay off. Wealth enables the future; poverty obliterates it. As it was in the late fourteenth and early fifteenth centuries, so it is today.

The base source of wealth of Europe's largely agricultural economy was farming and the taxes levied on it. The economy of the Middle Ages, despite the emerging merchant, was still mostly about aristocrats and the Church squeezing money out of peasants. The annual tithe or rent was a stream of income, the root of most pre-industrial finance. Land was the bedrock. But land is illiquid, and part of money's alchemy is turning inert wealth into liquid income. The Romans solved this problem by pawning land. Germans were about to experiment with a product that is still with us today – the mortgage, the *mort* bit meaning 'dead' in French.

In medieval Germany, wealthy landowners wanted cash. They pledged their land to the moneylender, typically the monastery, and with the collateral in the bag, the monks – who got some of their money from the collection box – lent out the lump sum to the squire. The squire paid a rate of interest to the monastery for the pleasure of getting the cash lump sum. The income from the land, those rents extracted from the peasants, went to the monastery. At the end of the term of the loan, the monastery looked to be repaid. As aristocrats are notoriously bad with other people's money, defaults were regular. In the event of default, the lender took the title and thereby acquired the land. (How do you think the Catholic Church became one of the biggest landowners in the world?) The contract thus had default (or death) built in, hence the name mortgage, or death contract. However, it still left the moneylender, the monastery, with a liquidity problem. Although land was valuable, it wasn't liquid, and why would a monastery, which also needed cash for candles, salt and the like, want yet more land?

What if there was another way? Rather than mortgaging their entire estate to the monastery, could aristocrats mortgage smaller bits of their land to someone else, with the monastery acting as the broker? In this way, the monastery wasn't left holding the baby, but still received a fee, and the aristocrat could free himself of the Church by borrowing from many smaller lenders. In a sense, the Church and the squire freed each other from each other by finding alternative lenders in medium-sized farmers, craftsmen or artisans who had a small amount of money under the mattress, which could instead be gaining some interest on a loan. By spreading the risk across many lenders, the overall interest rate faced by the aristocrat might be lower, but the small lender would still get some income, in the form of interest. And thus the annuity was born. As long as the harvest was good and the aristocrat wasn't a complete rake, the system should work well. Even if he was a rake, a small default risk could be built in, so that the lender would still get his money back, because the underlying land was still profitable.

Secure in the knowledge that most annuities would be paid, they could be traded, used to cancel debts and ultimately passed on as inheritance to children. An artisan who might have had a bit of money squirrelled away could buy an annuity and this would give him a stream of income in the future, a pledge on future earnings from the land while the aristocrat received cash. Annuities made illiquid land liquid. A sign of the success of German finance was the dramatic fall in interest rates throughout the fourteenth century from around 12 per cent to 6 per cent per annum.

When the price of borrowing falls, obviously the amount of borrowing rises, resulting in an explosion in the trade of these annuities and in credit in general. The more annuities around, the more liquid the market, the more attractive these loans became for savers, and the more cash available for borrowers. Based on the success of agriculture-based annuities, German towns introduced another product called municipal finance, where towns borrowed from their own citizens to fund public infrastructure. The municipal bonds that the towns issued to these lenders ended up being traded as they constituted a stream of income. Germany was about to enter an era of easy money – a time of liquidity – and Gutenberg stood to benefit.

Saving souls

Although the world knows Gutenberg for his bible, the first profit-making opportunity that sucked money into Johannes' mitts was a grubbier, though lucrative, side-hustle: the business of saving German souls. An emerging urban Germany, ruled by an avaricious Church, was still beholden to faith and super-stition. The medieval Church remained the main money-making machine. No monarch or merchant came close to the cloister when it came to turning a buck. There was one power the Church had that trumped all others. It had the best origin story, giving it a licence to print money, not directly but indirectly, by turning faith into money via donations. Annual tithes were paid to the Church and the population was a captive audience, easily tapped up every now and then when the Church faced a revenue squeeze.

As well as the whip-round, the Church had another unbeat-able revenue-raising trick that Gutenberg, ever the opportunist, was eyeing up. In a miracle of wine into water proportions, the Church professed to save your soul in return for a small fee. Transforming heaven into money was quite the party trick. A finer extortion racket would be difficult to conceive. The deal was simple. People could buy a 'letter of indulgence' for a dead or dying relative confirming that their sins would be forgiven, allowing the soul to avoid hell, irrespective of their behaviour on earth. Because of this, the Church had a never-ending stream of income. The relatives of the dead or the soon-to-be-dead stumped up cash in return for a straight pass directly to the kingdom of heaven. Imagine having just read Dante's *Inferno*, which by then had been in circulation for a century – you'd do anything to avoid the nine circles of hell with their abominations and befoulments.

Selling indulgences turned sinners into ready cash. What better business could there be, leveraging the unconditional love of a family member to save the soul of the bereaved? For the Church, stuffed to the gills with indolent monks and other hangers-on, selling indulgences was a money-printing bonanza, like having the sovereign mint within the walls of the cloister. The twenty-first-century descendant of the letter of indulgence is the Mass card in today's Catholic world. Devout mourners buy a 'greeting card' issued by the Church to 'offer up' a Mass for the recently deceased. Mass cards adorned the mantelpiece in our house after my father's funeral. Each card represents a payment from the living to the Church hoping to ensure safe passage for the soul of the faithfully departed.

A potential bottleneck for the Church in this free flow of cash was the process of writing up the letters of indulgence. In the early fifteenth century, as had been the case for a thousand years, writing began with killing an animal to use as parchment, before employing the expensive services of a scribe. The business was costly as it demanded abattoirs, calligraphers and a complex production process. For the Church, the more efficient the printing production line, the more money it could make. And this was Gutenberg's opportunity. He would corner the market for making indulgences with his new printing machine and in the process enrich himself and the boss, the Archbishop of Mainz (an office we will return to before the end of our story).

A goldsmith and signwriter by trade, Johannes convinced the archbishop that a rudimentary printing machine could make money hand over fist, producing more indulgences than a meticulous monk with an unhurried quill. Like the Italian bankers who lent out multiples of an original deposit via their fractional reserve banking, Gutenberg could generate multiples of the slow-writing scribe by printing. Showing a salesman's aptitude for human psychology, Gutenberg produced generic letters that cleverly left an extra-large space for the bragging indulgence-sponsors to sign so that they could highlight their generosity. Gutenberg's insight was that what motivated people wasn't so much saving souls as acquiring the status in public of being the most generous sponsor.

Indulgences were only the beginning. Gutenberg had his eyes on the bible. Unlike common indulgences, bought by those with a few extra bob, bibles were only purchased by the wealthy and were gifted to monasteries in return for prayers for the soul of the munificent donor. Selling indulgences was small beer in comparison to selling bibles. The bible Gutenberg planned to flog with the help of his new printing machine would be no ordinary bible. The more beautiful the bible, the higher the price – Gutenberg wasn't going into the bible business for God, but for money. Everyone needs luck, even the pushiest of hustlers, and in 1453 Gutenberg got lucky.

A vain pope

Pope Pius II was quite the character – a carouser, womaniser and boozer. He fathered at least two children, one in Scotland on an early business journey. Although he vowed never to return to that 'place unvisited by winter sun',[1] his half-year in Scotland was spent productively (and reproductively). He was in danger of making it a habit when, a few years later in France, a second child was born, the product of yet another foreign jaunt for our vigorous young pope. Apart from his eye for the ladies, Pius quite fancied himself as a writer of bawdy comedies. He is the only pope to have the additional accolade of erotic novelist, and his poem 'The Tale of Two Lovers' is not what you might expect from a man of the cloth.

Despite his carnal weakness, Pope Pius became a significant author of the time and presided over a strong papacy. Never letting his own inner libertine dominate his dogmatic public position, he supported the Crusades and advocated the primacy of the papacy over uppity archbishops. He even managed to stitch together an alliance with that other paragon of virtue, Vlad the Impaler, to protect the Christian eastern Balkans from the Muslim Ottomans. What were a few heads on spikes when European civilisation was at stake? When he wasn't making alliances with his old mate Count Dracula, Pius was writing – straining his eyes by candlelight – as he worked through his thirteen volumes of essays, the 'Commentaries', a diary of his life and times.

Like any self-respecting pontiff, Pius had a fondness for a bit of luxury, enjoying fine wines, paintings and architecture. With republican Florence and its merchant bankers setting the pace, building the most beautiful city in the world, the papacy had to react. Not to be outdone, Pius tried his hand at urban design. He razed the village he was brought up in, a place called Corsignano in Tuscany, and built a miniature Florence in its stead, replete with Duomo, various palazzi and a few Gothic churches. He humbly consecrated it by changing its name to Pienza – the town of Pius. Working tirelessly with draughtsmen, builders, architects and artists, added to all the late-night scribbling, took further toll on his eyes. This vain lothario hated having to wear glasses in public, but when a pope is expected to read to his congregation from a delicately hand-inscribed bible, such vanity can be a bit tricky. He needed a bible he could read without glasses – and Johannes Gutenberg provided the solution.

The design king

Gutenberg's training as a goldsmith attuned him to intricate work and aesthetics. He intended to dazzle his audience with design. His printed bibles would not only be cheaper and quicker to produce than the handwritten prototypes, but they would also be more beautiful. Understanding that it would be easier to navigate the text with clear chapter headings and spacing, Gutenberg set about completely reimagining how books were presented. His layout would delight the reader. Accustomed to finery, his customers – bishops, cardinals and the pope himself – must be enthralled. First impressions matter.

His design trademark was a scarlet chapter heading, propped up by a bold division down the middle of the page, with a column of easy-to-read text on either side that was lacquered and raised in varnish. By using varnish, Gutenberg gave a unique and sumptuous feel to his bibles. The two columns of text were decorated with beautiful borders of animals and plants in gold and various other bright colours.[2] The design was stunning and modern. It felt like the future and was completely different to the handwritten manuscripts that had preceded it. The result was wonderfully readable and it impressed one important influencer of the time, the short-sighted Pope Pius II, who wrote of Gutenberg's pages, 'You could read them without your glasses.'[3] God's printer, Johannes Gutenberg, was on his way.

One of the defining attributes of an innovator is an ability to combine various previous inventions and harness them into a new product through a process of trial and error. Much is made of the engineering genius of the printing press, not to mention its efficiency: Gutenberg could print several bibles in the time it took a scribe to write one. The bibles were also exquisite to look at and to touch. His designs were clear, crisp and eye-catching. Quite probably, Gutenberg's background as a goldsmith working with precious metals influenced his attention to detail. Once you saw a Gutenberg bible you would never forget it. It felt like jewellery.

The innovator had watched the locals around Mainz make wine with large presses that squeezed the grapes in vats, pushing down the press via a mechanical corkscrew that ensured all the grapes were pressed at the same time and with the same pressure. This was an old Roman technology. Perhaps, after a few glasses in a Mosel vineyard, Gutenberg experienced his Archimedes moment. Until then, printers had constantly smudged the ink because they didn't apply the same pressure on all the letters across a page consistently. Why not adapt the wine press technology for his printing machine? If Mainz hadn't been a hub of both metalwork and wine production, would Gutenberg have arrived at this solution?

Innovation tends to emerge from a confluence of factors that determine why and where an innovation develops. Mainz, like Florence, was a cluster of economic activity, largely based on its location on the Rhine, at the point where it connects with the River Mosel and the River Main. Mainz had capital, and without this, the perennially bankrupt Gutenberg would never have financed his machinery. The printing press was an expensive piece of kit. With its intricate iron casting and moveable typeface, the complex machine demanded deep pockets. A complete set of manufactured letters cost the equivalent of four to ten years' wages of the average artisan.[4] In fact, the technique for making the letters was considered so valuable that when one of Gutenberg's business partners died, Johannes sent a servant around to his home to dismantle the press, retrieve his components and 'destroy the evidence of their collaboration, lest these materials fall into the hands of his heirs'.[5] Without the explosion in annuities and municipal bonds that recycled savings and made investment capital available for adventurers like Gutenberg, it is unlikely that the printing press would have come from Germany when it did.

The buzz

The printing press electrified public debate, unleashing a thirst for knowledge. Better-informed citizens are garrulous citizens. The financial implications of the printing press were obvious: the general demand for books began to soar and as demand rose, prices fell. Economies of scale kicked in. More demand drove more supply. The Mainz printers operated at full tilt, keeping costs down, pocketing profits and supplying more books more cheaply. Between 1450 and 1500, the price of books fell by two thirds. In 1460, when Johannes printed his first bible, the price of a book amounted to about 100 days' average wages. By 1600, a book cost less than one day's worth of wages.[6] Printing would change the way we thought. Literate people could read a printed book on their own, as a solitary pursuit, and this individual study allowed for deeper reflection and analysis.

A revolutionary new design entered the scene: the pamphlet. A one-sided polemic that could be turned around quickly, digested swiftly and read out in the market square by a literate town crier, the pamphlet disseminated ideas to a population that was still largely illiterate. Printing didn't only change our way of thinking; it changed our way of working. With printing, the merchant was exposed, maybe for the first time, to the magic of productivity gains derived from mechanised production. Printing works were among the very first iteration of what would become the factory model of industrial production. The merchant was on his way to becoming an industrialist and Gutenberg's workshop wrote the opening sentences of the story that would become the industrial revolution. The printing press also introduced a third key factor of production into economics: capital. It was one of the first examples of a machine that profoundly affected the productivity of workers, boosting profitability per worker, the fount of all capitalism. Books also changed labour from sweat to skill, beginning the process of differentiation in workers between skilled and unskilled industrial labour. Both these developments – capitalism and skilled labour – would have profound impacts on society and politics in the centuries ahead.

Municipalities pooled resources to buy printing presses. The link between the establishment of a printing press and subsequent economic growth is unambiguous. Between 1500 and 1600, European cities with printing works established in the late fifteenth century grew 60 per cent faster than cities without printworks.[7] Intellectual freedom and commercial freedom went hand in hand. Once they got a printing press, cities in Germany and other parts of Europe that had no prior industrial, trading or financial advantage experienced higher levels of economic growth and a surge in literacy. People devoured books, pamphlets and journals, displaying a clear bias for new, future-looking pursuits like zoology, anatomy and botany.

This was good news for teachers and anyone working in education. The average university professor saw his salary rise from the same as the average skilled artisan to twice that in fifty years. People's interest in tomorrow and the possibilities of science took off. We can see this bias in the salaries of various types of professors during the early sixteenth century. Those teaching the sciences, maths and astronomy enjoyed larger pay increases than professors of law, theology, rhetoric, grammar, poetry and Greek.

Much as Italy had been in the fourteenth century, Germany from the sixteenth century on became the fulcrum of European innovation and thought – from Böhme to Hegel, via Leibniz, Wolff and Kant. Germany was suited to the dissemination of information and early adoption of commercial and technological innovations because the late Holy Roman Empire was a decentralised network of small cities and territories elbowing each other for prestige. Had Germany been one large, unified empire with a vertical structure of power, there would likely have been censorship from central government. The printing press, with its potential for producing revolutionary material, would probably have been monitored and controlled more closely. The Chinese had figured out printing centuries before Gutenberg but their mandarins, ever alert to a technology that might undermine the authority of the centre, were quick to shut down the diffusion of printing presses and adamant about censoring incendiary materials. In Germany there was no centre. The polycentric nature of the map, with its competing cities and towns, was the perfect breeding ground for intellectual and mercantile sedition. The scene was set.

Luther

Printing, the financial innovation that financed the Church in the mid-fifteenth century, would be the one that tore it apart in the sixteenth century. Martin Luther was a product of the printing press. But he was also a product of money.

He grew up in the silver-mining area of Saxony and his father was a mining entrepreneur, as were his brother and three brothers-in-law. Mining was an expensive business and the locals who started mining created a *gewerk* – an early type of joint-stock company – to pay for increasing up-front capital costs. The deeper into the mountain you dig, the more expensive the process. The Luther family, like other shareholders, invested before the digging started. Every quarter, investors either paid in more to keep the mine going or were given a payout in proportion to the shares they owned. In the 1490s, these shares began to generate returns in large, high-quality silver coins.[8] Martin Luther himself held some mining shares. However, between roughly 1500 and 1530, possibly as a result of too much prospecting, a mining slump prompted a credit crunch and severe regional depression in Saxony. The Luther family suffered financially while the Church continued to enrich itself creating money from indulgences. Could it have been this disparity between the sudden reduced circumstances of the silver mine owners and the ongoing opulence of the Church that, at least in part, prompted Luther's indignation?

The timing of his protest coincided with a monumental Vatican-run shakedown. In October 1517, an indulgence-selling roadshow rolled into Saxony, offering get-out-of-purgatory pardons in exchange for money that would supposedly be used to rebuild St Peter's Basilica in Rome. However, some of that money was actually intended for the Fugger banking family (Germany's equivalent to the Medicis), who were owed 21,000 ducats by the successor to Gutenberg's old boss, the Archbishop of Mainz. He had used the money to bribe the pope to grant him the bishopric, a valuable post because it was one of only seven electors of the Holy Roman Emperor.

Money, banking, bribery, corruption, lies and salvation: a cocktail to trigger a man like Luther.

His first post – nailed to the door of Wittenberg Cathedral on All Hallows' Eve, 1517 – was printed in bullet points rather than sentences because a short set of bullet points could be quickly reprinted on Gutenberg's machinery. Luther's points were conversation starters rather than definitive conclusions, allowing others to get involved in the debate.

The 'Ninety-five Theses' were an overnight sensation. The printing press was the disruption that allowed Luther to take his war against the Roman Catholic Church from the cloistered tower to the crowded market. The hierarchy was about to feel the power of the network. By the end of 1517, copies of the theses were being printed and reprinted in Leipzig, Nuremberg and Basel. Luther's literary output was immense. He wrote thirteen treatises which sold over 300,000 copies between 1517 and 1521.[9]

His pamphlets were written to be read out loud, in German rather than Latin. They were usually six to eight pages long, which made them easy to digest, and easy to hide. They contained drawings, vile caricatures of sleazy monks, corpulent bishops and corrupt lusty popes. Designed to shock as well as make people laugh, the pamphlet was the weapon of choice for Luther and his rebels.

In time, his anti-Roman ideas spread, and his rebel pastors began gaining positions in urban parishes and larger free cities, consolidating the network. Luther, the creator, was at the centre, churning out ideas, and the network of pastors were communicating these thoughts to their congregations, who in turn spread the word. Each discussion, whether in the back of an inn, at a toll turnpike, in the market square or among the artisans' guilds, mandated people who had never previously been asked their opinion of anything but the weather. Being mandated would have given the feeling of group participation. Wives talked to husbands, bakers argued with butchers, goldsmiths with moneylenders. The topics centred on the eternal questions of life, morality, the afterlife and, of course, salvation.

Luther's breakout publication was his 'Sermon on Indulgences and Grace', written in a German that everyone from Saxony to the Rhineland could understand. It was reprinted fourteen times in 1518 alone. It is estimated that 7 million pamphlets were printed in the period from 1517 to 1530, and more than one quarter of these were penned by Luther. The priest was a publishing sensation, and as success begets success, every up-and-coming publisher wanted to publish him – a Lutheran missive would keep the printworks busy.

It wasn't all about morals; money also drove Protestantism. A major attraction of this new religion was that a converting monarch could steal the assets of the old religion. England's Henry VIII, known also as the Great Debaser, a very poor money manager, found the idea of confiscating Church lands extremely tempting. Kings and princelings all over Germany followed Henry's example, expropriating Church property. From the perspective of a bankrupt king, Protestantism was like winning the lottery. And for the local prince, confiscating Church land was a surefire get-rich-quick scheme. Who wouldn't go for such an option?

Money also played a part lower down the hierarchy. Luther had stumbled on a cheaper way to salvation than buying indulgences. By living a good life, the saved could avoid the tax that was paying for an indulgence and yet guarantee the same outcome. You could almost say Protestantism was a tax avoidance strategy!

The rebel religion constituted a break from older forms of Christianity in another fundamental way: Protestantism celebrated acquiring money through hard work and good deeds, and involving oneself in enterprise. For Calvinists, with their radical brand of Protestantism, being rich and saving wealth were even earthly signs of your predestined place in heaven. This interpretation flipped traditional Christian thinking about money, wealth and poverty on its head. It could be said that from now on money had a religion.

In Germany, city after city flipped Protestant and the printing press played a crucial role. Cities with at least one printing press were more likely to convert than those without, while cities with multiple competing presses were even more likely to turn Protestant.[10] Luther went on the circuit giving lectures, and wrote letters relentlessly. Wittenberg was ground zero for the revolution, an academy of sedition, where rebellious priests came to hear the maestro in person. Infused with his radical message, these disciples headed back to the newly converted free cities to spread the message.

Maritime money

In the winter of 1519, as Martin Luther was cranking out his pamphlets, a meeting occurred between two men that would change the course of human history. Twenty-six years earlier, in pursuit of money, specifically Chinese money, Christopher Columbus had accidentally stumbled upon the Americas. In the subsequent years, all sorts of independent Spanish adventurers set off across the Atlantic in search of their fortunes and, in particular, in search of gold – which they found in enormous quantities. On the morning of 9 November 1519, Hernán Cortés, a Spanish clerk turned conquistador, walked up a causeway to meet, for the first time, Moctezuma II, the emperor of the Aztecs. Moctezuma bestowed gifts and hospitality upon the Europeans; it's fair to say that the generosity of the Meso-Americans towards the Spaniards was not reciprocated, either then or ever. Within months of this meeting, the Europeans set about destroying the great Aztec city of Tenochtitlan, killing Moctezuma and enslaving his people.

Many reasons have been given to explain why the Spaniards were more technologically advanced than the Aztecs. In their toolkit, the Europeans had ships, guns, wheels and steel. They also had compasses, maps, horses, cannons, vicious dogs that terrified the Americans and, maybe most significantly, they had immunity to a variety of diseases that would decimate the locals, including smallpox and the flu. The yawning technological gap evident at this fateful meeting between two civilisations has been described as Renaissance Europe coming face to face with the Sumerians.[11] Historians put the relative underdevelopment of the Meso-American civilisation down to a variety of structural causes, such as the Europeans being settled farmers for a much longer period, allowing greater settled and urbanised populations to develop. Rarely mentioned, however, is the fact that the Aztecs had only a very rudimentary form of money.

As we have been observing, money is a great enabler of innovation. Could the absence of a well-developed system of money and finance in Aztec civilisation explain why the Europeans were, technologically, so far ahead? In contrast to their agricultural prowess and undoubted architectural and mathematical abilities, the Aztecs had a pretty elementary form of money: they were using perishable cocoa beans for small transactions. Evidence suggests that, although they traded intensively, they relied on a system of bartering, gifting and tributes to do this. The Europeans, meanwhile, were the recipients of a tradition of monetary experimentation that stretched back to the Sumerian era, and had been using coins since the time of the Lydians. In trying to explain the differences between the New and Old Worlds, money surely deserves a mention.

The Aztecs might not have had sophisticated money, but they did have gold and silver, lots of both, and the Spaniards grabbed what they could. One estimate suggests that during the 1500s, the total stock of European gold and silver was five times bigger than it had been in 1493.[12] Vast armed armadas laden down with bullion left the New World for Spain, financed by freelance opportunists. Armed profiteers, the conquistadors, plundered the Americas wholesale.

The Spaniards were ransacking the mines of the New World, but this mania for gold and silver was a celebration of the past; the future of money would be a new form of money, paper money, with its financial handmaidens, the stock and bond markets. Money in the form of heavy bullion weighing down the stout Spanish galleys was history; the future would be feather-light paper in the hands of merchants.

A new age of commerce and colonialism was upon us and the oceans opened up the world. Maritime nations, rather than those with large landmasses, stole a financial march. By the seventeenth century, Holland, the smallest country in Europe, was the biggest winner.

PART 3:

REVOLUTIONARY MONEY

INVISIBLE MONEY

An unexpected visitor

In 1697, disguised as a ship's mate, the Tsar of Russia, Peter the Great, arrived in the richest city in the world. Built on marshland, Amsterdam was a free city of elegant houses, commercial quays and a network of busy canals, financed partly by a thriving stock market. This trading city was founded on the twin religions of Protestantism and commerce. Welcoming dissenters and religious refugees, it was home to the largest merchant navy in the world and formed the beating heart of a mercantile empire that stretched from Holland to Cape Town, Zanzibar and Malacca. Its harbour, with hundreds of masts piercing the overcast lowland sky, was its citadel, the source of Dutch power.

Russians, particularly landlocked Muscovites, had little knowledge of the sea, but Peter knew that the world was changing. People who understood the sea understood trade, and they were pulling ahead commercially from the rest – first Portugal in the sixteenth century and then Holland by the end of the seventeenth. Both maritime powers had rewritten the map of the world, following the trade routes, each creating trading outposts at critical points in Atlantic Africa, around the Cape, up the Indian Ocean and further east to Asia. They had managed to circumnavigate the globe, avoiding the Ottoman stranglehold on the overland Silk Roads. The now ascendant Dutch were involved in a global game of arbitrage, sourcing and buying items – like pepper, cinnamon and other spices – cheaply in the East and selling expensively in the West, pocketing the difference.

Russia was being left behind and this didn't sit well with the young Romanov tsar. Determined to unlock the secrets of Holland's success, Peter landed a four-month internship at the famed shipyards and from there he watched and learned, absorbing everything that Amsterdam had to offer. The world's largest landowner travelled to the world's largest shipbuilder to learn the ropes. Undercover, he lived in a tiny wooden artisan's house, where he made his own bed, donned the garb of a Dutch carpenter and lived like a local. When he had finished his internship, his Calvinist supervisor noted he was 'a good and skilful carpenter'.[1]

His stay in Amsterdam would change his life and the history of both Russia and Europe. When he built his new capital city, the tsar modelled it on the Dutch capital, even taking a Dutch name, 'Sankt Pieter Burkh', rather than a Russian equivalent. The greatest city in Russia imitated the greatest city in Europe: it was built on marshes and shaped around canals. Struck by the commercial and cultural vibrancy of cosmopolitan Amsterdam, Peter invited foreigners to set up shop in St Petersburg.

The autocratic overlord of the largest land empire in the world was not a man hemmed in by convention. According to one of his biographers,[2] the tsar was an imposing giant of a man who drank copiously, philandered indiscreetly and in the rest of his free time is rumoured to have enjoyed carrying out autopsies. Alert to treason within his own circle, Peter was amazed at the lack of privacy and nonchalant attitude to security he found in Holland. Wealthy Russians barricaded themselves behind militarised fortresses; in contrast, rich Dutch bankers, merchants and lawyers lived in homes with huge clear windows in full gaze of the commoners. This struck the tsar as extremely modern. The apparent social proximity of different classes rubbing shoulders must have been unsettling for a man who owned more slaves than anyone else in the world.

Like many Russians, Peter the Great was both impressed and unnerved by western European sophistication and technological prowess. This conflict between seeing the West as a beacon and a threat has long been a conundrum for Russian intellectuals. As has been the case for many years, ambitious Russian leaders regularly embrace cosmetic Western characteristics, but baulk at the deeper inconveniences actual Western liberal politics can impose on the powerful. On his return to Russia, Peter insisted that Russian aristocracy shave their long beards, adopt Western fashion and behave more like modest, hard-working Dutch burghers, rather than the serf-owning aristocracy that they were. Those parts of the Dutch set-up that didn't appeal to him, such as the Hollander king's subservience to the country's parliament, were left on the banks of the Amstel.

Although Peter wanted the fruits of Dutch money – the innovation, the wealth, the naval power – he wasn't too keen on the democratic and institutional compromises the Dutch establishment made to achieve them. Encouraging debate and accepting people who might not agree with you on everything wasn't for him, but sometimes you can't have one without the other. Dissent and creativity often contribute to the great adventure of commercial enterprise. Dutch tolerance, Dutch wealth and Dutch financial genius appeared to go together.

Given seventeenth-century Amsterdam's commercial energy and dexterity with money, is it any wonder that a curious and pioneering Russian monarch would arrive in the Dutch capital incognito looking to unearth the secrets of wealth? Holland was perplexing. How could a country so small have this power and prosperity when a country as large as Russia was poor? In the Russian world, might was right and power required scale. How did this tiny country emerge at the centre of European commerce? What alchemy was at work? Whatever the Dutch were drinking, Peter the Great wanted some.

Feather-light money

The printing press created a demand for paper, which had previously been the preserve of the clergy and court; most ordinary people in Europe would rarely have encountered paper or parchment in their daily lives. After Gutenberg, that changed. People wanted the written word on paper – posters, pamphlets, books and copybooks. An entire new production process emerged involving forestry, milling, washing, bleaching, pulping, stretching and drying. Where there were printing presses, there were paper mills. Literacy rates took off in a new age of enquiry and discovery. If the Church could be questioned and the established religion replaced, what else might be up for grabs? If paper could be used extensively for the Reformation's incendiary pamphlets, what else could it be used for?

Money, in all its forms, was about to undergo its own sort of Reformation. This thoroughgoing reassessment of what constituted money required some major leaps of faith, and possibly the most gymnastic of these intellectual jumps was the notion that a piece of paper could represent value far above its intrinsic value. Up to this point, we have seen various forms of money: Lydian gold, Greek silver, Roman copper, silver and gold, German silver and the golden florin. Money then evolved into letters of credit and German annuities, but these were always tied to particular merchants, merchant banks, municipalities or pieces of physical land; in a sense, letters of credit and annuities had a 'memory' – they could be traced to somebody or something.

Imagine a piece of paper representing money with no memory, no trace other than the faith in the money itself and the institution that prints it. The next iteration of money would be mass acceptance of paper money: pieces of paper issued by a centralised bank that could not be traced to anybody or anything except the credibility of that centralised bank, the issuer. Such an evolution in money required an evolution in society. It required deep levels of trust between people who did not know each other. And this is what the Dutch moved towards. Paper money would be a revolutionary chapter in the story of money. With a government stamp and an intricate design, a mere piece of paper can be magically transformed into money, legal tender to buy and sell real things.

As with printing, paper money had in fact been invented centuries before in China. Initially, paper money, at least at street level, derived from receipts of pawn shops. Pawn shops turned property into cash. People in China pawned their clothes or jewels and the pawn shop gave them a receipt, written to the value of the goods pawned. This receipt was then used to exchange goods up to the value of the property written on the paper. People understood the pawn shop was good for the money. During the Song dynasty (980–1280 CE), paper became the primary instrument of state money, mediating all transactions between the treasury and the bureaucracy.

This money was printed on mulberry bark paper using four-colour copper plates – the first item ever produced using this technology – and could be passed from hand to hand without smudging or perishing.

In Europe, paper money issued by a central bank first materialised in Britain in 1695 with the establishment of the Bank of England, but this could not have happened without the foundations that were laid in Amsterdam decades earlier. In 1609, the Dutch set up the Wisselbank, a centralised bank, owned by rich merchants, operating under a royal charter. Why the Dutch first? This was Peter the Great's question.

There are a number of reasons why the Wisselbank emerged in Holland. Small countries are hemmed in by the tyranny of geography. When the home market is small, the only way that small countries can grow quickly is by trade, acquiring market share in bigger regions. Once a small open economy breaks free of its geography and begins to trade way beyond its borders, it faces a monetary dilemma. What to do with this new money that is flowing in from abroad? If the trading state doesn't manage this new money, its own exchange rate will rise, destroying the very competitiveness that brought the money in to begin with. (Today, small successful trading countries like Singapore, Ireland and Switzerland face a similar conundrum.) Monetary economics in trading economies is a balancing act.

In the Dutch case, the more its merchants traded abroad, the more money flowed back into Amsterdam. In the early seventeenth century, this money would have been in the form of various coins – Spanish and British silver, Florentine florins and so on. There would also be bulk bullion. The more trade, the more currencies. To function smoothly, the Dutch economy needed a single currency, standardised by some institution, and one function of the Wisselbank was to soak up all these various coins and swap them into the Dutch currency, the guilder, backed by the gold in its reserves so that the money could be used in Holland.

Financing the navy was another central motive in setting up the Wisselbank. Although the Dutch, unlike other European colonists, largely preferred isolated trading outposts to large-scale territorial conquest, guns played an undoubted role in the expansion of Dutch commerce. Much is made of Dutch tolerance at home, but Dutch riches came from a smash-and-grab exercise visited upon the peoples of Africa and Asia. The state borrowed from merchants to fund the expanding navy. In turn, the navy protected merchant ships returning to Holland with bounty from East Asia and America. As trade increased, there were more ships, the navy got bigger and more money was needed to fund it – but this also led, of course, to more money flowing back into Amsterdam.

A tiny country with an outsized commercial empire, Holland was turning into the republic of money.

The republic of money

By the late 1580s, Holland was experimenting with long-term bonds, borrowing far into the future to finance investment today, giving the country an edge over competitors. New companies financed by shares that could be owned by citizens were underpinned by an evolving legal system that set the rules for trade all over the Dutch Empire. While they were plundering abroad, at home the republican Dutch looked at combining their resources and sharing the opportunity to invest in the colonial project. They decided to create a wide investor base and the world's first shareholding society, at least for the smaller merchant classes. In 1601, the Dutch East India Company (VOC) was founded, a financial behemoth financed privately by many shareholders. Its trading profits were so steep that the VOC would become the biggest company the world had ever seen, surpassing (in the money of the time) even Apple in valuation.

By 1602, the VOC was so material to the fortunes of Amsterdam that the government decided to grant it a monopoly on trade in the East Indies. A major reason for this was risk mitigation. A ship financed by Dutch investors was an all-or-nothing affair. If the ship was lost, all was lost. If the ship docked, the profits were so monumental that investors made a fortune. But how do you streamline the risk? You give the company a monopoly. This means that all the shareholders pool the risk, mitigating exposure and creating a more stable profit stream out of a precarious but profitable business.

By effectively tying the fortunes of the company to the state, the government encouraged shareholding, coaxing in people who would otherwise never have owned shares. They were creating an investment opportunity out of a speculative venture, and that investment would generate a stream of income for a broad section of the population, embedding financial capitalism deep in the Dutch psyche. Holland was on its way to becoming a shareholding culture mediated by money. The first one ever.

Amsterdam's cityscape evolved quite differently from how one might expect the richest place in the world to have looked. No broad avenues, no pompous squares for imperial displays and no outsized aristocratic villas – public modesty, despite the underlying wealth, characterised the capital city. Along the canal banks, the Dutch built attractive terraced townhouses, allowing boats to dock alongside, landing various goods from all over the world. These narrow merchants' homes were designed with warehouses at the bottom and shops on the first floor, leading to the home and office above. Amsterdam's burghers borrowed this model from the money-making democrats of Florence.

What Florence had been, Amsterdam became. Florence of the fifteenth century was a magnet for the curious, who were drawn to a city governed by the more egalitarian and accessible medium of money rather than a tight feudal class system. By the early seventeenth century, the ambitious from all over Europe headed to Amsterdam to make their fortune. In an intolerant and violent world, Amsterdam welcomed Sephardic Jews, expelled from Spain and Portugal, who brought commercial skills, financial savvy and knowledge of the Mediterranean and North African trade routes. Later, the French Protestant Huguenots found refuge in Holland, bringing banking experience to the obliging Dutch. Bankers for the French Crown for many years, these Calvinists learned their banking trade in the fairs of Lyon and Avignon, borrowing know-how from their spiritual cousins the Calvinists of Geneva. The first governor of the Bank of England, John Houblon, was a Huguenot, and in banks like the blue-blooded Cazenove their legacy is evident in the City of London today. Indeed, the word refugee, which comes from the name for the Huguenots fleeing France, the *réfugiés*, entered the English language in the late seventeenth century.

The Dutch economic miracle was the talk of Europe. Holland was trading wood from Scandinavia, sugar from the West Indies, furs from French Canada, tobacco from the British colonies in North America, and cinnamon, pepper, ginger and silk from Borneo. By the late sixteenth century, 100 years after Columbus had arrived in America, the indigenous populations of Latin America had been so decimated by disease and violence brought by the colonists that the Spanish had run out of indigenous people to enslave. The Dutch, prominent in the slave trade, sold Africans to the Spaniards. Tolerant at home, the Dutch chose to look the other way when it came to the high seas. If there was a pie, a Dutchman had his finger in it. The country oozed commerce and, in a way, Holland could be described as a multinational company – the East India Company – with a country stuck onto it, rather than the other way around. Imagine a corporation with a private army and you get the picture.

But there was something else going on, something that Peter the Great was trying to understand. It eluded him because it wasn't something physical, it was sociological. In fact, it was an idea. This idea was linked to the way Dutch people and their mercantile immigrants saw themselves and their prospects. As money reached deep into Dutch society, it altered the way the Dutch saw the future. For example, Holland came up with the concept of the perpetual bond. This is a loan where the capital is *never* repaid. By buying perpetual bonds, a lender would not get his lump sum of capital back but instead receive an income stream into perpetuity. Can you imagine how much trust in money there must be in a society for people to finance a loan that they know is never actually going to be repaid and yet consider this to be a prudent form of saving? It's a mind-boggling abstraction. This is the magic of money: notions that seem fantastical are accepted and even become humdrum.

For a society to willingly finance projects with money that would never be paid back, something must have changed in its belief system. In Renaissance Florence, only sophisticated traders, with their intricate network of fellow merchants, might have agreed to lend to each other accepting that the capital would never be repaid. But in early seventeenth-century Holland, regular municipalities were building dykes and sea fortifications by borrowing into perpetuity from ordinary local people, who used their perpetual bonds as a form of savings. The level of financial trust established in Dutch society suggests that the mercantile traits we spoke about in earlier chapters – such as a belief in commercial innovation, an openness to risk, an understanding of finance – must have extended deep into society.

Such mercantile or bourgeois values reflect a society moving from a top-down command and control economy to a horizontal network economy. The Dutch had no material advantage: no coal or iron deposits, unlike Britain; no industrial-scale woodland, unlike Scandinavia; no geographic edge, unlike medieval Italy; no vast overseas territory, unlike imperial Spain. Holland did not have a huge population like France or a huge land mass like Russia. In fact, its land mass was the smallest in Europe, and much of it was waterlogged. But the Dutch had an idea: mass commercial participation underpinned by an agile financial system that got the most out of money.

People would not have bought perpetual bonds unless they believed in a prosperous future. With this belief in the future, people came to believe they could change their own circumstances. For upward social mobility to be possible, society must have ennobled commercial effort, offering a degree of dignity and encouragement to the small person to dream big. Why would you take a commercial risk if the prevailing attitude of the nation was to demean and sneer at such endeavour? This scornful attitude is the default position of the aristocrat. But through its encounter with money, the Dutch mind had changed.

Peter the Great failed to grasp this essential link between personal liberty, the dignity of commerce and a buzzing, innovative, networked economy. The Dutch had no raw material except the most potent of all, the one between our ears: a free and enquiring mind. Without this human energy, there could be no sustainable economic growth because there would be no consistent innovation.

Experimentation in commerce and art regularly go together. While Dutch merchants were expanding trade, Dutch artists were innovating during a period that would come to be known as the age of the Dutch Masters. Portraits by the likes of Rembrandt, in contrast to earlier flamboyant Italian portraits, were austere and absent material ostentation, reflecting the Dutch preference for understated wealth. That's not to say they weren't signalling their status: for example, many of the subjects were dressed in black clothing, which appears modest until you learn that black was the most expensive dye at this time. The Dutch mind was pushing the boundaries, rejecting the old and embracing the new in all sorts of ways. The perpetual bond and a painting by Vermeer come from the same place: the human imagination.

Trading on the wind

The Dutch nudged the possibilities of money forward, founding their stock market, the New Exchange, in 1610. By the 1620s, many modern financial instruments were being used daily by the Dutch, including futures markets to bet on possible outcomes years away, margin financing to leverage a hunch, and the buying and selling of options to allow gambling on a bonanza or a catastrophe. Almost every possible combination of future events could be priced in money in the

Amsterdam of the early 1600s. Is it any surprise that the Dutch got carried away?

As more capital sought out Holland as a safe home and a cauldron of opportunity, interest rates fell, house prices took off and the value of shares, even in companies without any profit, soared. The early seventeenth-century Dutch referred to this phenomenon as *windhandel* trading, meaning 'trading on fresh air'. Money was invisible. With *windhandel* generating paper profits, wealth was rising and people's appetite for risk was expanding. Between 1630 and 1639, shares in the Dutch East India Company more than doubled and the Amsterdam stock index rose from 229 in 1630 to 500 by 1640. All markets were rising. Traders and investors, who made money on housing, stuck a few guilders into shares, including shares in the VOC. Sometimes, the worst investment decisions are taken in what appear to be the best of times. Effervescence and giddiness reigned. Each new height prompted more gossip, and stories of great fortunes coaxed more people to get involved in a market that kept rising. Getting rich was never easier, and when people get rich, they want to tell others.

Good gossip is hard to beat. Gossip can be innocent and it can be dangerous – and most of us love it. As Aristotle observed, we are social creatures. We underestimate the influence of gossip in economics and finance, particularly when the crowd gets hyped up by rumour and fear of missing out. The business cycle is nothing more than the collective expression of human nature, vacillating between optimism and pessimism. We get giddy together; we get depressed together. The 'together' bit is the key.

I like to use the term 'economics of gossip' to outline the way asset prices react when we, the social animal, respond to new information and pass it on, infecting others with our mood. Classical economics, as taught to undergraduates around the world, assumes people are rational and unencumbered by emotion or gossip when it comes to making decisions about money. Have you ever met a human like this? It is foolish to regard humankind, beautifully flawed creatures that we are, as rational, and ignore the role of our moods. Financial patterns are repeated throughout history, in recurring boom–bust cycles, largely because money is social. Speculation is money at its most social, bringing together people who might not otherwise know each other or have anything in common except a particular joint project – the project of making easy money. When we are excited by easy gains, we are more likely to be 'momentum' investors who go with the flow, rather than 'value' investors who go against the grain. Most of us behave like the herd.

In the crowd, the laws of economics are shaken up. Classical economics contends that when prices rise, demand falls. Is this the case? It's more accurate to say that when some prices rise, like the price of certain assets, people who own these assets feel rich and they talk about it. A potential buyer, spooked by this gossip, panics at the signal that asset prices are rising. Believing that today's price is a bargain and if he waits it'll cost more tomorrow, he buys today. Price increases beget more price increases, bringing forward demand. One of the fundamental laws of economics is not a law after all.

A second fundamental law contends that when prices rise, supply will rise. But is this always accurate? In a rising market, a would-be seller has second thoughts. She thinks, with prices rising, she'd be mad to sell now, when she could sell next year and make more money. She shares this observation with her friends. They all wait for a better price tomorrow rather than selling today. But rising prices do not always cause supply to rise; they can, in fact, cause supply to contract, squeezing the price skywards on a journey from boom to bust. Classical economics tells us that price is some mechanical instrument that signals sterile 'equilibrium' between supply and demand, where the economy is stable. Only blackboard economists think of prices like that. In the real world, rising prices are financial aphrodisiacs. They tell us how much profit we can make, on paper at least, and lure us into markets, urging us to gamble on tomorrow – the opposite of stability. For economists, price is only a number; for real people, price is a feeling.

Tulipmania

In the late sixteenth century, tulips were introduced to Amsterdam by the ambassador of the Ottoman Empire. (In Turkish, tulip means turban, the shape of the flower's distinctive crown.) The most exotic flower of the era sparked the interest of the horticultural and botanical community. The windows of Herengracht – bragging walls for Amsterdam's high society – displayed beautiful floral arrangements every spring.

In a highly speculative society, characterised by *windhandel*, why not take a punt on the future price of tulip bulbs? With prices going up, bulbs sown today would yield a capital gain come what may. Compared to shares or houses, bulbs were cheap and allowed smaller investors to get in on the gamble. For a decade or so the prices of tulips rose steadily. Due to the depth and sophistication of Dutch capital markets, tulip contracts were accepted in everyday business. A merchant could pay for goods with a tulip contract and then cash in when the flowers emerged in the spring and pay back the loan with the proceeds, in the run-of-the-mill way that collateral is used today. This might seem normal to us, but at a time when most Europeans had never stepped outside their village, the cosmopolitan Dutch were trading collateralised debt obligations based on tulips.

Initially, the market was made up of Dutch florists or well-off amateur bulb collectors. By late 1634, however, Haarlem flower traders noticed a new type of person bidding for bulbs, some from as far away as Paris.[3] Speculators were becoming attracted by stories of earning easy money in the bulb trade. *Tulpenwoerde* or Tulipmania took hold in the summer and autumn of 1636. As prices were bid upwards, professionals opted out, leaving the tulip market to an inexperienced but enthusiastic hoi polloi. The merchant princes of Amsterdam, preferring to stick with bills of exchange, the posher homes in the city and central bank-backed notes, watched from the sidelines as the mania unfolded. As more people became involved, tulip brokers started to take payment-in-kind as security. Cows, tracts of land, paintings, a dozen sheep, oxheads of wine, a silver beaker and 1,000 pounds of cheese are all recorded as collateral that was used to secure a certain number of bulbs.[4] Holland was mortgaging its real wealth on the ephemeral *windhandel* promise of making money from a handful of tulip bulbs.

In the winter of 1636, when the average annual wage was between 200 and 400 guilders and the average townhouse cost 300 guilders, an average tulip bulb, of the third-rate type, rose from 25 guilders pre-boom to 220 guilders. Further up the rarity tree, a Generalissimo tulip that fetched 95 guilders in early 1636 traded at 900 guilders only a year later. By then the rarest tulip, the Semper Augustus, traded for 6,000 guilders – over twenty times the average annual salary.[5]

Thousands of speculators were now involved; taverns were overflowing with people pooling their resources and mortgaging possessions in search of more exposure. The giddiness of the crowd, egged on by tales of fortunes made, drove the madness until 3 February 1637, when panic to buy was replaced by panic to sell. Bankruptcies were widespread. The herd moved from greed to fear, euphoria to panic, and the price, the signal that galvanised the masses on the way up, crushed their dreams on the way down.

Tulipmania was a popular phenomenon in the sense that it involved the average person and small-time dealers. Unlike many future monetary financial boom–bust episodes, the financial elite, Amsterdam's established bankers and intercontinental merchant princes, didn't really dirty their hands. Critically, because all the collateral was real as opposed to debt-financed, there was a one-off short shock to the economy rather than a long-term crisis. The opposite happens when a boom is financed by credit (as we will see later). After the shock of the collapse of tulip prices, it didn't take long for the Dutch economy to recover.

Holland continued to trade and lead the world in finance. By the time Peter the Great rocked up in his artisan disguise, there was still a lot for him to learn. From the close of the seventeenth century, following the Dutch army's invasion of England in 1688, many of Amsterdam's financial tricks passed across the North Sea to London. Dutch bankers and financiers followed King William of Orange to England, fertilising London with Amsterdam's monetary DNA. Holland was the first country to experience, in a widespread fashion, what we would call today the rise of a financial bourgeoisie, a class whose agility with money allowed this tiny republic to galvanise its own resources and those of the globe to such an extent that Amsterdam became the richest city in the world, and Holland could orchestrate a coup d'état on its far larger neighbour.

One of the innovations that spread from Amsterdam to London at this time was a centralised merchant bank not unlike the Wisselbank. The Bank of England, established in 1694, would issue paper money, leading to deep capital markets, perpetual bonds, listed companies that could raise equity from investors, and limited liability companies that enabled risk pooling, essential for financing Britain's overseas commercial expansion.

From the establishment of the Dutch East India Company in 1602 to the Dutch coup d'état in Britain, also known as the Glorious Revolution, constant innovation with money had propelled Holland forward. The seventeenth-century Dutch were the princes of money, inventing many of the financial instruments we continue to use today. The same country that had adopted Luther's Protestant message with such enthusiasm was quick to imagine that a share price written on a piece of paper could have value, and for this idea to take hold, something had to change in people's heads.

While the Dutch monetary century revealed what can be achieved via money and trade, with Tulipmania it also exposed the madness of crowds whipped up by money. And while the great arbitrage trade – buying goods cheaply all around the world and selling them expensively in Europe – enriched the merchants of Amsterdam, it came at a brutal cost for colonised peoples all over the globe. This cost would continue to be borne throughout the following centuries. The pursuit of money, a liberation to some, also directly resulted in the colonisation, maltreatment and degradation of millions. The technology that enabled so much human progress and innovation also facilitated terror and suffering. The story of money, once again, is the story of us – for good and ill.

11

THE FATHER OF
MONETARY ECONOMICS

Murderer on the run

In April 1694, things weren't looking great for hell-raising Scot John Law. He'd just blown a decent inheritance on gambling, and possibly other delights of the night. His disappointed mother had to bail him out, and now he was going to break the news to her that no mother ever wants to hear: he had just killed a man. Only twenty-three, born reasonably well-off, John Law was doomed. Or was he?

He had killed Edmund Wilson in a duel with an impulsive lunge of a sword to the belly. Apparently, Law and Wilson loved the same woman. That wasn't all: the woman, Betty Villiers, was also the king's lover. A complicated and dangerous ménage-à-trois. Maybe at that point, like the hero of 'Bohemian Rhapsody', he wished he'd never been born at all, but Law sidestepped the hangman in one of the many improbable scrapes of his life. Murderer, gambler, philanderer, art collector, casino impresario, seducer of women and generally all-round good-time-Charlie, the father of monetary economics was far from the dull, stereotypical economist. He was a hoot, and a highly intelligent one too. A man who could keep a secret, of which he knew many, Law's life was one long, hair-raising adventure after another.

Some might say, given his later escapades, that Law would do anything for money, which is only half wrong. In time, he would revolutionise money itself and his legacy is scrawled, like intellectual graffiti, over present-day central banking. John Law was the father of what would become known as fiat money – money issued by central banks that is not tied to gold. While the Dutch continued to anchor their system around the golden guilder, Law's system was constrained by nothing but trust. As we will see, the man who slipped the noose in 1694 was driven by the urge to escape constraints both in his personal life and, more importantly for our purposes, in the management of money. Law wanted to set money free. He wasn't everyone's cup of tea, either during his life or afterwards, but as the political economist Joseph Schumpeter put it, Law 'is in a class by himself . . . He worked out the economics of his projects with a brilliance and, yes, profundity, which places him in the front ranks of monetary theorists of all time.'[1]

Around the time he murdered Wilson, Law was swanning around London in his finery, eating, drinking and generally causing mayhem absent any sign of legitimate income. Duels were going out of fashion, but for a couple of young men about town, Law and Wilson, puffed up by vanity and insecurity, a duel was still a way to preserve honour. Not that the pair in question had much of that. Law's defence was that it was a crime of passion. On finding out that Wilson was also in Villiers' bed, he challenged his amorous competitor to a duel. That was the story doing the rounds in London in the summer of 1694. But there's another, more titillating possibility, which is that Law was in fact hired as a hit man. Rumour had it that Wilson was a kept man. Here's where the story gets even more scandalous.

Many years later, in 1723, an alternative and scurrilous explanation for Wilson's luxurious lifestyle emerged in a forty-nine-page pamphlet entitled *Love-Letters Between a certain late Nobleman and the famous Mr. Wilson discovering the true History of the Rise and surprising Grandeur of that celebrated Beau*. The pamphlet suggested that Wilson had been kept in silk and sauce by a male lover. The nobleman, allegedly, had become tired of Wilson as a lover – maybe he had become excessively demanding from a financial viewpoint or, more likely, he was threatening to spill the beans. In this story, there is no crime of passion, no spurned lover, no king's mistress sharing two younger bucks. The killing of Edmund was a simple hit – and John Law was the paid assassin.

A *cause célèbre* for historians of early gay literature, such as Rictor Norton, the letters hint that the nobleman in question was Charles Spencer, the 3rd Earl of Sunderland, a direct ancestor of Winston Churchill, Princess Diana and Prince William, the next king of England. If this hypothesis is correct – the evidence for it is still somewhat circumstantial – then the two men most directly involved in the killing of Edmund Wilson on Bloomsbury Heath in April 1694 were John Law and Charles Spencer. Twenty-six years later, in 1720, at the height of the stock market bubbles, these two possible criminal accomplices would meet again, one as France's Controller-General of Finances and the other as Britain's First Lord of the Treasury. They were still keeping secrets, and secrets would save both their hides in another story involving money, lovers and royalty. We'll return to that later.

Law escaped not only the death penalty but also incarceration. Documents at the Public Record Office in London show that the government arranged his escape from prison.[2] Was this because of the special pleading of Law's well-placed Scottish connections or was it part of the guarantee given to Law when plans were made for him to kill Wilson in the duel? Having friends in high places can come in handy, especially if you have information that might compromise them. After his 'escape' in 1694, Law spent the next decade travelling through France, Holland and Italy, essentially on the run. He used his mathematical skills, first noticed at school in Scotland, to make a fortune in the casinos of Europe. Deploying the laws of probability, he amassed vast wealth, later estimated at between 1.5 and 2 million French livres by the 1720s.

The first monetary theorist

While gaming gave him a rich and louche lifestyle, banking and the possibilities of paper money intrigued Law, perhaps a result of him spending time in Amsterdam. Seeing what money did to people, the energy it releases, the animal spirits it liberates, Law couldn't accept that human endeavour should be limited by the amount of gold in the ground. He saw gold, silver and copper as ancient, anti-scientific impediments to the economic possibilities that paper money afforded. Despite being a convicted murderer still technically on the run, the Scotsman sent a plan for a completely new banking system, based on paper money, to Lord Godolphin, the English Lord High Treasurer.

His 1704 proposal (belatedly published for the first time in 1994 as *John Law's 'Essay on a Land Bank'*[3]) is remarkably modern in tone, showing a clarity of thought on monetary issues that is quite superior to the contemporary writings on money. Think back to our Chinese pawnbroker example in the previous chapter, where property was turned into liquid cash. In early eighteenth-century European societies, there was plenty of property to use as collateral, but there was always a squeeze on money because people wanted the reassurance of gold or silver underpinning the value of cash. Despite Dutch financial innovations, the dead hand of gold still exercised a limit on the money supply. For Law, this was a failure of imagination, not finance. What if he could come up with another base for his paper money? At this stage in his thinking, that base was land, the traditional source of all income in pre-industrial societies, and a stable and reasonably liquid asset.

For Law, there was an obvious connection between the amount of money available in the economy and the growth rate. This connection represented a major step forward in economic theory. For the first time, he drew a link between money, its supply and the vibrancy of the economy in general, which he termed the demand for money. The nub of his thinking was that a supply of new money would generate economic energy and vibrancy, creating an increased demand for money. For example, someone wants to set up a bakery and, given enough money to do so, will establish that business and start selling bread. People will buy that bread – with money. The demand for money to buy the goods will then increase as the supply of the goods increases. As long as the money supplied is used to invest in real businesses, like the bakery, the output of the economy increases (as there is more bread). Precisely because there is more bread, the price of bread will not rise dramatically. Demand will always raise the price, but if supply responds, the price increase will be modest.

Law believed new money would generate economic activity, and thus more demand for money. Demand and supply of money would increase together, pushing the economy to grow faster, thereby bringing about an enhanced level of general prosperity. From Law's idea flows all modern central bank thinking. Even today, the US Federal Reserve's mandate to manage the money supply and achieve both growth and inflation objectives stems directly from Law's observations.

The New World

Godolphin, the English Lord High Treasurer, rejected Law's proposal. Undaunted, Law ploughed on, trying to cajole anyone who would listen, hustling his revolutionary monetary ideas around Europe. He got his breakthrough in France, then the richest and, Russia apart, the biggest and most populous country in Europe. The free-spending Sun King, Louis XIV, who had died in 1715, had almost bankrupted the country. The regent, Philippe Duc d'Orléans, knew that France needed an injection of economic magic. In desperation, the regent listened to Law. France was faced by two crises. First, they had a shortage of silver and gold. This was made more acute by a second problem: the very high level of state indebtedness. Law's monetary thinking could kill both birds with one stone.

To address the first crisis, Law, as Controller-General of Finances, suggested replacing metallic money in the form of gold and silver with paper money issued by a new bank, the General Bank, which was established in May 1716. Modelled on the Bank of England, itself based largely on the Dutch Wisselbank, the new bank would coax France's richest nobles to buy its shares. Law omitted to tell the world that the two largest shareholders were himself and the regent. This private bank, operating under royal charter, then issued paper money, initially fully convertible into gold and silver, but later backed only by the state's bona fides, financed by tax revenue. The General Bank solved France's first problem, as paper money circulated freely in the economy, motivating French traders, entrepreneurs and business folk to take more risks, bring more products to markets, and finance new trade routes.

To address the national debt, Law knew he must appeal to the speculative side of human beings, a side that was – at least in him – highly attuned. Having observed gamblers in the casino, Law came up with the idea of a massive debt-for-equity swap. In simple language, this means betting on tomorrow to solve the problems of today. Like all salesmen, Law needed a spellbinding story about the future. And in the early eighteenth century, the future was the New World, which promised untold profits (on the back of stolen land and unpaid workers in the form of slaves) for those visionary enough to take the plunge.

The discovery of the New World was a highly disruptive event in European history and, like all disruptions, it caught the imagination. In America, land was cheap (it was stolen from the First Nationers) and the soil was productive. With its broad rivers, endless horizons and enormous forests, America would provide the engine of growth for France for centuries to come. The French had watched with jealousy as Spain to the south, in truth a country the French looked down on, became fabulously wealthy on the gold and silver of Central and South America. Parisians were aware of the potential wealth of the New World as French trappers were sending home furs, pelts and lumber in abundant quantities from the American plains, while the Caribbean colonies sent rum, rice and tobacco.

At this stage, the colonies and their vast wealth were limited to colonists, the people who were over there. What might happen if Law could enlist tens of thousands of French people into the potential of the colonies via the sale of shares in a company, like the Dutch East India Company? Who wouldn't want a slice of that action? With the money raised by selling shares, Law's scheme would pay off the national debt, atoning for the sins of yesterday with the promise of tomorrow.

In August 1717, Law took over the Compagnie d'Occident (Company of the West), which had been given monopoly trading rights by the king over French Louisiana. French Louisiana was not the same as the present US state of Louisiana: it covered a much bigger area, almost half the size of the USA today. It was an enormous tract of fertile, irrigated land, ready to be harvested not just for agriculture but for minerals. With the Company of the West, Law put his debt-for-equity idea into place. Rather than take cash from new shareholders, Law offered existing holders of government debt a swap. They could exchange their French government IOUs (*billets d'état*) for the new company's shares.

Excited by the prospect of large capital gains from further exploitation of French Louisiana, many jumped at the idea. Law, ever the student of human psychology, made the new shares available at a deep discount to what he thought was their true value, meaning the shares would bounce on purchase, and the winners would do what they always do – brag and gossip about their new riches, persuading more reticent owners of government debt to have a flutter on the New World. Gossip infiltrated the cafés of Paris, Marseille and Lyon, creating excitement leveraged by greed. As the share price of the Company of the West rose, Law used these valuable shares as currency to finance a series of spectacular takeovers of other companies, heightening the sense of easy riches available to anyone who'd back him and his genius ideas.

Mississippi burning

Law glued the state onto his ventures by persuading the regent to turn the General Bank into the government's bank, meaning the formerly private bank was nationalised. From this point, all taxes were paid to and all state spending disbursed from this bank. Law now had the state's central treasury and every taxman in the country working for him. France was experiencing a one-man leveraged management buy-out, and no one was any the wiser. There was only one manager, Law, and it was the French people who were providing the money. In 1718, as the Company of the West continued to expand, the General Bank was renamed the Royal Bank, showing the extent to which Law was in the regent's inner circle. The Crown and the murderer were in it together.

Law repeated the same trick over and over, buying shell companies in the French colonies and bundling them together, all with mandates to exploit future bounty. The parent company came to be known as the Mississippi Company, a sufficiently vague name for an entity that covered everything from sugar to slave trading. In the early 1700s, European colonists were harnessing the greed of local investors to exploit the lives, land and mineral wealth of those they subjugated. With the support of these local bigwigs and the backing of a private army (like the Dutch VOC's), the Mississippi Company was a behemoth. To finance his acquisitions, Law, the arch manipulator, continued the ruse, offering the shares at deep discounts to investors so that the share price would bounce, exciting yet more speculators. France was agog with trading fever. Mothers, daughters and granddaughters joined in. And why wouldn't they? Wasn't everything going skywards?

With share prices skyrocketing, the stage was set for a major stock market boom. All the while, Law was reducing France's national debt, exchanging government securities for shares, swapping the low-risk for the high. The sheer magnitude of this operation was breathtaking. Awash with money, his next move was to refinance the entirety of the Crown's debt, pushing out maturity dates and lowering the rate of interest.

The share price of the Mississippi Company, 500 livres in May 1719, had jumped to 5,000 livres by September of that same year.[4] In the environment shaped by this rapidly rising share price, capital gains drove investors scatty. Who cared about boring old dividends when you were making many times your money on the share price appreciation alone? Share dealing on the narrow and winding rue Quincampoix was so intense that there was no room for tables to exchange contracts; at some point during this tumult, an entrepreneurial hunchback hired out his hump so that transactors could use it as a writing desk.[5]

Law's novel approach to money had succeeded in completely transforming the French financial system, turning the country into a boom-time economy brimming with paper money. A highly speculative company sat at the centre of the French financial system, sucking in the real resources of the country and turning them into promises of future profit, dependent on the fantastical notion that colonies – in many cases no more than a couple of tobacco or sugar plantations – could make a huge population in Europe rich into perpetuity. What was once public (the tax system) became private, and what was once private (the savings of the populace) became public.

France had caught the trading bug and the world was watching. People who had got in early saw themselves as visionaries, and those still to join felt unfairly locked out. To satisfy the frenzy – and to raise more funds – Law issued more and more shares. Issue followed issue and within a three-week period in the autumn of 1719, the Mississippi Company issued over 300,000 shares at 5,000 livres a share, amounting to 1.5 billion livres. Ensuring that the mania percolated right down to those who couldn't afford to buy shares outright, Law introduced payment by instalment, the classic 'buy now, pay later' strategy. People were putting down money they often couldn't spare. Small down payments and an ever-increasing demand for shares pushed the price of shares to over 9,000 livres in that same autumn of 1719.[6]

Twenty-five years after he escaped the hangman, it looked as if Law had performed another miracle by saving the French economy's finances and reinventing French money. A new era of money was upon us: money backed by nothing more than the promise and credibility of the state. In addition, the state's debts had been converted into equity of the Mississippi Company. The economy was thriving and John Law was the French equivalent of prime minister. Not bad for an escaped Scottish murderer.

End game

By the end of 1719, Europe was swept up by Mississippi mania. Speculators flooded to Paris to buy and sell the Mississippi Company's shares, which reached a high of 10,000 livres by December, valuing it at 6.24 billion livres. Firing on all cylinders, the share price drove the demand for money, driving the issuance of more shares. This was facilitated by the Royal Bank, which printed money hand over fist. New money created surged to 1 billion livres by the end of 1719. The company was driving the bank, which in turn was driving the company. (Today, we see the same phenomenon with property booms, where property prices increase developers' profitability so they become even better bets for the banks, which lend more money to the developers, which further drives up property prices, kicking off an entirely new cycle of credit and money creation – until it stops.)

The greatest compliment the English could give the French was imitation. Usually quick to look down their noses at the French when it came to money, Britain introduced a variant of the Mississippi Company in January 1720 when the South Sea Company proposed to take over most of the government debt. The proposal was accepted by our friend the Earl of Sunderland, Charles Spencer, the man who – allegedly – hired Law to kill Edmund Wilson, and who was now Britain's First Lord of the Treasury.

The British saw the French and raised them. Exchange Alley in London hosted the world's second stock market boom, the South Sea Bubble of 1720, with enormous crowds flocking there to purchase shares not only in the South Sea Company, but also a variety of 'bubble' companies with charters that varied from the serious to the bizarre. The serious included charters for insurance companies, some of which exist today, while the bizarre included a company producing square cannonballs and even a company for 'a project to be announced at a future date'. (This may seem ludicrous but the twenty-first century has seen the advent of SPACs (special purpose acquisition companies) – special investment funds set up blind, where the investor will be told what the investment is . . . at a later date! These SPACs were offered by Wall Street's bluest of blue-chip investment firms as recently as 2022.)

Back in France, in February 1720, the market, deep in the mania phase, began to wobble. Ultimately, any valuation can only be sustained if income underpinning the valuation rises. Law was facing an Emperor's New Clothes moment. Various reasons have been cited for the wobble, ranging from a plague in Marseille to inflation taking off in busy French ports. Whatever the catalyst, the pendulum swung and buyers disappeared, their place taken by desperate sellers. Share prices in the Mississippi Company began to plummet. People's paper wealth vanished. In panic, everyone wanted gold, not Law's paper promises. In December 1720, not for the first time, Law was forced to flee a country. And not for the first time he scarpered with the help of the establishment.

After the South Sea Bubble collapsed in Britain, Charles Spencer was brought before the House of Commons and charged with using South Sea shares to bribe politicians and members of George I's entourage, including, yet again, the king's mistress. This corruption threatened the Hanoverian monarchy and protecting the king may have encouraged some MPs to vote in Spencer's favour to keep it quiet. After stormy debate, Spencer was acquitted. In exile, Law watched on as, once again, the lives of Charles Spencer and John Law were mired in money, mistresses, maybe not murder, but certainly malfeasance.

Legacy

Despite the collapse of the Mississippi Company, Law's experiment opened the door to a new type of relationship between the state and money. His innovations laid the foundation for the form of money we use today. This is Law's legacy: money issued by the central bank on behalf of the state, deriving its strength from the institutional credibility of the state and, indirectly, made whole by the state's tax revenue. Law showed that money can be unchained from gold and silver, foreshadowing the influential twentieth-century English economist John Maynard Keynes, who would famously oppose tying the currency to gold.

Law also understood that money drives trade and, if the economy is weak, printing money will kickstart it. This observation is an essential part of the catechism and the creed of modern central banking, and it follows that Law is the spiritual father of quantitative easing (more on that later). Law appreciated the alchemy of money, that it is a kind of magic, motivating people to strive, to innovate, and ultimately to change their own personal circumstances and thereby change the world.

Law had considered using land as his base asset, which makes sense: backed by land, paper money can be given an anchor. However, Law pushed things too far in his attempt to reduce national debt. His financial engineering, involving debt-for-equity swaps, wiped out the wealth of those who swapped state debt for the vague promise of enormous wealth. Law turned the wealthier French subjects from investors, happy to be paid steady returns from government debt, into speculators, excited by the prospect of a get-rich-quick scheme. Had he relied exclusively on a land-backed paper money, rather than a speculation-backed paper money, his system might have succeeded. As we will see, centuries later, and in more prudent hands, money issued by the central bank and backed by a government promise would end up underpinning the most successful monetary regime the world has ever seen: the fiat system.

In the years immediately after the collapse of the Mississippi Company scheme, French finance went backwards. The upper and middle classes saw their savings decimated and this led to a rejection of innovations in money during the rest of the eighteenth century. As a result, France was bedevilled by monetary crises and deployed an unsustainable tax system — and we know where that led to in 1789. John Law's experiments, at least in part, laid the foundations for the French Revolution. And that's not all. American patriots, fifty years later, cited the corruption of Charles Spencer and his cronies back in London as one of their many reasons for breaking away from the orbit of Britain. The proximity of the king and members of the cabinet to the financial skulduggery of the South Sea Company revealed to the American revolutionaries the rot at the heart of the British system, which they compared to the corruption of the Roman Empire. Pamphlet after pamphlet was published in subsequent years using the South Sea Bubble as proof of British venality. Could Law, with his alleged accomplice Spencer, have encouraged not one but two revolutions?

THE BISHOP OF MONEY

The limping devil

You must be some almighty class of scoundrel if Napoleon describes you as 'a pile of shit in silk stockings'. Can you imagine the number of people who must have crossed Bonaparte? Think of all the charlatans, sycophants, arrogant aristocrats on their way down and cut-throat Jacobins on their way up. As insults go, it's quite evocative. You'd be almost proud of it. What type of a creature would prompt such a vivid description?

Charles-Maurice de Talleyrand-Périgord was a bishop, politician, financier, foreign minister, revolutionary agitator, serial lover, inscrutable diplomat and political survivor.[1] A nimble operator endowed with talent and mendacity in equal measure, his limp did not hold him back. He survived several bosses and held powerful positions in the court of the king. Outliving the beheaded monarch, as guillotines were falling all over France, Talleyrand reinvented himself as a radical. The story of how he became Napoleon's foreign secretary would fill an entire book, but he went on to abandon Bonaparte, jumping ship at the last minute, clutching personal victory from national defeat, and resurfacing as chief negotiator for defeated France at the Congress of Vienna in 1814. With an extraordinary ability to sense which way the wind was blowing, Talleyrand switched sides from Church to parliament, from the parliament to the king, from king to Jacobin revolution, from revolutionaries to exile, from exile to Napoleon and from Napoleon back to the king. To do this without losing his head is impressive enough. To do this and amass a personal fortune, numerous mistresses, vast estates, sumptuous art collections and still turn up on the winning side during possibly the most convulsive revolutionary three decades in French and European history requires extraordinary cunning and ruthlessness. Is it any wonder that the bishops, his former ecclesiastical allies whom he double-crossed, referred to him as '*le diable boiteux*' ('the limping devil')?

In the aftermath of the collapse of John Law's financial system in 1720, innovation in money became taboo in France. Despite the calamity of the South Sea Bubble, France's sworn enemy, Britain, continued to innovate financially, learning from the speculative mistakes of 1720 to create deeper markets, with more options for financing, leading to more economic vibrancy. Britain's mastery of money was one of the critical factors in propelling the industrial revolution; it would not have taken off so spectacularly had it not been for the availability of investors and capital markets to finance the new technological innovations. Industrialisation – with its factories and machines, dredging of canals, deep shaft mining, not to mention the building of new cities – demanded money. The industrial revolution was as much a feat of finance as engineering.

Britain's bond markets enabled risk assessment, while its insurance industry mitigated jeopardy. A variety of financial products gave investors a path to participation in the great industrial upswing and the monetary muscle of the nation lifted it onto a different growth path. Proper risk management makes more capital available, and the prospect of capital gain coaxes money from under the mattress and into the path of investment. If managed properly, each financial product begets more financial products and capital seeps further into the economy, pushing down the cost of doing business and pushing up returns. The British adapted the Dutch attitude to money, refining and improving on the Hollanders' techniques, and London in the eighteenth century was to finance what Amsterdam had been in the seventeenth: the pre-eminent centre for global money. Winning three naval wars against the Dutch probably helped the British cause too.

While Britain innovated, France turned its back on monetary creativity. Since Law, anyone involved in finance was regarded as deeply suspicious. New banks didn't even call themselves banks and instead used the expression *caisses*, meaning deposits, so besmirched was the banking industry's reputation. This meant that France laboured under a primitive monetary system. The Crown borrowed at high interest rates from locals and foreigners, notably Calvinist banks in Geneva. Excessive taxation covered the shortfall. France's eighteenth-century financial dilemmas were succinctly explained by Jean Colbert, Louis XIV's finance minister, who described the art of taxation as 'plucking the maximum feathers from the goose with the minimum of hissing'.

Global trade demands deep pockets, and a country that turns its back on money and monetary inventiveness runs the risk of becoming a lumbering giant, outwitted by more financially savvy competitors. A century and a half after the nimble Dutch were issuing perpetual bonds, floating companies and sharing risk, France, the most powerful country in Europe, with the continent's largest population, was bridled with a primitive tax system that wasn't too different from that of the Babylonians. Financial instability characterised the French economy and, as is always the case when money is tight, political fragility was ever present. A constant pressure on the public finances was not helped by successive kings' weaknesses for war and parties. Although some European countries were beginning to distance Church and state, in France the clergy and the monarchy were enmeshed. Kings were anointed by French cardinals and the upper clergy held a defined role in the monarchy. In aristocratic families, the first son inherited the family estate, and typically the second son was sent to the Church to become a priest. One of those aspirant priests would become the monetary mastermind of the French Revolution.

The monetary dilemma

The French Revolution was a revolution about money, and specifically about taxation. Because the French hadn't innovated with money, the financial system was extremely blunt: when the king needed money, he taxed the poor. Eventually, the poor got fed up with it.

But revolutionaries also need money. For the apprentice revolutionary, a crash course in banking and monetary economics might be more beneficial than Marxism, Leninism and agitprop. No cash, no coup. Behind all the exalted rhetoric, most revolutions are about money and revolutionaries usually promise to give money back to the people. Revolutions weaponise the unfairness of taxation by the rotten, soon-to-be-overthrown regime, where the little man is fleeced to finance the rich man's lifestyle. Equality is never far from the lips of rebels, be they American, French or Russian. Revolutions usually centre on the questions of who has the money, why don't we have more of it, and how do we get our hands on all of it?

After the excitement of storming the barricades, revolutionaries must focus on the mundane, including working out how to pay for everything. In power but desperately short of money, the new cadres cannot rely on the old tax base – that's what they were revolting against in the first place. The first act of the newly established French National Assembly on 17 June 1789 was to declare all existing taxes illegal. But without tax, where does the state's money come from? The revolutionary French state couldn't borrow because capital left the country before you could say 'Liberté, Égalité, Fraternité'. They could print money, but even though they changed the national anthem, the underlying logic of money still remained the same: print too much and you get inflation. And if you print too much when your resources are tied up fighting a war, you get hyperinflation.

Money is and always has been a social contract between government and citizens. We, the citizens, will use the new currency as long as you, the government, maintain its value and you undertake to give us whatever underlying asset backs the currency if we choose to demand it. Usually, when people use paper money, they forget it is backed by an asset. They come to accept the paper money as being a store of wealth – nobody seriously thinks about the promise on their dollar bill. Today, the note itself is enough of a stand-in for the promise. The road travelled by all paper currencies is the same: from incredulity to credibility, to habit, to was-it-ever-any-different?

The French revolutionaries realised they needed the alchemy of Law's paper money, but they needed far more than a promise based on a speculative company with land in a faraway continent. To back the new revolutionary currency, they needed a foundational asset closer to home that people could understand. This is where the limping devil comes in.

The sublime operator

Although Talleyrand was a first son, born into the aristocracy and well educated, he could not have a military career because of an infirmity in his left leg. Reluctantly, he accepted his parents' ruling and became a priest. The ambitious Talleyrand lost little time in agitating to become a bishop, encouraging his dying father to persuade Louis XVI to make him Bishop of Autun, despite his own mother imploring the Church not to elevate him from priest to bishop. With mothers like that, who needs enemies? The king decided to nominate Talleyrand, assuring the back-stabbing mother that the son had time to improve his behaviour. An astute judge of character Louis XVI was not.

By the revolutionary year of 1789, Talleyrand had managed to become not only a bishop but also Agent-General of the Clergy. In this role he carried out an in-depth survey of the Church's assets and activities. Such knowledge of the Church's underlying balance sheet and his attention to accounting detail ensured that Talleyrand was the man who had calculated the net worth of the French Catholic Church, an extraordinarily valuable piece of information, in the right hands and at the right time. You could say Talleyrand was the Bishop of Money.

Representing the Church in affairs of money, he worked closely with the Controller-General of Finances, Charles Alexandre de Calonne, who taught Talleyrand a great deal about banking, finance, fiscal policy and debt management.

He also taught Talleyrand the art of using haute cuisine to persuade people to your way of thinking. Calonne's head chef, Olivier, employed a team of sauce makers, pâtissiers and other culinary specialists to prepare gargantuan dinners during which the policy makers would discuss Calonne's new approaches to fiscal policy. Talleyrand learned that extravagant dinners prepared by top chefs helped bend the ears of rulers, diplomats, money men and the people in power. What twenty-first-century corporate deal maker doesn't use the same trick? Years later, as Napoleon's foreign minister, Talleyrand remarked that 'he had a greater need for cooks than diplomats'.

Between banquets, the Bishop of Money also picked up an intricate knowledge of the inner workings of the French economy. A new ideology, that of '*laissez-faire, laissez-passer*' ('freedom to produce and freedom to trade'), had emerged from the economic thinking of writers such as Vincent de Gournay and François Quesnay. Regarded as an important subset of a larger philosophical movement proclaiming the rights of political liberty and freedom for scientific research, these economists were central to what came to be known as the Enlightenment. Economics and liberty were revolutionary bedfellows, obvious enemies of the conservative Church. And where do you think our establishment bishop might have had the opportunity to rub shoulders with such potentially revolutionary minds? He hung out with the economists in a Freemasons' Lodge. Yes, never missing a trick, Talleyrand, the bishop and gourmand, was also – secretly – a leading member of the Freemasons. Lodges at this time were a hotbed of revolutionary ideas. Condorcet, Roederer and Turgot, an outstanding trio of economists who promoted liberal ideas about France's future, were members of a lodge called the

Trente. Mixing with them gave Talleyrand the edge in economics. Not to mention the right contacts and network.

The great survivor

In May 1789, two months before the storming of the Bastille, Talleyrand took his own place in parliament as was his right as a bishop. He envisaged his future outside the Church, and the revolution provided him with his opportunity. By October 1789, with France engulfed in chaos and the parliament deeply divided, the uber-confident Bishop Talleyrand presented himself as the consensus candidate, a safe pair of hands for the position of finance minister. Talleyrand had sensed power slipping from the *ancien régime* of king, bishops and aristocrats. He needed to jump, but which way? One false move and he was a goner. He knew France needed to clear its national debt and that would demand a new currency. The 35-year-old bishop produced a judicious plan. His proposal was simplicity itself, namely the enforced confiscation of all ecclesiastical property in France. His fellow bishops didn't see this coming; they only felt the knife between their shoulder blades after it was plunged.

Apart from the Church, who wouldn't like the plan? The king was off the hook, the aristocrats felt the financial noose loosen somewhat, and for the people, it was radical enough, identifying the plump cardinal, fattened by fine wines and creamy camembert, as the villain. Mimicking Henry VIII two centuries earlier, Talleyrand's idea was primarily a debt management proposal, converting the proceeds of the enforced sale of the Church's property into money to pay off the government's debt. Once he had brought down the amount of government debt, interest rates would fall and, more significantly, he could raise new financing and issue new state bonds. The risk of default, which was driven up by the sheer amount of government debt, would now diminish as the existing debt had been paid back using the proceeds of selling the Church lands.

Cleverly, he attacked the Church but not the clergy, many of whom were still popular at a local level. Talleyrand, a numbers man, believed that the clergy could get by on 80 to 85 million livres, made up of Sunday collections. He proposed that every *curé* be given an annual government stipend of 1,200 livres along with free accommodation, while the Church's property would be used to fill the hole in the state's budget. A win–win for everyone – bar the bishops, whose very aloofness and pomposity made them easy targets.

Talleyrand's proposal that 'national goods' (*les biens nationaux*) should be given back to the nation was brought before the National Assembly in November 1789. It was seconded by his friend, Comte de Mirabeau, one of the leaders of the early phases of the revolution. A powerful orator, Mirabeau's support ensured that the Assembly voted in favour of nationalising the Church's land. Talleyrand was off and from there events moved at revolutionary speed.

The revolutionary bond

The instrument that financed the French Revolution was a monetary innovation called the *assignat*. As has been the case throughout our story, critical moments often turn on financial innovations. The hand of money is rarely far from momentous events. By December 1789, the enforced nationalisation of Church lands had provided the revolution with enough collateral to back the issue of 400 million livres of assignats, a new monetary instrument. Purchasing an assignat would give the holder the right to buy Church land when it came up for sale. Punters wishing to buy Church lands bought assignats with gold and silver, coaxing hoarders of precious metals to bring them into circulation, thereby freeing up French capital that was being stashed away for a rainy day.

There was a lot of Church land in France; obviously, as a nationwide scheme, selling all this land would take time. But the revolutionaries didn't have time. They needed money immediately. That's why, to encourage the purchase of assignats, the state paid a 5 per cent rate of interest on each assignat so investors would be paid while they waited for the conveyance to go through. Gold and silver paid no interest, but the assignat meant an investor would receive an annual income of 5 per cent on his capital. The assignat, essentially an IOU from the state, backed by appropriated Church wealth, operated like a bond, allowing Talleyrand's treasury to manage the country's debt mountain. Issued only in high denominations, the intention was that assignats weren't available for everyday spending. Once the investor had bought their Church property and the contract of conveyance had been completed, the plan was that the assignat, the piece of paper, marking the first part of the contract, was to be burned.

Enormous swathes of Church property were transferred to the private sector. New owners of land became inevitable supporters of the revolution. Talleyrand, now eyeing a position of serious power, was building a constituency in support of both himself and further revolutionary moves. He created a new landowning rebel class. Talleyrand knew how to play the masses. In agricultural France, moderately well-off farmers became a significant power base for the revolution, which up to then had been an urban and intellectual affair. Fusing both power blocs was a stroke of genius.

The early revolutionaries were bourgeois rebels, who emphasised the need for prudence, arguing that the sale of Church property could *only* be used to reduce the national debt. At that early stage, the revolution could be interpreted almost as a middle-class reform movement orchestrated by responsible liberal citizens whose attitude to money tended towards caution. These Jacobins were the merchants of our last few chapters, who yearned for political representation but baulked at the financial anarchy that traditionally follows rebellion. Financially, the revolution had so far been more of a changing of the guard, a palace coup, than a rabble uprising. In these opening months, Talleyrand's financial plan benefitted those who might be termed insiders, people with a stake in society, a far cry from the *sans culottes* of revolutionary yore. So far, so stable.

However, as the revolution became more radical due to the emerging civil war and the threat of invasion by Europe's monarchist regimes, these mercantile revolutionaries' attitude to money changed. How were they to pay their soldiers? At this point, the role of the assignat – which had thus far acted as what we would now call an asset-backed security – switched from debt management to monetary creation. Without new taxes, the French revolutionary state was desperately short of money. Unsurprisingly, the budget deficit exploded. Printing yet more assignats seemed to be the answer. With a bit of luck, the revolutionary authorities might have been able to pull the wool over people's eyes while they still assumed that assignats would be underpinned by Church land.

Talleyrand was opposed to using assignats as money to pay for everyday expenses, but the revolution was now in the hands of radicals, who were less concerned about paying off the debts of the king and more concerned with funding and fighting an ideological war. The likes of Robespierre were not thinking about the rate of interest. Talleyrand's plan was upended and the revolutionaries abdicated the debt management approach to concentrate instead on using the new paper money to finance daily expenditure. The instrument that initially financed the revolution would mutate into pieces of paper printed at will simply to keep the revolutionaries themselves from being guillotined. The printing presses whirred.

Money and the Terror

War is never good for money. By late 1792, revolutionary France was about to enter a hyperinflationary spiral. Sensing the revolution was escalating and becoming dangerously radical, Talleyrand slipped out of town for London just ahead of the guillotining of the king in January 1793. As the country descended into a vicious civil war, inflation had reached 12 per cent per month and by 1795 would spiral to 80 per cent per month.[2]

The Jacobin government attempted to suppress these inflationary forces by introducing price and income controls. At first glance, this makes sense. If prices are rising, you try to control them by capping them. But why would a farmer, whose costs are rising because of inflation, sell goods at a price that is capped? It guarantees that he will lose money. Obviously, he chooses to sell on the black market, where he will get a fair price – in his eyes. Quickly, the supply of most goods to the state and in the controlled market disappeared. The black market flourished. Price caps, introduced to curb inflation, led to food shortages, driving up inflation even further. Nothing undermines a revolution more than starvation.

Failing to anticipate this economic dynamic, the revolutionary government introduced the *Loi du Maximum Général* in September 1793, establishing price limits for thirty-nine staple articles including meat, butter, salted fish, beer, cider, coal, wood, candles, oil, salt and soap. Prices of these products could not exceed their 1790 prices by more than a third and wages were fixed at their 1790 level plus 50 per cent. This move was met with open rebellion, as the fixed prices did not sufficiently compensate people in the face of rampant inflation. Money was dividing the country yet again, and inflation was leading France towards the Terror.

Price caps forced peasants to hide their crops and flocks so as not to sell their products at a loss. Supply tightened, pushing up prices yet further. Speculators hoarded stock and food shortages ensued. To stamp out hoarding, the government incentivised spies to denounce the hoarders and then guillotined those found guilty. Robespierre cranked up the terror machine. It could be said that suspect money – rather than suspect politics – greased the guillotine, in an environment of food shortages, denunciations and worthless currency. Thousands of people were publicly executed while incipient revolts in Brittany and the Vendée were put down.

Robespierre himself was executed in July 1794, and the Terror brought to an end, but the printing presses continued to work overtime to pay soldiers and spies: by the end of 1794, 6 billion livres of assignats had been issued; by July 1795, 13.5 billion had been issued, rising to 23.5 billion by December 1795; and that amount had increased by February 1796 to a whopping 40 billion livres. To put this in context, in 1789, when Talleyrand came up with his scheme, total French GDP was estimated to be 6.5 billion livres: the revolutionaries were printing multiples of the total French annual income in worthless paper money. The official figures actually underestimated the amount of paper money in circulation due to mass forgeries – even within French prisons, collusive jailers smuggled in printing equipment for inmates to forge currency.[3]

As was the case in Weimar Germany many years later, paper money meant nothing. When money dies, trust and stability in society break down. One of money's many psychological qualities is that it simplifies our complicated world. It is an organisational technology that imposes discipline. Functioning as it should, money means prices can be trusted. Prices contain a vast array of information about value, scarcity and relative worth. Apart from their economic impact, prices serve as psychological anchors. Money provides a short cut, allowing us to absorb this information in a trustworthy number or a series of numbers. Kick away the crutch of dependable money, and society is unmoored, which is something France's enemies in Britain appreciated. The British establishment, fearful of the message of the French Revolution, would utilise any means to destroy it. Why not money?

In 1793, a Scottish writer and engineer, the beautifully named William Playfair (who, incidentally, produced the world's first economic graphics, using line, bar and pie charts to analyse economic data), had conceived the idea of orchestrating a major counterfeiting operation from Britain. He presented his plan to the British home secretary, Henry Dundas, and with the tacit permission of prime minister William Pitt the Younger Playfair started to print French money. (As we will see in the next chapter, it was not the first time Britain had employed dirty tricks to destroy a foreign currency: between 1776 and 1780, it flooded America with counterfeit Continentals, the currency of the American revolutionaries.) As Playfair had written to

Dundas, there were two ways of combatting the revolution – by military means or through money – and Playfair argued it was better to destroy assignats rather than shed the blood of men.[4]

Go west

From London, Talleyrand watched the French monetary disaster unfold. But he didn't stay long. Urged by his British hosts to leave a deeply anti-French England, he arrived in the United States in 1794 with a letter of introduction from Angelica Church, the sister-in-law of the revolutionary Alexander Hamilton. Hamilton and Talleyrand would become firm friends. And Hamilton, like Talleyrand, would use currency reform to catapult his career. Hobnobbing with America's revolutionary leaders did Talleyrand no harm at all for his next move: a triumphal return to France in 1797 to position himself for the post-revolutionary rule of Napoleon Bonaparte. His British and American contacts would be helpful as France needed to rebuild relationships.

Amazingly, through all this, he had remained a bishop, in name at least, but multiple affairs and children paved the way for him being laicised by Pope Pius VII in 1802. Free of his clerical association, Talleyrand could serve the secular Bonaparte as foreign minister. Later, he would abandon Bonaparte, switching sides, once again at the right time, returning to support the monarchy. Over the tempestuous period from the revolution in 1789 to the 1830s, Talleyrand, the *diable boiteux*, served Louis XVI, various regimes of the French Revolution, and Napoleon, as well as the restored Bourbon monarchs Louis XVIII and Louis Philippe. Towards the end of his life, Talleyrand became the French ambassador to the United Kingdom between

1830 and 1834, and he was instrumental in establishing the new state of Belgium, a buffer zone between France and its continental enemies.

His assignats, although ultimately rendered worthless by excessive printing, provided the financial launchpad for the French Revolution. Had Talleyrand not confiscated Church land and sold it off, it is unlikely that the Jacobins would have gained a critical mass of popular support. Talleyrand's plan, like Law's before him, aimed at liberating France and its giant economy from the tyranny of gold and silver. Had later revolutionaries not debased the assignat, it would have been seen as the miracle instrument that not only financed the revolution but also allowed for the reasonably smooth transition of assets from one power base to another.

In the last few decades, revolutions or mass transitions have occurred in many countries of central and eastern Europe. All faced the same dilemma as Talleyrand: how do you protect the money of a nation as it moves from one regime to another? In the 1990s, in former communist Europe, establishing a credible currency was an essential building block for the transition from socialism to the market. Central banks received large dollar or other hard currency loans from the International Monetary Fund to anchor and maintain the value of the new currencies. These loans backed new currencies that had no track record, in countries that had, in reality, been using the deutschmark and the dollar as parallel currencies. Although the US and its allies were backstopping the system, even with this global financial architecture in place, many transition countries experienced hyperinflation.

Consider Talleyrand, who was trying to execute something similar in France, except he had no outside support and, worse still, the old regimes of Europe were plotting against France.

When seen against this background, the initial achievements of the Bishop of Money should not be underestimated. And one man who appreciated this was Talleyrand's counterpart in revolutionary America, Alexander Hamilton. The same challenge – a huge economy hamstrung by insufficient money – stymied the American revolutionaries. Or at least it did until Alexander Hamilton plotted a pathway for a new currency that would change our world forever: the US dollar.

13

MONEY AND THE AMERICAN REPUBLIC

A bullet to the gullet

Talleyrand, despite his manoeuvrings and manipulations, died peacefully in his own bed. The same pleasure was not afforded to his American hero, the brilliant revolutionary and financial wizard, Alexander Hamilton. [1] Talleyrand may have been a man without a moral compass, whom the left saw as betraying the revolution and the right condemned as betraying God, but by weaving his way through the different administrations, occupying key positions and helping stabilise France at critical moments in the post-revolutionary period, he was clearly a good judge of character. He'd seen the greats up close and of Hamilton, Talleyrand remarked, 'I consider Napoleon, [British Whig statesman Charles James] Fox, and Hamilton the three greatest men of our epoch and, if I were forced to decide between the three, I would give without hesitation the first place to Hamilton.' [2]

When we think of revolutionaries, we tend to have in mind the romantic figure of the daring rebel. But following convulsions, revolutions need stabilisers, those who consolidate and bring order, including accountants and financiers. Talleyrand was such a man. So too was Alexander Hamilton, one of the Founding Fathers, who played a key role in supporting George Washington in the creation of the United States.

According to Duff Cooper, Talleyrand's biographer, Talleyrand and Hamilton were both realist politicians who 'despised sentimental twaddle whether it poured from the lips of a Robespierre or a Jefferson'.[3] During Talleyrand's exile in America between 1794 and 1796, these two stabilisers became friends – and, when setting up the US dollar and the new financial architecture of the American republic, Hamilton would learn from the French Republic's mistakes.

On a cool July morning of 1804 in Weehawken, New Jersey, overlooking the Hudson River, Hamilton found himself in a duel with the vice president, Aaron Burr. As they'd say in prison, both men had a bit of 'previous' – in fact they could not stand each other – but it is hard to fathom how a former Treasury Secretary and the standing vice president came to be facing each other, locked and loaded. In the end, Hamilton aimed to miss – or so we assume – allowing Burr to extract life-long vengeance on his more brilliant adversary. Alexander Hamilton, the man who introduced the dollar, and through this probably did more than any of the Founding Fathers to create a federal United States of America, took a bullet to the gullet. He died a few days later.

On a subsequent visit to Napoleonic France, Burr sought a meeting with the then omnipotent Talleyrand, foreign minister of America's revolutionary ally. Talleyrand's secretary relayed Talleyrand's withering message: 'I shall be glad to see Colonel Burr but please tell him that a portrait of Alexander Hamilton always hangs in my study where all may see it.'[4] They didn't meet.

Birth of the dollar

Twelve years before Hamilton's murder, and as the value of Talleyrand's assignats was tanking, the American revolutionaries passed the Coinage Act on 2 April 1792. This made the dollar the currency of the USA and tied it in value to the Spanish dollar, a ubiquitous currency at that time. Treasury Secretary Hamilton, the stabiliser, learned from the monetary chaos his friend in France had unwittingly unleashed and tied the dollar to a recognised and credible coin – currency needs an anchor.

The Americans had experienced their own version of the assignats. The Continental was the paper currency the revolutionaries used to finance the war. Unable to borrow abroad because their chances of success against the imperial British were seen as slim, the revolutionaries were compelled to borrow from their own supporters. But, just as the French did with the assignats, as the War of Independence dragged on, they printed far too many Continentals. How else could they pay for soldiers and army supplies?

The Continentals plunged in value, leading to the American expression 'not worth a Continental'. The financial cost of American independence was borne by US savers, who were wiped out by the collapse of the Continental, not helped by mass forgeries from London. By 1792, with independence won, but the fledgling republic still fragile and in constant fear of British invasion, Hamilton realised that the moment for monetary experiments was over; it was time for consolidation and certainty. As the first Treasury Secretary, he anchored the American financial system to a solid currency via the Coinage Act, and this changed the course of money – and American history. It's almost impossible to imagine the

United States of America without the dollar. Indeed, from the perspective of the twenty-first century, it's impossible to imagine the world without the dollar. The man who introduced it might have become president had he not been murdered.

How did this man, born on the Caribbean island of Nevis, make the journey, almost destitute, to holding one of the highest positions in America? Abandoned by his Scottish trader father at the age of eleven and left parentless by the subsequent death of his Huguenot mother, the French-speaking Hamilton was financially supported by locals and friends, who noticed his early promise, and paid for him to attend college in New York. Unlike many of the well-to-do federalists, he had been born poor, but his intellect and considerable bravery on the battlefield – he fought alongside General Washington and played a critical role at the Battle of Yorktown – enabled him to ascend the heights of American revolutionary power.

The split

In Ireland we say that the first item on the agenda of every Irish revolutionary movement is the split. The American Founding Fathers were afflicted with the same weakness for separation, jealousy and rancour. Thomas Jefferson and Alexander Hamilton clashed regularly and held contrasting views of how to fashion a new independent America. Hamilton, the modernist, federalist, urbane thinker, wanted the US to develop into a capitalist state, competing with the Europeans in industry, finance and commerce. Jefferson, an anti-federalist republican, together with other American greats James Madison and Samuel Adams, had an elegiac, almost primitive view of finance and commerce, preferring an arcadian vision of rural – and largely isolated – America uncorrupted by money, markets and trade.

While Jefferson was country and western, Hamilton was hip hop. Jefferson held a homespun, Mom's apple pie view of the world – not unusual in nationalist revolutionary leaders. Hamilton, on the other hand, envisaged a muscular American federation fully involved in the global economy, with a strong central federal government raising taxes in its own hard currency, backed by a federalist army defending the Constitution against enemies within and without. It's not hard to see where some of today's Republican Party thinking originated, with 'small government' Republicans agitating for lower taxes and less federal interference in the local affairs of each state. Blame Jefferson.

Back then, these divisions were only emerging as the new republic tried to figure out what to do after they'd kicked out the British. Typically, once any revolution has achieved its goals, unity is fractured and, in the absence of an enemy, the revolutionary coalition begins to disintegrate. In this case, the division emerged along republican and federalist lines.

Three fifths of a human

The split between the federalist and the non-federalist wings of the American revolutionaries materialised almost as soon as the War of Independence was won. How could the thirteen rebel states create a new country out of the ashes of the British defeat? Their currency, the Continental, wasn't, as the saying goes, worth anything. Like the French revolutionaries, they had printed paper money to fund the war. Now independent, many of the states feared surrendering their new power and sovereignty to a powerful federal government. But if such a transfer did not occur, the government wouldn't have the wherewithal to defend the United States from its enemies or leverage the country's enormous resources.

Here is where Hamilton the soldier became Hamilton the writer, thinker and orator. A national constitution would promote a unified view of what America stood for – more or less the creed of the country. But constitutional aspirations, while easy to proclaim as broad goals, are harder to hammer out in detail. Philadelphia was the site of the Constitutional Convention where, in May 1787, with bigwigs George Washington and Benjamin Franklin in attendance, various plans were presented and discussed. Individual states feared a federal takeover, while proponents of a federal style of government feared that the centralised authority would be given insufficient power. A clear division had emerged.

An agreement that became known as the Connecticut Compromise brought some sort of resolution, which is why in the USA, perplexingly to us foreigners, each state has equal representation in the Senate (two senators each) irrespective of its size. In contrast, the House of Representatives reflects population size. But in 1787, how did the Founding Fathers assess population size? In the traditional way, you'd think: by counting the people. But no. In one of the most shameful chapters of American history, Black slaves were counted not as one human but as three fifths of a person, while Native Americans (because they weren't 'property') were not counted at all – and they were denied any right to vote in elections to the House of Representatives. This three-fifths rule would subsequently enable the big slave-owning states to greatly increase their representation in the House of Representatives. Slaves were being used to enhance the 'democratic' legitimacy of the very people who were brutalising them.

The Constitution, signed in Philadelphia, required the ratification of at least nine of the thirteen states. Enter Hamilton, the writer. Along with James Madison, and to a lesser extent the lawyer John Jay, Hamilton organised a campaign to influence public opinion. His chosen marketing method was the press. On 27 October 1787, he published the first of a series of newspaper articles in favour of the Constitution. These would become known as *The Federalist Papers*. The papers were also published in book form, and would ultimately contain eighty-five articles, of which fifty-one were attributed to Hamilton, twenty-nine to Madison and five to Jay. So great was the power of the press in this age of the political pamphlet that Hamilton's reasoning won over public opinion. In fact, he accomplished that task with such brilliance that a huge float, the Federal Ship Hamilton, was pulled through the city by delighted New Yorkers in July 1788 and serious proposals were presented to have the city renamed Hamiltoniana.[5]

Building support for the Constitution was one thing; Hamilton would turn his attention to a symbol that would remind Americans daily that they lived in a new federal republic – the new American dollar. Nobody thinks about their country's constitution every day, but what better reminder of federalism than the money in your pocket?

First, however, he would have to subdue opposition using a slightly blunter instrument.

The Whiskey Rebels

For a nation supposedly founded by Puritans, Americans love a drink, and one of the first tests of post-revolutionary harmony emerged over booze. In revolutionary times, rural America was full of pot-still whiskey distilleries. Locals manufactured their own whiskeys with varying degrees of quality and purity. Moonshine in all but name, these distilleries sold hooch throughout farming communities and in the local towns and cities. In 1791, Treasury Secretary Hamilton was short of money and, as finance ministers would do time and again, he decided to tax that 'old reliable', whiskey.[6] Every treasurer knows taxing grog is a no-brainer. But the local backwoodsmen weren't having it. Whiskey insurgents in western Pennsylvania formed militias, armed themselves and attacked some local officials attempting to raise the tax, posing a direct threat to the fledgling federal government.

Faced with the prospect of armed rebellion from former patriots, George Washington, appreciating the fragility of the situation, understood that the new state was in a bind. They had won the War of Independence based on the principle of not paying taxes to the remote Crown, so they could hardly turn around and levy taxes to finance a remote centralised federal government. But, as with the French Revolution, once the excitement of the barricades had passed, the government's concerns had shifted from rousing slogans to empty coffers. Without tax revenue, government couldn't operate. Faced with these uppity whiskey-driven militias, the federal government was in danger of becoming a joke. Washington dithered. Foot dragging in the face of an open rebellion and mass refusal to pay federal tax further besmirched the new state's reputation among its unruly citizens. Who would blink first?

Hamilton urged Washington to face down these pot-still insurrectionists. Reluctantly, Washington acceded. Accompanied by Hamilton, who organised the logistics of provisioning the troops, Washington led the new US army into Pennsylvania in 1794, against its own people. The revolt was quickly put down, and the ringleaders imprisoned. Washington later pardoned most of them, but the federal army's rapid suppression of the militia made everyone realise who was boss. The feds moved against the states and the feds won. In its first test, its first insurgency, the central government stood up. America, the country that would later introduce Prohibition, was forged by the reaction to a booze rebellion.

It was Hamilton who masterminded this federal show of strength, understanding that creating a federal republic is done piece by piece. You first quell local opposition and then you unify the country around a federal currency. With money, citizens' allegiance to the federation can be attracted willingly. Having shown the crude end of its power with the military, the federal government would display something more nuanced and more impressive, and that was the power of money. If war was Hamilton's rapier, money would be his balm.

The dollar

The finest economic brain among the Founding Fathers, Hamilton knew that talk of human rights and the pursuit of happiness was all very well, but something tangible was required to hold the United States together. Without some binding organisational tool, the republic and its competing states might unravel. That tool would be money. And central to the legitimacy of the new federal republic would be a new currency.

Throughout history, going right back to Alexander the Great, money has symbolised something bigger than mere exchange. Money is political power and all across Alexander's vast empire, his subjects knew who the boss was when they saw his face on the coins. To this day, money symbolises the nation, as is the case with sterling, or a greater supra-national political project, as with the euro.

For the founders of the American republic, the currency

would be emblematic of the new country and a new beginning. Because money is tangible, and we use it every day, it serves as a gelling agent for other institutions, such as the tax system, which further bolsters the state. For a nation the size of the American republic, money created an allegiance to the new country in a more mundane and yet powerful way than a constitution. While the Constitution may have been the creed, money was the sacrament – or you might say, as the great French chronicler of the early United States, Alexis de Tocqueville, was to observe a few years later, that money was the religion of the new republic.[7]

Understanding that the new currency needed to be credible, Hamilton linked the US dollar to the Spanish dollar, which was then a type of global standard. It is important to appreciate that, under the British, the region we would now refer to as the northeast of the United States suffered constantly from a lack of coins: local commerce centred around a grocer, publican or other trader who extended credit and took a cut when all these debits and credits were settled every few months. As colonies, these states were using British coins minted in London – if they could get their hands on them – which would only find their way to the US via trade. For there to be a surplus of coins in the colonies, the colonies would have had to run a large and ongoing trade surplus with the coloniser – but, of course, the aim of the colonisers was to extract resources cheaply from the colony. As the British were trying to buy cheap stuff from America while trying to sell the colonised expensive stuff in return, there was always a flow of coins out of America to Britain, leaving the colonies starved of hard currency. In the late seventeenth century, the British went one further and prohibited the export of gold and silver from Britain, further tightening the monetary noose around its American colonies. But here's where the Spaniards came in.

For the preceding two centuries, Spanish America had been the source of most of the coinage in the Americas more widely, and most of the new silver in the world. Spain had turned Mexico and Peru, with their silver deposits, into giant mints, making silver coins: the mine of Potosí in Peru was referred to in Spanish as 'the mountain of money',[8] and between 1556 and 1783 it produced almost 50,000 tons of pure silver. The coins were originally known as *reals* (after the Spanish for 'royal'), and were traded all over the world. (Today, the currencies of a number of Arabic countries as well as Brazil are still called the *real* or *riyal*, a derivative of the old Spanish term.) By the eighteenth century, these Spanish coins were the most widely used in the Americas and were called the silver dollar – a Germanic name ultimately derived from Joachimsthal, the site of Europe's most productive silver mines, which produced millions of 'thaler' coins between the sixteenth and eighteenth centuries.

During the eighteenth century, the northern states of what would become the US ran a trade surplus with the West Indies – selling wheat, pork, pipe staves and pitch – which meant there was a good number of Spanish silver dollars in circulation. The new US government stipulated that the new American dollar would be equivalent to this Spanish silver dollar. Under Hamilton, a new mint was instituted and, as the American colonies had no access to silver or gold of their own, the mint melted down Spanish currency already in circulation and restamped it. During the minting process, Hamilton found that the coins contained a rather bizarre amount of 371.5 grains of silver, and from then on every American silver dollar contained that same unusual amount.[9] The Americans quite pragmatically didn't bother re-minting every single Spanish dollar; right up until around 1850 they allowed the Spanish coins to circulate because everyone knew they were worth the same as the US dollar. The silver dollar remained the American standard coin until after the Civil War.

Hard money and debt

Having witnessed the hyperinflation of the Continental currency, Hamilton appreciated that paper money was a risky proposition for the new state, and should be avoided, at least at the outset. The citizens of the new republic needed to have confidence in the value of their new currency, even if it meant that the US would have to live and die by trade. Without any real domestic sources of silver and gold, Hamilton knew they couldn't maintain the value of the new currency without earning it.

Monetary discipline forced the Americans to become unusually innovative in finance, and Hamilton was at the forefront of these innovations. Before Hamilton, each state had its own approach to finance, issuing debts, trading in the bankrupt Continental and thereby completely undermining the citizens' trust in banks and finance. Hamilton wanted to encourage the thirteen states to buy into the bigger picture of establishing a more powerful economic entity at the federal level. There were considerable differences of opinion between the heavily indebted states and those who had borrowed less as to how and when the burden of the total debt should be allocated. Behind these disagreements there was the additional issue of what type of taxation could be imposed on a people who had taken up arms against the British on the very issue of taxation. 'No taxation without representation' had been their battle cry. Now they had representation, they had to determine the appropriate structure for taxation to repay the debts accumulated during the war.

Hamilton, greatly influenced by the contemporary British and Dutch approaches to this issue, believed that funding the national debt was essential to the stability of any country: if the country's debt was well managed, with no fear of default, this would be the cornerstone of the national finances. He calculated precisely that there was $75 million of debt outstanding and annual interest payments of $4.6 million.[10] To inject credibility into the American debt markets, Hamilton made two audacious moves. First, he decided that the debts of the thirteen individual states should be lumped together into new federal debt. Second, the federal debt would be repaid in full even though he didn't have to do this – in effect, this was a gift to lenders who didn't expect to get all their money back, particularly after a war. By subsuming all the debts into federal debt, he ensured that America would not have state debt competing with federal debt on the international money and bond markets. Symbolically, it also underpinned the primacy of the federation over the states. All of this served to accelerate the centralisation process that Hamilton saw as crucial to the political and economic development of the United States.

Having established the dollar and created a federal tax system with a centralised federal debt market, the energetic Hamilton moved to establish a central bank. Like the Bank of England, it would be privately owned, with 80 per cent of the $10 million of seed capital held in private hands. Hamilton also created a sinking fund to assist in the management of the national debt. Ostensibly, the role of the sinking fund was to put aside money to pay off the national debt over time, but it did more than that. As a country with little gold or silver, Hamilton knew the growth rates he anticipated for America would demand some borrowing internationally. Having a 'rainy day' fund, locally financed, would increase the attractiveness of US government securities because investors, both domestic and foreign, would know there was always a buyer of last resort: the Bank of the United States and its sinking fund.[11] Having a centralised sinking fund was like having an adult in the room who could stabilise the market when it got jittery. Under the cover of the fund, Hamilton was also able to authorise the Bank of the United States to act as lender of last resort when financial markets ran short of liquidity – a dangerous phenomenon that we have seen multiple times in this story of money.

Money and the American DNA

From the chaos of the War of Independence and the hyper-inflation that followed it – not to mention the birthing pains of a new republic – the economic performance of the United States in the following decades was remarkable. Income per head surpassed Britain within forty years. And remember this wasn't the Britain of today – this was the Britain of both the industrial revolution and empire, when vast swathes of the globe were coloured red.

Infused with a sense of the economic destiny of the United States, Hamilton told Talleyrand that he foresaw 'the day when – and it is perhaps very remote – great markets, such as formerly existed in the old world, will be established in America'.[12] It's not too far a stretch to say that he built the financial architecture to achieve this dream. Without the groundwork laid by Alexander Hamilton during his frenetic five years at the Treasury, it's unlikely that the United States' economy would have taken off quite so impressively. That is not to say it wouldn't have happened, but possibly it wouldn't have happened when it did and so quickly. The day Hamilton walked into the Treasury, the country was bankrupt; by the time he left he had sorted out America's government debt, the public finances were stable and the country had a strong new currency, giving savers security while allowing borrowers to finance their investments.[13] America also had a proper securities market and was able to sell its bonds to foreigners, who trusted the new state to pay its way. The resulting inflows of capital were used to finance expansion.

The Americans, revealing their love of money and profit so regularly commented on by European visitors, displayed an uncanny ability to form companies and take a risk. This created an economic excitement that enticed Europeans to leave the old world and have a go in the new one. Hamilton's sinking fund ensured that investors knew the US would support the government debt market, encouraging capital as well as talent to flow into America. While Europe became engulfed in the ideological wars of the early nineteenth century, America, in splendid isolation, with a functioning banking system and a de facto central bank, got down to the business of making money.

A capitalist republic, red in tooth and claw, America of the early 1800s was an economy on steroids. Alexis de Tocqueville observed in 1831 that, 'As one digs deeper into the national character of the Americans, one sees that they have sought the value of everything in this world only in the answer to this single question: how much money it will bring in.'[14] Money's promise was, and still is, the possibility of personal upward social mobility. In Europe, such individualism threatened the social contract – the monarchies, the class system and the social ceiling beyond which a smart man or woman would find it difficult to climb. In America, this was less true: with money a person could obliterate their origins and create a new reality. For Europeans, America was the country of the self-made man. Like the millions of my own countrymen and women who left Ireland for America, this promise of money must have been unbelievably seductive and Hamilton, himself once a poor migrant, appreciated this.

Yet Hamilton only understood his compatriots up to a point. While their expansive view of money differed from that of cautious Europeans, Americans – for a nation of slave owners – had unusually puritanical ethics in other areas, as Alexander Hamilton was about to find out.

The sex scandal

Like many talented politicians, Hamilton, the man who could have been president, created as many detractors as admirers. Seen as an obvious successor to George Washington, this monetary genius was outmanoeuvred by his federalist colleague John Adams, who pointedly didn't ask him to run in the 1796 election as his vice president. Of course, Hamilton was also disliked by Jefferson on the other side, leader of a new party called the Democratic Republicans, more agrarian and less committed to commerce. So far so normal in politics.

But in 1797, after his unimpeachable time in the Treasury, Hamilton gave his detractors what they wanted: popular outrage. He found himself at the centre of America's first public sex scandal. He'd been having an affair with Maria Reynolds – a married woman. And, in a bit of classic intrigue, Reynolds' husband, aware of the illicit relationship, had been blackmailing Hamilton. Hamilton's ambitions for the highest office in the land were thwarted by his inability to keep his trousers zipped. Attitudes to sex in eighteenth-century republican America were very different to those in republican France, a contrast which endures to this day. Hamilton's friend Talleyrand flaunted his indiscretions as a Parisian badge of honour. In fact, the philandering bishop probably benefitted from his various illicit dalliances, as has often been the case with powerful French men.

In 1804, Hamilton, always vituperative with the pen, wrote a series of pamphlets denouncing one of his many rivals, Vice President Aaron Burr, during a particularly vicious election campaign for governor of New York. Burr accused Hamilton of slandering him and claimed only a duel would settle things. It was widely expected that both men would only go through the motions. But Burr had different notions. He aimed to kill, and on 7 July 1804, the vice president of the United States murdered the former Treasury Secretary.

Only in America.

PART 4:

MODERN MONEY

14

EMPIRICISM AND THE EVOLUTIONARY ECONOMY

Money and measurements

Joseph Roth's novel *Weights and Measures* begins in 1857 in Galicia, a province of the Austrian Empire, sandwiched between what is now Poland and Ukraine. Home to Poles, Jews, Ukrainians, Ruthenians and the odd smattering of Austrian bureaucrats, Galicia was governed for over two hundred years by Vienna, until 1918. Designed as a buffer between the Austrian and Russian empires, Galicia's frontierland attracted a mix of peddlers, draft dodgers and contraband dealers – not a place that would necessarily welcome an agent of the state, particularly one whose job it was to second-guess the locals' commercial integrity.

Roth's protagonist, Eibenschütz, was charged with overseeing the transition from imperial measurements to decimalisation introduced by the Austrians to standardise the empire's monetary and measurement systems. As Roth describes it, Eibenschütz's role, aided by armed policemen, was to punish cheats. For the locals, having traded with each other for years, there was no need for this decimalisation innovation. What was it other than some bureaucratic intrusion? In Roth's words:

A long time ago there had been real measurements, now there were only scales. Cloth had been measured with the arm, and as all the world knows, a man's arm from his closed fist to his elbow, measured an ell no more and no less . . . in these parts there were many folk who had no use for weights and measures. They weighed in the hand and measured with the eye.[1]

In money and measurement, as in science, the nineteenth-century world was moving from guesswork and reputation to precision and objectivity. Eventually adopted by the Austrian Empire, decimalisation owes much of its impetus to Hamilton's revolutionary America.

The US dollar was the world's first completely decimalised currency, enshrined in 1792 by Hamilton's Coinage Act. Citizens of the new US wanted to reinforce their separation from imperial Britain and erase any trace of it from the new republic. Crowns, farthings and sovereigns sounded too English, so the Americans introduced a new decimal currency with the dollar divisible into 100 cents (from the Latin for a hundred).[2] The dime came from the old French expression for one tenth, which would have been used within the vast French-speaking areas of North America.

Decimalisation was a revolutionary statement and was seen as such by the old regimes in Europe who, despite decimal's logic, were not about to bow to these new kids on the block, at least at first. No matter how convoluted their monetary system, no bewigged monarchist entertained the thought of changing their currency denomination.

The Napoleonic Wars were a battle for ideas: on the one side, republicanism, representing the modern; and on the other, monarchy, representing the past. In the convulsive cauldron of the eighteenth and early nineteenth centuries, arguments about currency denomination reflected the political, social and intellectual fault line between conservatives and radicals. The essence of conservatism is to conserve, as the Irishman who coined the term, Edmund Burke, espoused. For conservatives, tradition is valued, and progress is a process of building on small gains, preserving that which works and genuflecting to heritage. Along with preserving arcane currency denominations came a suite of other conservative beliefs including hereditary peerages, established churches and, naturally, monarchies. Conservatives are by implication backward-looking, deriving legitimacy from what went before as opposed to embracing what might be to come. But in the innovation-driven world of science, the tyranny of tradition can be detrimental for progress and discovery. In the nineteenth century, radicals would agitate for the new and the possible, while conservatives would hanker after the tried and tested. The battle for money was no different.

If revolutionary America had embraced decimalisation when it came to money, revolutionary France adopted it with fanatical zeal. The French decimalised everything and exported this logical and easy-to-comprehend system all over Europe – from Italy to Germany – via Napoleon's revolutionary army. To the French, decimalisation was an expression of democracy and liberty, smashing through the awkward inheritance of the old monarchical system. And they didn't limit the decimal revolution to money and weights alone. In the French revolutionary calendar, a week was changed from seven to ten days (to be called a 'decade'), and the day consisted of ten hours. A revolutionary hour was 100 minutes and a minute, 100 seconds. The year still contained twelve months but began in October. All references to religious feasts or Roman emperors or deities were removed and replaced with references to the prevailing weather at that time of year. The French took what used to be August and named it Thermidor, meaning the hot month, replacing the old reference to Augustus, the Roman emperor. The immersive decimalisation of all things French lasted for over ten years and although some of the more experimental aspects were abandoned, decimalised coins, weights and measurements persisted.

The convenience and ease of calculation in the decimalised system proved compelling for scientists and revolutionaries alike. The beauty of the metric system based on tens and hundreds is that it makes standardisation and comparison easy. It also puts empiricism to the fore. Mechanics, technicians and businesspeople were particularly taken by the metric system as it allowed for precision and, ultimately, increased productivity. Over time, country after country adopted it. As science and enquiry took off in the nineteenth century, metric became an international grammar understood by everyone. While the British held out (it was a monarchy after all), in monetary measurements most other countries would fall in line with revolutionary America and France. Despite France's losses on the battlefield, and America being isolated beyond an ocean, their revolutions occupied nineteenth-century minds. Decimalisation would affect not just how we traded but how we thought.

Money's mind games

The commercial revolution of the eighteenth century gave way to the industrial revolution of the nineteenth century, itself a function of the age of scientific discovery which co-evolved with it. Money played a significant role in this shift, not just as the mediator of economic expansion, but also in the way it altered human psychology. Money and how to manage it became increasingly important in everyday lives. The growth of industry and the accompanying spread of industrial wages meant a greater number of people were using money, and more things in daily life were now connected and defined by money: for example, it might occur to an industrial worker that the money they can earn through eight hours' work equals five days' rent, or the price of that overcoat they have their eye on.

Decimalisation of money made more people numerate, and the more numerate the population, the more likely the population is to accept scientific breakthroughs backed by measurement. A similar process to what we observed with the introduction of zero was occurring but on a much broader scale. Everyone who had a coin in their pocket could more easily divide and multiply by ten and a hundred. It may be hard to understand today just how big a change this was in the way people thought. New parts of our brain were being used: pre-decimalisation, the average person would have 'calculated' in quantities such as farthings or guineas having learned by rote the relationships between the various coins without much understanding of the calculus behind it. That all changes with decimalisation, which in the nineteenth century co-evolves with great leaps in scientific discovery, all of which are grounded in inductive reasoning and the collection of empirical data. One man who was gathering data and observing all sorts of relationships in nature was Charles Darwin. His discovery would rock the world.

When Darwin met money

In the summer of 1848, Charles Darwin was following news of a typhus outbreak among Irish immigrants at the docks in Boston, Massachusetts. The unfolding human tragedy took Darwin's mind off the stock market, where his losses were ratcheting up. The stocks of railway companies, the transformative technology of the Victorian age, were the subject of wild speculation. Evolution, Darwin's theory of how life had emerged and developed on earth, with its dictum of natural selection, should have warned him that not every company involved in the railway business would succeed. In fact, most companies set up hastily in the giddiness of the railway mania failed spectacularly. By mid-1848, his bet on railway stocks was unravelling. Like Isaac Newton before him – who lost his fortune in the 1720 South Sea Bubble by making the mistake of applying the predictable laws of physics to the messy world of money – Darwin was financially undone. He might have been a prodigy who changed our understanding of the world, but when it came to money, how it worked and how the average person's mood was affected by it, Darwin was as gullible as the next lad. As the Romans taught us, money is mercurial – you think you have a handle on it, but it can slip through your fingers.

Darwin wasn't only interested in money for the sake of speculation. A decade earlier, it was economics that had given him the concept of natural selection, and from there everything had flowed.[3] Darwin's theory of life on earth was revealed to him not in a biological treatise, but in an economics book. He wrote in his diary:

In October 1838, that is fifteen months after I had begun my systematic enquiry, I happened to read for my amusement 'Malthus on Population', and being well prepared to appreciate the struggle for existence which everywhere goes on from long-continued observation of the habits of plants and animals, it at once struck me that under these circumstances favourable variations would tend to be preserved and unfavourable ones to be destroyed. The result of this would be the creation of a new species. Here then I had at last got a theory by which to work.

The full title of the book, by the economist and Anglican minister Thomas Malthus, is *An Essay on the Principle of Population, as It Affects the Future Improvement of Society*. In 1838, Darwin was desperately in search of a theory to explain his observations of the natural world. During his famous voyages, he took copious notes about which animals and plants had thrived and which had become extinct. In the Galápagos Islands, he noticed some animals thriving that were extinct elsewhere. He examined flowers and plants and how they fought with each other for light and nutrients. He studied how the ones that survived seemed to adapt to their environment and he called this constant struggle the 'warring of the species'. Darwin concluded that some plants struggle in a changed environment while others thrive, and that the same principle might apply to humans. He had data but no framework – until he read Malthus. Once he digested *An Essay on the Principle of Population*, Darwin had his theory and he spent the 1840s applying his data to his new life-on-earth thesis, one that was largely based on the key Malthusian insight of 'positive checks', which Darwin called natural selection.

Malthus suggested that as industry expanded, incomes from

industry became more secure, and people had more children. For Malthus, the population boom, driven by the industrial boom, would inevitably slam against the ability of the land to provide enough food. The world would be caught in what became known as a 'Malthusian trap'. Before that moment, farmers would default to one crop or a narrow set of crops that might provide a staple for an increasing population, meaning more people would become more and more dependent on fewer crops, increasing the fragility of existence. (This is what would happen in famine-afflicted Ireland in the 1840s.) For Malthus, increased populations would inevitably succumb to privation, whether it be food shortages, crop failure or contagious disease, as rising populations put pressure on the earth's natural resources. Less adaptable populations would succumb, leading to catastrophic population collapse.

Most importantly for Darwin, Malthus wrote that people would adapt their behaviour when faced with the limits of the land to sustain ever-growing populations. These were the so-called positive checks. Darwin immediately saw the relevance of these behavioural adaptations for his own theory of life on earth. The species that deployed positive checks, adapting to their environment, would survive; those that didn't adapt would die out. For example, after the Irish Famine, marriage rates plummeted, emigration continued and the trauma of seeing their neighbours starve changed the behaviour of coming generations. The population on the island of Ireland fell from 8 million in 1841 to less than 4 million by 1941, as the Malthusian positive checks kicked in. Adapting their behaviour was the key to survival. In the 1850s, about 990,000 Irish people emigrated to the United States – 83 per cent of all migrants to the US in that decade. My ancestors adapted. It wasn't so much survival of the fittest as survival of the most adaptive. As he observed the traumatised Irish refugees in 1848, their experience would have provided further evidence for Darwin of Malthus' theories and how these economic observations could apply to biology.

The adaptive world

Darwin concluded that positive checks were the sociological equivalent of nature's natural selection process. In a sense, Malthus was the first evolutionary economist, arguing that a form of natural selection governed the relationship between people and the planet, and that this relationship was never static. His ideas were not limited to food supply. Malthus suggested that great towns would see a much higher incidence of plagues and epidemics wiping out large numbers to keep a lid on the population and, at the same time, human behaviour would adapt, using social distancing, quarantine and other behaviours to keep people apart. What Malthus did not foresee was that human ingenuity would mean that our positive checks would involve breathtaking improvements in sanitation and public health, as well as scientific and technological advances that boosted agricultural output and made his Malthusian trap idea seem quaint and outdated as the population surged. Malthus underestimated humankind, but today's climate change crisis shows us that nature continues to set the terms of engagement. The world remains in a state of evolutionary churn.

As the economy in Britain and America started to expand, the science that would become economics began to grow in popularity. Beginning with Adam Smith in the late eighteenth century, intellectuals started to consider the economy as a subject in itself. Up until the industrial revolution, the notion of the economy was an abstract idea, but with the advent of the empirical society, industrialisation, wages and profits, intellectuals and scientists started to explore the concept of 'the economy', a system consisting of a complex web of profoundly consequential relationships. People began to ask how the economy works, where innovation comes from and what role money plays within this system.

Victorian economics gave Victorian biology its greatest breakthrough: the theory of natural selection. It is difficult to overstate how the theory of evolution affected the way Victorians thought. Everything they had believed up to then about their place in the world, including how we got here, was upended. Evolution undermined social hierarchy as well as religion: if nature evolved, how could you have a society that stood still? The creation of so much doubt, where there had been certainty, generated dissent. This disquiet is reflected in the art and literature of the Victorian age, as people tried to come to terms with new ways of looking at the world. Science threatened superstition; dogma and received wisdom were questioned. Tradition was assailed by the modern, leading to an explosion in scientific enquiry and technological innovation. Germ theory, stemming directly from a growth of interest in biology sparked by Darwin, would fundamentally change the field of medicine. The development of anaesthetics, X-rays and microscope technology was accompanied by the invention of the light bulb and the telephone. These inventions needed money, and an enthusiasm for science released enormous investment.

Economics gave Darwin his template and, in turn, Darwin's template offered a way of understanding how the economy worked. As Alfred Marshall, regarded by many as the father of modern economics, noted, 'the Mecca of the economist lies in economic biology',[4] meaning that the economy is characterised by similarly volatile evolutionary forces to those found in nature, because it too is a complex and interrelated system. And the source of the volatility in economics is the wonderfully unpredictable animal at its centre, the human being. A political event in India would evidence this complexity, underscoring just how difficult it is to predict the path of the ever-adapting economy.

The cobra effect

As Darwin was beavering away on the final proofs of *On the Origin of Species*, more shocking news from the colonies rattled Westminster. This time, it wasn't Ireland but India. In 1857, British-occupied India rebelled. British textbooks still refer to the uprising as a 'mutiny', as if Indians agitating for freedom was a display of disloyalty. Facing widespread insurrection, the British feared losing the colony. India had become a looter's paradise, far too valuable to abandon. When the British arrived, Indian GDP was close to 30 per cent of the world's total global income, but by the time they left, India's GDP was reduced to less than 3 per cent of world income.

After the 1857 rebellion, Britain changed tack and set out to bribe enough people in India into believing that occupation was good for them. Britain continued looting and plundering while carrying out the official policy of 'killing home rule with kindness'. This meant benign public works projects, like building train tracks with Indian taxes, putting up the odd library or two, and building an entirely new trading city, the cosmopolitan entrepot of Bombay, out of which the wealth of the Indian interior could be funnelled. Each meagre effort was held up as an example of enlightened foreign rule or, as they said themselves, 'bringing civilisation' to a civilisation that pre-dated the British state by 4,000 years.

The British thought they might win a few propaganda brownie points in the administration of the sprawling city of Delhi. A few years after the 1857 rebellion, an opportunity presented itself. The British High Commission received reports of a cobra infestation in the warren of Old Delhi. Thirty minutes is all a person has before a cobra bite will cause asphyxia. Not surprisingly, the city was panicking. Here was the chance for the British to display to Indians how lucky they were to be ruled from competent London. The British would chase the snakes out of Delhi.

Back in Whitehall, the India Office considered how to co-opt the local population in the drive to eliminate the deadly cobras. They offered a financial reward on the production of a dead cobra at a specific point in the old city. The locals, spurred by money, would take control of the snake menace and in no time Delhi would be cobra-free.

At first, Delhi's intrepid snake charmers got to work. Lots of dead cobras started turning up at the drop-off points – the cobra population was being decimated. The locals collected their rewards. The British were chuffed. But within a few months, reports filtered back to London that all was not well on the cobra front. The number of dead cobras being delivered was *increasing*. What was going on? The law of unintended consequences had kicked in. By putting a price on the cobra's head, the British had turned it from a venomous menace into a valuable commodity and, by extension, into a stream of income. Money talks. The entrepreneurs of Old Delhi reacted not by killing wild cobras, but by breeding them! The domesticated cobra was easier to kill than its wild cousin and a production line of profit for enterprising locals was developed.

At the stroke of a Whitehall pen, the menace was turned into a vibrant business. The British were perplexed. There *were* fewer wild cobras on the streets, but money was flying out of government coffers to pay for a surge in dead cobras. Eventually they twigged what was going on and raided the burgeoning businesses, these new cobra farms. Incensed at having been duped, the British ended the reward scheme. The Indian entrepreneurs promptly reacted to the collapse in the value of cobras by releasing their stock into the city. Why keep them if they were worthless? The city became infested with cobras again, worse than before the scheme.

Money and the evolutionary economy

The cobra tale reveals that money nudges the economy, which works like a giant and unpredictable evolutionary organism. In the economy, products come and go; sometimes great ideas don't catch on while lesser ones do. No one really knows why. With more and more money in the economy, more ideas are turned into products and services. Each begins life with confidence, yet only a few will survive. Have you ever been at a doubting or self-conscious product launch? Every new design is going to change the world, until it doesn't. The best-laid marketing plans rarely survive their impact with the market. Like our Delhi cobra charmers, the market is unpredictable.

Where genetic evolution is gradual, economic evolution, mediated and propelled by money, is incredibly fast. The more money, the more products, the more energy and the quicker the evolutionary process. As in the natural world where a diverse ecosystem is a healthy one, the more diverse an economy – the more interactions, people, networks and capital – the more ideas, products and services are produced. A healthy economy is vibrant; the more exuberant the better. As the economy evolves, rolling with various punches, the most diverse region succeeds because it doesn't become overdependent on any single thing.

Monoculture in the natural world is highly fragile. Think about Darwin's musing on my Irish ancestors, who were dependent on one crop, the potato. Monoculture in evolutionary economics works the same way as it does in the animal world. It's the road to poverty. With the exception of petrostates, economic diversity is the road to riches. Diversity offers more options, combinations and novel possibilities for commercial cross-pollination. For example, when Gutenberg invented the printing press in the thriving ecosystem of fifteenth-century Mainz, commercial diversity was his friend. He combined his know-how in print technology, stemming from his artistic background as a goldsmith, with the wine-pressing technology used in Mainz for centuries. Combining these capabilities was the key to the innovation.

New products are usually fashioned out of things that are adjacent or close at hand. The entrepreneur is the person who puts these things together, and they do this with money. The more money, the more risk, the more diversity and the quicker the economy evolves. New products replace old ones, and no one has any idea what will be spawned by what. Like the cobra example, one initiative which is expected to lead to one outcome can lead to something quite different and often contradictory. We cannot forecast with any accuracy the ripple effects of an innovation.[5] Once launched, the printing press spawned vast unexpected changes in many areas of life, from education and industry to finance and religion, leading ultimately to the Reformation.

The world economy in Darwin's time was buzzing with ideas, discoveries and new products. It wasn't so much growing – simply getting bigger – as evolving. The products that survived were those that adapted. There was no grand creator anointing one product or another: the economy was a design without a designer. The frenzy of speculation in railway shares that ensnared Darwin was only one of many during this period. The discoveries of oil and electricity sparked enthusiastic gambling on which resource would be the winner in the great evolutionary battle.

Money was both the fuel and the arbiter of this new world. If a product or company was making money, it survived. If not, it became extinct. In effect, money as profit is the evolutionary economy's way of telling the world whether a new product is a winner or not. Although not yet defined in the words of twentieth-century political economist Joseph Schumpeter, the great nineteenth-century economic takeoff was driven by 'gales of creative destruction', or what Keynes termed 'animal spirits'. The economy isn't static, or mechanical, or modellable. It's *alive* and it *evolves*.

A growing middle class

By the mid-nineteenth century, money was making the world smaller. New consumer products increased the demand for raw materials, which landed at the ports of Europe and America to be deployed in new factories that were producing an astonishing array of goods. Wages and profits from these factories generated income for workers, while the factories required clerks, lawyers, accountants and managers – those who made up the new middle classes, and would later become known as white-collar workers. Banks, set up to take in the savings of this class, needed to earn money on these savings. They lent to entrepreneurs, creating a commercial class of investors who were constantly looking for the next big thing. The period saw an explosion in credit and financial innovation, leading to the evolution of what we would now call the banking industry, whose reach extended all around the globe, wherever there was a demand for money. Driven by innovation, this vibrant banking system funnelled money and credit into the hands of industrialists and, ultimately, the bourgeoisie with their insatiable demand for products.

One such product was the bicycle, an invention so transformative that its impact would be felt all over the world. Nowhere more so – and more tragically – than in Africa.

MONEY ON TRIAL

Heart of darkness

'Are you an assassin, Willard?'
'I'm a soldier.'
'You're neither; you're a grocery boy, sent by grocery clerks to collect the bill.'

As put-downs go, this one from the rogue Colonel Kurtz (Marlon Brando) to Captain Willard (Martin Sheen) is devastating. The scene with a bald Kurtz lathering his head while psyching out young Willard should have been enough on its own to win an Oscar. Familiar to cinema lovers worldwide, Francis Ford Coppola's *Apocalypse Now*, set during the Vietnam War, sees the young assassin Willard venture up the Mekong River in search of Kurtz, who is holed up in his jungle fortress behind a macabre fence made up of severed heads impaled on spikes. Coppola's storyline is borrowed from a Polish writer's account of real-life events in the Belgian Congo. That writer is Józef Teodor Konrad Korzeniowski, better known to the world as Joseph Conrad. His 1899 novella *Heart of Darkness* revealed to a literary audience the true nature of King

Leopold of Belgium's so-called free trade zone, which strad-dled the vast Congo River in Central Africa (the same trading route where the Ishango Bone was unearthed).

In 1890, the 32-year-old Pole was working aboard a ship delivering railway sleepers to the Congo. Roger Casement, an Africa veteran who had worked as a surveyor of railways, map maker and labour recruiter, took the young writer under his wing. Night after night, Casement informed Conrad of the industrial-scale human rights abuses that were being meted out further up the Congo River. Two years before Casement and Conrad met, in 1888, Casement had encountered a sadistic Belgian officer named Guillaume Van Kerckhoven who adorned his barracks with severed heads on stakes, precisely the tactic used by Mr Kurtz in Conrad's novella and his namesake in Coppola's film. Casement would later write a report about Van Kerckhoven that was politely received and filed away in London. Criticism of the Congo wasn't too welcome in powerful circles because too much money was being made.

Had he not lived an extraordinary life – and up to the age of forty there was little to suggest he would – Dubliner Roger Casement would likely have been buried in my local cemetery, close to where my grandparents lie. His brother is buried there and, by a strange twist of fate, he lies only a few plots from the resting place of John Boyd Dunlop, the man who invented the pneumatic rubber tyre. Dunlop's invention trans-formed the global economy and is critical to the story of money, rubber and the Congo. Had it not been for Dunlop's invention, it's unlikely that Casement would have ended up in the Congo in the first place.

In 1880, Dunlop, an enterprising local vet in Downpatrick, County Down, had stooped to listen to his five-year-old son complaining that his bike was uncomfortable to ride over the bumpy cobbled streets. Dunlop came up with the bright idea of pumping air into rubber tyres and fitting them round the wheels to soften the ride.

Rubber had been introduced to Europe in 1526 when Spanish conquerors brought a strange material back to Cádiz along with some captured indigenous people. A small but vocal anti-slavery section within the Spanish Church, hoping to reveal to the court in Cádiz the intelligence and sophistication of these 'Indians', invited them to play their own game, *ullamaliztli*, a forerunner of football. The teams had to get a ball through a hoop at either end of a pitch using only their hips, chest and thighs. What captivated the Spaniards was not so much the physical dexterity of the players as the ball itself. Made of a never-before-seen substance, its motion was so strange that the Spanish language didn't even have a word to describe its bounce.[1] Europeans couldn't figure out how a substance could be heavy to throw and yet bounce light as a feather at the same time. The substance, harvested from trees in the Amazonian jungle, could bend and stretch. It wasn't until the early nineteenth century that European chemists figured out that rubber stretched when heated (and could be moulded into boots which became an instant hit), but back in the Amazon, people had been adapting and utilising rubber for centuries. After the Amazon, there was only one other climatically similar region in the world – the ecosystem surrounding the great Congo River in West Africa.

Dunlop made his name in rubber tyres, selling his pneumatic tyre patent to the global multinational that subsequently bore his name, Dunlop Industries. Pneumatic tyres changed the world. Wheels rolled more smoothly and made the bike far gentler to cycle. The 1880s fad for bicycles turned into a global boom by the 1890s. Dunlop had reinvented the wheel.

His invention would also rewrite not just African history but global financial and economic flows.

In many ways, botany had long been one of the chief instruments of empire. Plants, first as consumer goods such as tea, sugar and coffee, drove much global trade during the commercial age of the seventeenth and eighteenth centuries, enriching European merchants. By the nineteenth century, while consumer tastes were still important for commerce, the medicinal and industrial properties of plants now fuelled globalisation. The botanist, regularly painted as a benign, intrepid scientist, was more often than not an agent of imperialism, while seemingly harmless botanic gardens were the research labs of colonialism. Thermochemical advances during the industrial revolution further transformed the place of botany in the economic system: for example, vulcanisation – a process whereby sulphur is added to latex to harden rubber – had dramatic consequences for the role rubber played in the global economy, as in its use as insulating and waterproof tubing for electrical wires. Rubber and rubber-growing areas became pivotal to worldwide industrial production, and by the late nineteenth century raw rubber became a crucial input into a whole host of new industrial and consumer goods, enmeshing Western consumers, workers, manufacturers and financiers in a vast colonial project.

Cycle mania

In the years following Dunlop's invention, the middle classes of Europe and America took to cycling with gusto. Less expensive than horses, bicycles were a free-wheeling alternative to the trains that only connected certain towns and villages. With the bike, you could go where you wanted. In England, parish records show a significant increase in intervillage marriages coincident with the cycle mania of the 1890s. People who might otherwise not have met each other hooked up thanks to the bike, expanding the gene pool.

In Cambridge, on 21 May 1897, when the university Senate was voting on whether to grant female students the right to receive a full degree, a group of angry male students brandishing signs reading 'Varsity for males' tore into an effigy of a woman on a bicycle. They ripped the mannequin apart, tore off her head and posted her remains – with her bicycle – through the gates of the all-female Newnham College. The woman on the bicycle represented everything that was scandalous about this invention. For traditionalists, the bike was a transgressive machine, a mechanism for women to assert their independence.

In 1896, at the age of thirteen, Christabel Pankhurst, daughter of the suffragette leader Emmeline, petitioned her father to buy her a bike. She and her sister Sylvia joined the Clarion Cycle Club in Manchester, an offshoot of the socialist newspaper *The Clarion*. By 1900, there were seventy Clarion cycling clubs in Britain, all admitting women, who used these clubs to cycle around towns and villages bringing the suffragette message to new parts of the country. The prudish conservative establishment lectured women about everything from the capacity of the saddle to rob their technical virginity, to the impact of 'bicycle face' on a girl's natural prettiness, and the scandal of female cyclists wearing bloomers. Nevertheless, the market for bikes took off.

In 1890, there were 27 factories in the US making 40,000 bikes a year. By 1896 there were 250 factories churning out 12 million bikes per year. Pope, the largest bike maker in the States, was making a bicycle a minute by the middle of the decade. The UK, the bike-producing centre of the world, had 700 factories. Money followed the craze as investors flocked to get some of the action. As production ticked upwards, prices fell. In the US, between 1890 and 1896, the price of a bicycle almost halved from around \$150 to \$80. Hoping to cash in on Dunlop-like success, one third of all patents lodged in the US patent office in the 1890s were bicycle-related.[2]

The money-go-round

The emerging middle class of the late nineteenth century was not only buying bicycles with their disposable income, but was also saving, a practice that was previously the reserve of the very rich. Most middle-class savers were conservative – they put their money into the bank for 'safekeeping', taking an annual interest rate and not really asking where this income came from. The banks sought income on these savings and they lent out to higher-risk investments to generate a return to meet the interest due to savers as well as make a profit for themselves. What better place to make money than the colonies?

Where there are savings, there will always be financial products to attract those savings. The late Victorian age was the imperial age and those savings products were taking a punt on companies all over the globe. The publicly traded company was the investment vehicle of choice, offering commercial opportunities for investments in a dazzling array of new sectors and regions. We have seen that the explosion in consumer goods meant a rise in demand for raw materials from all over the world, and this made the planet more integrated. We were in the first era of globalisation. A new global supply chain sparked by Dunlop's invention linked suffragettes in Manchester with bike manufacturers in Coventry, and steel producers in Sheffield with suppliers of rubber deep in the Belgian Congo. In the centre of this web was the publicly traded company that linked middle-class depositors to the entire venture. Their savings financed a seemingly innocuous bicycle industry but, as we shall see, that industry was under-pinned by a colonial heist and all the horror that entailed. Rubber linked the Congo to the streets of Manchester and finance linked it to the City of London.

European money was scouring the world looking for profit. Between 1855 and 1900, foreign investment out of Europe trebled from $4.6 billion to $13.8 billion. In 1870, foreign investments accounted for 7 per cent of all European income, but by 1914 they had climbed to 20 per cent. The British spent the most – averaging 4 per cent of its annual GDP – financing exploitative ventures across the world in the forty years to 1900.[3] About a third of all British savings were redirected out of the UK to finance far-flung companies and projects, meaning that a vast swathe of British upper- and middle-class people were financially complicit in and profited from the colonial project. *Active* investors held their noses and committed money because investment in empire tended to yield higher returns than domestic investments. *Ordinary* savers were probably unaware that their money was being recycled into the global economy and colonial schemes. The British Empire was a money machine. But it wasn't just Britain.

Nineteenth-century Belgium wanted a colony too, and at the 1884–1885 Berlin Conference on Africa, King Leopold II convinced his cousins, the other European monarchs, that his goals in the Congo were philanthropic, and included ending the slave trade – as a result, in November 1889, an anti-slavery conference of the major powers was held in

Brussels.[4] The British, French and German governments acquiesced to Leopold's claim to remote Congo in order to avoid conflict with each other, as they were busy chopping up the rest of Africa among themselves. Belgium, the buffer state in Europe, also became a sort of buffer state in Africa between the French, British and new German colonies. And that, more or less, is how the Congo Free State became the personal property of King Leopold II. When his agents in the Congo told him about abundant wild rubber vines growing along the riverbanks, Leopold was quick to recognise the bonanza that Dunlop's innovation might yield. However, he needed money to make money. The domestic Belgian capital market was constrained in comparison with commercially ambitious London, the venture capital headquarters of the Victorian age. British financiers' risk appetites for far-flung places, whetted by looting India, were more adventurous than those of staid Belgian prospectors. The British could see the big picture because they'd stretched the canvas.

Leopold looked to London to solve his financial dilemma. He persuaded an Englishman, Colonel John Thomas North, whom he had met at a horse race in Ostend, to invest £40,000 in a new company that would systematically exploit the rubber of the Congo's Maringa-Lopori basin. The result was the formation of what would become one of the world's most profitable companies, the Anglo-Belgian India Rubber and Exploration Company, known as ABIR, on 6 August 1892.

The company structure, devised first by the Romans, reinstated by merchants in Florence, and tweaked by Dutch and British financiers, was a perfect mechanism for transporting money from one jurisdiction to another. The Victorian public company – with its legal protection for investors and its tradeable shares that could access a deep and liquid capital market – was partly responsible for nineteenth-century colonialism's spectacular success in fusing the financial interests of the few in the exploitation of the many.

ABIR's memorandum and articles of association detailed the protection offered to its shareholders but had little to say about the conditions of the workers in the Congo. In one moment of financial sorcery, a company that brutally enslaved hundreds of thousands of locals in a hellscape of blood, shit and death could be transformed into a clean balance sheet, a tidy share document, a sterile share price bobbing up and down in crisp newspaper reports measuring the rising wealth of investors. The beauty of the public share company is that it broke the link (in most investors' minds) between the value of their share portfolio and the repellent origin of this wealth.

ABIR sold licences to control the rubber trade in sections of the enormous territory called the Congo Free State. The licensees acquired the rights to exploit all the products of the forests in the Maringa-Lopori basin for thirty years. The Belgian state would supply guns, ammunition and soldiers to protect these colonists from the locals whose land they had stolen. This land included the second-largest rubber forest in the world (after the Amazon) and rubber would be extracted there for fourteen years, from 1892 to 1906.[5] With a share certificate in one hand and a machine gun in the other, the Belgians went about the business of multinational trading on stolen land, backed by a private army – a model made irresistibly profitable by the British East India Company and the Dutch VOC before them.

Although time-intensive and physically demanding, unlike most other natural resources, such as diamonds or minerals, harvesting rubber required minimal capital investment and did not involve much training of the labour force. It was pure profit. If Leopold could orchestrate a system whereby the newly conquered locals could pay their 'taxes' to Belgium by working for the rubber company, he could make a fortune.

Mutilating for money

Far from the factories of Manchester and the cycle-filled streets of the world's great cities, Roger Casement watched as the Congo Free State filled up with rubber plantations, speculators and agents. The local people were about to suffer terribly. With the Belgian militia behind them, the rubber companies would turn the colony into a killing field. It is estimated that up to half the population, between 5 and 10 million people, died in the Congo Free State between 1885 and 1908. The price of rubber doubled from 1894 to 1905, and much of it came from the Belgian Congo. Each rise in rubber prices meant more suffering. With the world now on two pneumatic wheels, the demand for rubber from the Congo rose steadily from 77 tons in 1895 to 452 tons by 1898 and reached 1,048 tons by 1903. ABIR's profits were astronomical.[6]

Enslaved in work camps, the locals toiled day and night to achieve quotas. Those who failed to meet theirs were subjected to physical violence, including whipping by the *chicotte* (a whip made of hippopotamus hide), burning with gum copal, and sometimes a bullet to the head. Each ABIR agent commanded a force of twenty-five to eighty soldiers armed with Belgian-made rifles to punish recalcitrant villagers. This militia force was given the rather glorious-sounding name of the Force Publique. In truth it was a killing squad. In 1903, one outpost imported 17,600 cartridges, 22,755 loads for cap guns, 29,255 caps, 33 rifles and 126 cap guns – all this not for a warzone, but an unarmed, defenceless region.[7] As the cost of labour was zero, the Belgians' main expense was these munitions, and this led them to a most unspeakable cost-cutting strategy.

Most of the Force Publique were local sadists, boozed up, under the command of small-time Belgians. Assiduous in their cost control, word came in from Brussels that too much ammunition was being used and budgeting was required. Brussels suspected the local militia were stealing bullets and selling them on. To avoid waste and prevent theft, soldiers were required to provide evidence that each bullet had gone towards killing a dangerous local. The evidence demanded was a severed human hand. Consider the type of bureaucrat who came up with that idea. These hands were smoked for preservation, and collected in baskets by European agents who matched the number of bullets with an equivalent number of severed hands.

On the docks in Antwerp, E. D. Morel, a French-English clerk in a Liverpool-based shipping company, watched as cargo from the Congo was unloaded. King Leopold claimed to the world that the Congo Free State was a thriving hub where rubber and ivory were being traded with the locals in exchange for the finest Belgian goods. But the only goods leaving Belgium for the Congo were ammunition and guns. Morel began to suspect that Leopold wasn't telling the world the whole story of the Congo Free State. He wasn't the only one.

The secret

Throughout much of the 1890s, Roger Casement had been working to gather on-the-ground intelligence from Africa for the British Broad of Trade. By 1898 he was reporting to London in his new role as British consul, documenting the spiralling atrocities in the Congo. In April 1903, now amassing a clutch of enemies among the wealthy and influential British rubber barons, he received news of another kind from Paris that disturbed him. Major General Hector MacDonald, one of Britain's most decorated soldiers, had shot himself following the revelation of his homosexuality and his liaisons with young men in Ceylon. Casement wrote in his diaries after a sleepless night, 'Did not close my eyes. Hector MacDonald's death very sad.'[8] Casement knew he'd be toast if news of his own homosexuality were to get out.

Following a House of Commons debate in May 1903, Casement was instructed by the Foreign Office to travel to the interior to gather 'authentic information' about the alleged maladministration in the Congo. His world was about to change forever. When Casement left on his historic journey in June, he was almost thirty-nine years old, with nearly twenty years' African experience behind him. His friend Herbert Ward, with whom he had travelled in the Congo in the 1880s, wrote on the eve of Casement's emergence into the public eye: 'No man walks this earth at this moment who is more absolutely good and honest and noble minded than Roger Casement.'[9] Public opinion would change.

Casement headed upriver, taking his own transport because depending on official transportation would ensure that he saw only what the Belgians wanted him to see. As he advanced deeper into rubber territory, his worst suspicions were confirmed and more. He witnessed scenes of mutilation, castrations and other savagery in almost every village. Whole populations were devastated, and some terrified survivors revealed to Casement the specifics of the violence that had been inflicted upon them. The details King Leopold wanted to hide were about to be made public.

In October 1903, Casement returned to London bearing

Le bossu de la rue Quincampoix. Dessin de E. Morin, gravure de Delangle.

During the speculative mania around the Mississippi Company in 1719, share dealing on the rue Quincampoix was so intense that there was no room for tables to exchange contracts, and an entrepreneurial hunchback hired out his hump as a writing desk, as shown in this nineteenth-century illustration by Edmond Morin.

Described by Napoleon as 'a pile of shit in silk stockings', Charles-Maurice de Talleyrand-Périgord is depicted in this 1815 caricature as 'the man with six heads', a reference to the number of French regimes he had participated in.

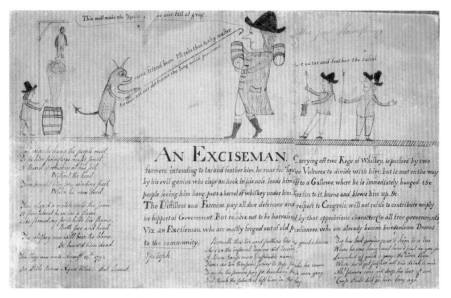

The first real test of federal power in the United States involved a whiskey rebellion over money – specifically tax. This drawing from 1791 shows an exciseman pursued by two farmers as they chase him to the gallows.

Alexander Hamilton knew that without some binding organisational tool, the American republic might unravel. That tool would be money and its main instrument the US dollar.

Irish emigrants to America fleeing famine in 1856. Charles Darwin's theory of the 'survival of the fittest' stemmed from the economic notion of the 'Malthusian trap', whereby humankind is locked in a constant battle with the environment and the latter always wins.

During the years of the Congo Free State, administrators in Brussels suspected the local militia in Congo were stealing bullets and selling them on. Soldiers were required to provide a severed human hand as evidence that each bullet had gone towards killing a dangerous local.

The trial of Roger Casement in 1916 was a box-office sensation. A figure of global stature, who had exposed Belgium's shame in the Congo, he was found guilty of high treason and sentenced to death. The trial is depicted here in a painting by the Irish artist John Lavery.

The Gold Standard (1850–1914) constituted a long period of monetary conservatism and small government. In this 1897 *Punch* cartoon, Britain, represented by John Bull, resists American attempts to replace gold with silver.

While most Americans see *The Wizard of Oz* as an innocent children's fairy tale, the film is based on an allegory about a culture war between the financial elite and the working man, which pitted the established US political parties against the Populists of the 1890s.

Writer James Joyce was also an entrepreneur, opening Dublin's first cinema in 1909. Artistic self-expression and commercial self-expression both spring from the human urge to create something new.

In the early twentieth century, Vienna was the fulcrum of modernism and experimentation. This 1911 poster features the radically modern architecture of Adolf Loos, which broke ranks with the more formal neoclassical pastiche dominant at the time.

Confident of victory, Germany exchanged people's savings for war bonds to finance the First World War – a scheme advertised by this poster. As everyone expected to be paid back, lending to the government was not only considered an act of national solidarity, but also prudent financial management. It didn't turn out that way.

Children playing with increasingly worthless banknotes in Weimar Germany. In August 1923, a dollar was worth 620,000 marks, and by November of that year, it was worth 630 billion marks.

Andy Warhol, *Dollar Sign* (1981). Fiat money is the most significant innovation in money since the Lydians minted their first coin, and at the centre of this system lies the US dollar.

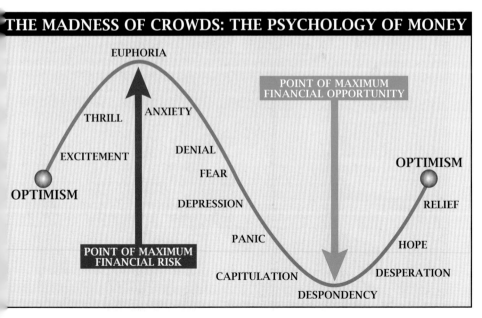

Due to the madness of crowds, sometimes the worst financial decision is taken in what appears to be the best of times, and the best financial decision is taken in what appears to be the worst of times.

Cryptocurrency was backed by celebrity endorsements and Wall Street's wallet, but it largely failed to live up to the hype because the problem it purported to solve wasn't really much of a problem to begin with.

Two Nairobi residents transfer money using M-Pesa at a shop. Today, there are 50,000 registered agents acting as tiny banks all over Kenya, and the system looks set to become a model for money in much of Africa.

this explosive material. With furious energy, he had produced in two weeks a sixty-page record of his journey complete with eyewitness statements. It was a report which, according to Morel – who had by now abandoned his job to expose the Congo Free State in various articles and pamphlets – was to 'brand a reigning sovereign, allied by family connections to half the courts of Europe, with indelible infamy . . . [a] report which, finally and for all time, was to tear aside the veil from the most gigantic fraud and wickedness which our generation has known.'[10]

Casement met Morel for the first time in late December 1903 in London. Morel's writings were attracting the attention of Church leaders, abolitionists and missionaries, as well as reformist Liberal politicians. With Casement's evidence and influence, these two moral dynamos became an irresistible force for change. Travelling to Ireland via Dún Laoghaire (where Casement's statue stands proudly today), they headed for the tranquillity of the Slieve Donard hotel in Newcastle, a Victorian seaside town at the foot of the Mourne mountains, only a few miles from where the pneumatic rubber tyre was invented by Dunlop. Their meeting was described by Arthur Conan Doyle as 'the most dramatic scene in modern history'.[11] With only their personal resources, these two men founded the Congo Reform Association. As Casement said, 'it was the unique character of the Congo wickedness . . . which called for the formation of a special body formulating a very special appeal to the humanity of England'.[12] Casement and the prodigious Morel turned themselves into evidence-gathering machines, documenting atrocity after atrocity and producing a vast body of incriminating facts that made clear the Congo was an international crime scene.

In a remarkable episode of double standards, Britain, the

world's most rapacious imperialist, the country that over the previous 300 years had plundered more money out of its colonies than any other, led the crusade against imperialist Belgium. At the head of the crusade was the Congo Reform Association, with Casement acting as Morel's chief advisor. Casement's official revelations, reported widely, condemned King Leopold and his slave colony to international opprobrium.

Given its position as the global coloniser-in-chief, Britain's motives for going after Belgium were not driven by some Pauline conversion to humanity and decency. By the turn of the century, the value of rubber to the international economy remained critical, but the industry was moving away from extraction and towards the much less onerous business of rubber plantations. Extraction involved enormous amounts of manpower and considerable tropical danger, as rubber forests remained inaccessible. Plantation, on the other hand, was a far cleaner, easier business. You required a tropical climate, flat terrain and a willing workforce. It might not come as any surprise that the ideal environment for this was southeast Asia, specifically the British colony of Malaya. Closing the Congo's rubber industry would mean the supply of rubber would have to come from elsewhere; Malaya was an obvious candidate. In addition, the Boer War of 1899 to 1902 and the intimidation and brutality meted out by British forces in South Africa was painting London in a highly unflattering light. The oldest PR trick in the book is to deflect attention from your own wrongdoing, and Casement's reports on the Congo served this purpose.

Trial of the century

Casement was knighted for his services, and it was as Sir Roger Casement that his own people, the Irish, came to know him. Always sympathetic to the Irish nationalist cause, he began to publish anti-British essays in 1911, resigned from the consular service in 1913, and became a full-time revolutionary. By 1916, Casement was in Berlin, attempting to gather arms for the coming rebellion in Ireland. As he headed back to Ireland with modest munitions aboard a submarine, he landed in Kerry a week before the 1916 Rising. Condemned by, among other things, a Berlin metro ticket in his breast pocket, he was picked up by the police.

Casement was charged with high treason and brought to London under heavy guard, via Dún Laoghaire harbour, a mile from where he was raised in the tiny seaside village of Sandycove. George Bernard Shaw, at that time one of the world's most famous polemicists, offered to write his defence, and Arthur Conan Doyle was a keen supporter. Declining Bernard Shaw's offer, Casement penned his own defence. The trial was a box-office sensation. Casement, a figure of global stature, the man who had exposed Belgium's shame in the Congo, a symbol of the anti-colonial struggle that was just beginning to coalesce, stood accused. He was found guilty and sentenced to death. But he presented a dilemma to the British cabinet: dead, he would be a martyr; alive, he could be imprisoned and later used as a negotiating pawn with the Irish rebels. London came under significant pressure internationally and domestically to commute the sentence. In the early summer months of 1916, there were extensive discussions, and no fewer than five times Casement was discussed at cabinet level.

The cabinet continued to prevaricate until extracts of Casement's diaries – which were purported to evidence his sexual relations with young men – happened to find their way into the hands of people in power, including the US ambassador to London, senior churchmen, newspaper editors and those with influence in Irish-American circles. Arguments that the diaries were cleverly concocted forgeries have never gone away. Forgeries or not, the so-called Black Diaries sealed Casement's fate: the deeply homophobic, morally conservative press had a field day. Treason was bad enough, but homosexuality tipped middle England over the cliff. Rescinding the death sentence of a revolutionary when Britain was at war was one thing; rescinding the death sentence of an Irish homosexual traitor was beyond even the most liberal members of the cabinet. On 3 August 1916, Casement was hanged in Pentonville Prison.

Endgame

In a world where the narrative tended to be controlled by those who amassed great fortunes in the first era of globalisation, Roger Casement was a humanitarian activist who spoke about greater rights than the right of money to dictate outcomes. Jawaharlal Nehru, a young Indian, who had earlier come across Irish nationalism while visiting his cousin (who was studying medicine in Dublin), followed the trial and was influenced by the revolutionary message of the Irish insurrectionists. He mused that Casement's speech in court 'seemed to point out exactly how a subject nation should feel'.[13] Colonialism had reached its apogee and, in the decades to come, it began to be challenged further. Nehru, inspired by Casement's global vision, would lead India to independence in 1947 and become its first prime minister.

Lenin observed that colonialism was peak capitalism.[14] The pendulum had swung too far in the interests of those who expropriated, accumulated and hoarded money. The nineteenth century had seen a hundred relentless years of the march of money, which dictated who got what, who ruled whom, which nations were subjugated and which were victors. It was also a century where innovations in finance, stock markets and international flows of capital brought huge swathes of the globe into a worldwide monetary system. This period of globalisation came to a crashing end when the imperial countries of Europe set upon each other in 1914. An era that began with the unlikely expansion of mercantile Holland, driven by the prowess of Dutch finance, reached its zenith in the early years of the twentieth century with rampant and rapacious colonialism, and began to fall apart when faced with internationalist campaigners like Casement and nationalist liberation struggles.

In the subsequent years, that pendulum swung back towards a variety of -isms: communism, socialism, Marxism, Fabianism and the one we focus on here – anti-colonialism. Every era or ideology sows the seeds of its own destruction, and the hyper-capitalism of the late nineteenth century, although extremely successful if you were very rich, very white and very European, was a different story if you were colonised, humiliated and terrorised. No Marxist himself, Roger Casement was more of a liberal. A fair trade advocate, he believed that those who extracted commodities such as rubber – whether they be Congolese or indigenous tribes in Peru – should be treated humanely. He was against extractive capitalism and extreme exploitation. Part of a reforming tradition that was active at a grassroots level in both Ireland and Britain at the time, Casement was drawn to the possibilities of building a more socially just world. The anti-colonial movement he championed became one of the most significant political forces of the twentieth century, and its genesis lay in the atrocities of the previous three centuries, most carried out in pursuit of money. Although it was not obvious at the time, the trial of Casement was a pivotal moment.

In 1922, the year Ireland achieved independence, John Dunlop, the inventor who had sparked the rubber boom, was buried in Deansgrange cemetery in Dublin. Had it not been for Dunlop's innovation, there might not have been any Belgian atrocities in the Congo, Casement might not have become a global revolutionary and, instead of being hanged in Pentonville Prison, he might have died peacefully, buried in the family plot only yards away from Dunlop's resting place.

16

YELLOW BRICK ROAD

The Wizard of Oz

The Wizard of Oz remains one of the most watched American movies of all time. The staple of Christmas viewing back in the days when people sat in front of terrestrial TV, this American children's story is all about money. More specifically, it concerns the populist movement that fought to bring the US off the Gold Standard against the backdrop of late nineteenth-century deflation. While most Americans see *The Wizard of Oz* as an innocent children's fairy tale, the film is a highly political allegory. It is the story of class struggle and a culture war between the financial elite and the working man, the moneyed East Coast and the rural South and West, and the established political parties and an insurrectionist movement – the Populists – that emerged in the 1890s.

In the film, we can read Oz, the evil Wizard, as the embodiment of the banking elite and also a stand-in for gold, *oz* being the symbol for an ounce. The Yellow Brick Road represents the Gold Standard itself, a pathway made of gold bars. Dorothy is the farmer's daughter from Kansas, the state geographically smack in the middle of the country, representing that mythical place, middle America. The Scarecrow is the Midwestern farmer, put upon by falling prices, and the Tin Man is the industrial worker whose wages are also falling, impacted by deflation associated with the Gold Standard. The Cowardly Lion is the merged Democrat-Populist candidate in the 1896 presidential election, William Jennings Bryan.

Before Dorothy and her friends, working Americans, can enter the Emerald City, they are ordered to wear green-coloured spectacles. The conservative financiers who run the Emerald City, in other words, force its citizens to look at the world through money-coloured lenses. To satisfy the Wizard, the group must travel to the West and destroy his enemy, the Wicked Witch. The West represents the Midwest of America, the farming heartland and the source of the Populist move-ment. At every stage, Dorothy is being used by the Wizard to uphold the rules of the Emerald City and the interests of rich Americans who support the Gold Standard. At his behest, she kills the Witch and returns with her friends to the Emerald City confident that the Wizard will grant them their wishes. When they unmask the Wizard, however, they discover he is nothing but a fraud – as is the Gold Standard. Although Dorothy's shoes are red in the film version, in the novel that the film is based on her shoes are silver. To return to Kansas, Dorothy need only click the heels of her *silver* shoes together. The power to solve her problems – by adding silver to the money stock – was there all the time.

The political message behind *The Wizard of Oz* was that the average American, embodied by Dorothy, could be liber-ated by a move from the straitjacket of the Gold Standard to the looser jersey of a silver-backed currency. While this may seem obscure, the last US election of the nineteenth century was fought on this very issue: what backs money, silver or gold?'

Crucifixion by gold

Against a late nineteenth-century background of breakthroughs in science and medicine, technological advances across a range of areas and an empirical and rational revolution, you might expect that significant changes would have emerged in the way we organise money. Given the experimentation in the eighteenth century, and the revolutionary power of paper money in propelling and financing both the French and American revolutions, it would have been logical to predict that financial disruptors of the nineteenth century would have learned from former mistakes and continued to innovate with currency. This didn't happen.

Instead, we had the era of the Gold Standard, which lasted from approximately 1850 to 1914, a long period of monetary conservatism and small government. The political and financial establishment was wary of the paper money experiments of the revolutionary times, which had caused such tremendous instability. The Gold Standard was regarded as a bulwark against dangerous social and political change. This system, whereby all money was backed by the world's limited gold supply, became the central plank of global economic and monetary policy. A scheme that ties money to gold means that there will always be a shortage of money because there is always a shortage of gold. Such a system suits those who already have money. But what is the right amount of money for a growing economy?

Those who support the idea that there's already too much money out there are likely to be those people who already have plenty of money. In contrast, the people who advocate that there's not enough cash out there are likely to be those who don't have enough money. To understand the political landscape at the turn of the new century, and the two opposing camps that emerged to clash over the question of whether to tie the US currency to gold or silver, we need to go back and trace a bit of American monetary history and a momentous decision taken by the US after the Civil War.

In 1873, America tied the dollar to gold. The politics of gold in the US had been upended in 1848 by the California gold rush: up to then, America had no known natural sources of the precious metal, but after this discovery it became possible for the Americans to contemplate a monetary future based around gold. And yet for a country intent on taking in millions of immigrants, locking itself into a Gold Standard would mean that the amount of money that could be issued would fall per head as the population surged. America already had a well-understood currency in Hamilton's silver dollar, which remained in circulation. Up until the discovery of Californian gold, financial control and order was achieved with the existing silver standard, and this gave the US more flexibility because it could print more money, silver being cheaper than gold. After the gold rush, however, the price of gold fell against silver and this changed attitudes towards adopting the Gold Standard. In addition, American financiers were worried that international investors, addicted to gold, might regard an American silver standard as second-rate. That the USA, today's global superpower, felt the need to hitch its wagon to gold in the late nineteenth century, and didn't have the self-confidence to go it alone in the world, indicates where Washington saw itself in the global economic pecking order.

Gold has a fixed supply: if the economy grows, meaning the economy produces more things, the price of those things must fall in gold terms, because the supply of gold doesn't rise in response to the rise in the economy's output. Tethering a currency to gold is inherently deflationary. Falling prices sounds good, doesn't it? We are conditioned to think about prices in this way. It is good if the price of things you *buy* falls. But this cuts both ways. What if the things you *sell*, like your labour, also fall against gold? In a period of deflation, whose standard of living rises? The people with gold, of course. That means people in finance, people trading money or speculating on other commodities, those with access to money – the already wealthy. Currencies linked to gold will reward people with savings. Who in the late nineteenth century had savings? The same people who have always had savings: rich people, of course.

There is another dynamic that can reinforce this inequality. If the supply of money per head is declining, the price of goods and wages falls but something else happens to asset prices. When money is tied to gold and in short supply, how does the economy finance investment, building or speculation on the future? It does so via credit. The banking system adjusts accordingly to provide that credit. Now consider this at an economy-wide level. Credit markets expand dramatically, pushing up asset prices, which typically ensnare the economy in a credit cycle. As asset prices rise at a time when everyday prices and wages are stagnant, a speculator class becomes enormously wealthy, driving a wedge between the workers – those who depend on wages for their income – and the wealthy – those who depend on rents, dividends and asset prices for their income. A similar dynamic played out after 2008 in most Western economies as central banks made very cheap credit available to banks and those banks lent this to 'creditworthy' clients – namely the already rich who had invested in assets such as housing – driving up asset prices way above wages.

After the Civil War, the growing US economy was a magnet for European funds, but the vibrant silver versus gold debate planted doubt in the European mind as it threatened to devalue the currency. If the Americans wanted to print more dollars to ease financial privations and political tensions, dollar devaluation was a risk. The world was yet to be convinced that the Americans had the political stomach to remain on the Gold Standard. This lack of credibility implied that, despite its growth rates, America was risky, and so it had to offer higher interest rates to Europeans to encourage them to hold its debts. Expensive borrowing meant more reliance on running large trade surpluses with the rest of the world, which in the late nineteenth century more or less meant Europe.

Acts of nature saved the USA from perennial gold crises. In the late 1870s, a series of European crop failures and unusual weather patterns bailed out the Americans. In May 1879, it snowed in France, and similarly poor weather afflicted central Europe and Russia. For the first time in a decade, the port of Odessa, Europe's fastest growing trading centre, was not straining at the seams with Russian wheat to ship to Europe. The shortage pushed European wheat prices skywards, while across the Atlantic, a bumper harvest ensured that American wheat fed the world – at high prices. As wheat travelled one way, gold travelled the other. America's gold stock increased further the following year with the discovery of oil in Pennsylvania. US oil and wheat were travelling to Europe, helping the Americans maintain the Gold Standard without strangling an economy that at this stage was absorbing thousands of European immigrants per week, first Irish, then Italians and Jews.

Good harvests and good luck for the Americans meant that gold flowed in, but so too did these immigrants from Europe driven out by the same process: bad harvests meant emigration. While gold flowed west across the Atlantic, more and more people continued to arrive in America, causing the overall gold per person ratio to deteriorate. Even though the economy was growing, the fruits of this growth were not evenly spread, socially or geographically.

This situation can last for a while, particularly if there is no way for the workers to exhibit their displeasure. But democracies come with a device called the ballot box which has a way of dealing with such dilemmas. By the end of the century, a selective form of democracy (which didn't give women and certain minorities the vote) was the norm in the US and, in a democracy, a monetary system that favours the already wealthy becomes a central issue. The poor might not have a stake, but they have a vote. For Americans in the 1880s and 1890s, the Gold Standard would become the totemic issue. The poor wanted the US to move back to a silver system that would allow more money to circulate. The rich wanted the Gold Standard to remain in place, cementing their position at the top. The rallying cry of the 1896 election was 'Silver instead of Gold' – it was the working man versus the elite. As William Jennings Bryan (the Cowardly Lion in our *Wizard of Oz* allegory) said at the Democratic National Convention in Chicago, taking aim at bankers, financiers and gold bugs, 'You shall not press down upon the brow of labor this crown of thorns. You shall not crucify mankind upon a cross of gold.'

Dixieland

In the 1830s, the Bank of Louisiana issued a ten-dollar note. Due to the preponderance of Francophones in the region, the ten-dollar note was known by a French name, *dix*, meaning ten. But the English speakers didn't pronounce the 'x' in the French way (*'deece'* with a soft 'x') and so it became *dix* with a hard 'x'. Louisiana, home to the wealthy port of New Orleans, was a rich state, and printed the most credible currency in the South. The currency of the Bank of Louisiana, the dix, became widely used in the adjacent Confederate states. The impact of the dix increased dramatically during the gold rush because New Orleans was the first port that Californian gold was deposited in: difficult as it is to understand now, it was cheaper to transport Californian gold by ship all the way down round Cape Horn and up the other side to New Orleans. The more gold in New Orleans, the more banknotes printed. In time, the Confederacy became known as Dixieland.

The legacy of the Civil War remained central to American politics. Both the North and the South had needed money to fight and both resorted to issuing paper money, backed by loans from their own side. For instance, investors would invest in Union government IOUs and with this money in the Treasury, the Union government printed paper money with nothing to back it but the promise of victory. To keep money coming in, the Union government undertook to pay the interest on their bonds to the lender in gold coins, but paid their soldiers in notes, which became known as greenbacks.

It is estimated that the Southern Confederate government started the war with less than $40 million in real assets. How could you fight a prolonged war with such meagre resources?

The Confederacy did what all desperate financiers do: it promised to pay everything back on victory. Wealthy landowners, slave owners, cotton plantation owners and the ordinary middle class lent money for the war effort. The government used what hard currency it had to buy guns and ammunition and used a variety of loans, many collateralised by pledges of future cotton harvests. To pay the soldiers, it printed its own Confederate dollars. With all the resources of the Confederacy going to the war effort, inflation exploded. Just to give you an idea of how bad things were, in the Northern Union states goods that cost $100 in 1860 had increased to $146 by 1865; in the South the same goods that cost $100 in 1860 soared to $9,211 by 1865.[2]

After the war, there was no Confederate government to pay back Southern bondholders. The Northern side refused to redeem any of the now worthless IOUs issued by its former enemy. Losing the war condemned much of the South to bankruptcy. As well as suffering a humiliating defeat, the Southern states, which had been the richest part of the US before the war, based on land, agriculture and slaves, ended up being the poorest. Their infrastructure was destroyed, and they had no capital or any Marshall Aid-type plan to rebuild.

The resentment in the bankrupt South towards Washington and its cosy consensus of Republicans and the business elite is not difficult to comprehend. Wealthy Southerners who had given all their gold to the Confederate cause were now flirting with poverty. Meanwhile, Southern farmers, largely dependent on cotton, saw the price of their product fall. Not surprisingly, the South seethed. In the ensuing years, the people who paid most for this were the poor Black ex-slaves. Though technically liberated, they came to be governed by the racist Jim Crow laws that were introduced piecemeal over the 1880s. The impoverishment of the whites may even have exacerbated the terror visited on the Southern Black population in the decades after the victory of the anti-slavery cause.

In contrast, Wall Street boomed. This vast, unstable, violent country offered all sorts of opportunities for speculation. Immigrants made a go-getting society even more frenetic. This was an era when great fortunes were made and lost, the era of magnates like Cornelius Vanderbilt and Jay Gould, which became known as the Gilded Age. In his 1899 bestseller, *The Theory of the Leisure Class*, economist and sociologist Thorstein Veblen would document the excessive consumption of this new moneyed class, showing that as Wall Street splurged, rural America suffered.

In the Midwest, the combination of the railroads and the Gold Standard had a profoundly negative effect on farmers. The railway boom brought millions of acres of arable land under tillage. This increased the supply of corn and wheat, and pushed their prices downwards. Farmers who had borrowed for machinery and to purchase land found themselves increasingly indebted. Their debts were in gold-backed dollars, and the price of gold was rising, but their income was in crops, and as the supply of land expanded, the price of those crops continued to fall. In the country's agricultural heartland, the balance sheets of these farmers imploded while the wealth of the railroad bosses soared.

In 1870, farmers in Kansas received 43 cents for a bushel of corn; twenty years later, they were receiving 10 cents a bushel, less than it cost to produce.[3] An agrarian movement, the Farmers' Alliance, began as an organisation to increase the power of producers by negotiating with bulk buyers as a co-operative. The co-operative extended its role in the countryside by opening libraries and disseminating all sorts of radical (at the time) pamphlets on agrarian reform. Across the Midwest, the Farmers' Alliance gained members. Its manifesto centred on curtailment of the power of the railroads, federal loans to aid farmers in debt, and currency reform that entailed reintroducing Hamilton's old silver dollar alongside the gold dollar to ease monetary conditions, which would give debtors a chance to clear their loans. The Alliance also advocated for progressive issues such as the vote for women. Despite issuing platitudes, politicians, both Republican and Democrat, did very little to assuage the farmers' concerns. But when the wheat and corn farmers of the Midwest and the cotton farmers of the South united, a new political force would emerge. With a speculator urban class in the Northeast becoming wealthy and a rural farming class in the South and the Midwest caught in the monetary brace of the Gold Standard, American democracy was ripe for change.

Enter the Populists

The Gold Standard was an international system, which tied all major currencies to gold, and as a result, a crisis in one part of the world could affect another region rapidly. In 1892, a global financial crisis that began with a series of defaults in far-off Argentina and culminated with the bailing out of Barings, one of Britain's largest banks, had severe repercussions for the American economy. The transmission mechanism was the Gold Standard. To bail out Barings, which had lost tens of millions on its investments in Argentina, the Bank of England needed gold. It raised British interest rates, causing gold to flow into London – and out of the rest of the world, including America. The resulting credit crunch in America pushed unemployment up to 20 per cent and, with businesses failing all over the country, a new party, the Populist Party, which was determined to free the US dollar from the shackles of gold, began to mobilise as a third force in US politics.

Obsessed with maintaining confidence in the currency and advised by bankers, Grover Cleveland, the Democratic president, responded to the unemployment crisis not by spending dollars on public works, but by spending dollars buying up gold. He wanted to show the world that America was good for its credit and wouldn't let its reserves fall to a level that might undermine its commitment to gold. For the average farmer, the global financial crisis and the reaction to it crystallised the idea that an elite financial cabal was putting the interests of bankers above the interests of the working man.[4]

If Washington would not acknowledge what was happening in the hinterland, then the hinterland would come to Washington. A Populist politician, James Coxey, organised a march on the capital, called the 'petition in boots' or 'Coxey's Army'. Unemployed people from all over the country enlisted. In 1894, the first ever mass march in American history called on the government to hire unemployed men to build public infrastructure financed by a public deficit that would be enabled by a move from the restrictive Gold Standard to a looser silver standard. This would be precisely the policy followed by President Franklin Delano Roosevelt forty years later, but in 1894 the Populist Party's manifesto was considered impossibly radical by the Republicans and by most Democrats. As the Populists garnered increasing support, however, the Democratic Party's unity around the Gold Standard began to erode. They could see which way the wind was blowing and weren't in the business of politics to miss an opportunity. If they couldn't match the Populists on the ground in terms of mobilisation, they'd join them, literally.[5]

At the 1896 Democratic Convention all hell broke loose. The Democrats rejected their own sitting president, choosing a relatively unknown candidate, William Jennings Bryan, as their leader. More radically, they adopted the policy of jettisoning the Gold Standard in favour of a dollar backed by a combination of gold and silver. Jennings Bryan and his supporters called for the dollar to be convertible into silver, valuing 16 ounces of silver equivalent to 1 ounce of gold – a ratio far below the ratio then prevailing in the market, which was about 31 to 1. Such a move would have doubled the money supply overnight. Critics denounced the plan as wildly inflationary.

The Populists now faced a dilemma as their signature policy had been stolen by the Democrats. Would they split the radical vote or join forces with the Democrats and go for a dual assault on the White House in the upcoming election? The Populists opted for an alliance, promising a war on the plutocracy. The Populist programme of aid for farmers, the vote for women, income tax cuts for ordinary workers, the regulation of railroad barons, and of course public deficits to build infrastructure, would only be workable if the monetary brace of gold was loosened.

Despite his alliance with the Populists and his soaring oratory, Jennings Bryan was defeated by the Republican candidate, William McKinley. The American popular revolution against gold was over, for now.

We're not in Kansas anymore

In the summer of 1896, a few months before the Populist-Democrat defeat, thousands of miles away from Washington, an almost destitute First Nations woman, Shaaw Tláa, who had lost her first husband and child to influenza, was living with her second husband George Carmack. She would change the politics of money in the United States for a generation. In one of the many tributaries of the great Yukon River in Alaska, this couple eked out a precarious living fishing for salmon while hoping to find gold. One August morning, Shaaw Tláa saw something glittering in the water. By next spring, news of the first discovery of Klondike gold had made it to California and, before that year was out, 100,000 hopefuls had descended on this remote region hoping to strike it big. The Klondike, added to the discovery of vast seams of gold in Colorado and South Africa, almost doubled the world's supply of gold over the following ten years.

The Democrats got their monetary easing not by abandoning the Gold Standard but by the newly increased gold supply that allowed the global monetary brace to relax. Between 1897 and 1914, as more dollars were printed, prices in the US rose by nearly 50 per cent. Deflation was slain by the intrepid prospecting of a First Nations woman, Shaaw Tláa, or Kate Carmack as she was better known, who would die in the great Spanish Flu pandemic of 1920.

The issue of money and whether the dollar should be tied to gold or silver remained a central part of American economic and monetary discourse. Attachment to gold was seen as a priority of the financial and business elite associated with the Republican Party, whereas a preference for tying the dollar to silver, thereby permitting more money to be in circulation, was often associated with the working man, linked to the Democrats.

The Gold Standard lasted for another decade or so, but the First World War put a temporary stop to it, while the Great Depression sealed its fate. The war required financing and countries were not going to hamper their war efforts and imperil their security by keeping their currencies – and thus their ability to fight – tied to gold. The years after the war, the 1920s, were characterised by central bankers' efforts to get back to the Gold Standard, but the global political, demo-graphic and economic realities had changed, and the politics of money needed to reflect this. Dismissed by John Maynard Keynes as a 'barbarous relic', the Gold Standard limped on, wreaking needless havoc after the 1929 crash by exacerbating the credit crunch of the Great Depression, before eventually being consigned to history by Roosevelt in 1936.

If Shaaw Tláa represents one type of American heroine, Dorothy in *The Wizard of Oz* represents another, the wholesome farming girl from Kansas, the heart of the United States. In the crowd at that rumbustious Democratic Convention in 1896 was a journeyman journalist, L. Frank Baum, who had a number of careers behind him by that time. Like many millions of Americans, Baum was taken by the radical, unifying message of the Populists. Having experienced business failure and the various gold-related credit crunches, Baum was a true believer in bimetallism, a currency backed by a mix of both gold and silver. Bitterly disappointed by the defeat of Jennings Bryan, Baum turned his hand to writing children's books and penned an allegory, *The Wonderful Wizard of Oz*.

In 1937, just a year after Roosevelt had taken a traumatised US off the Gold Standard, the success of Walt Disney's first feature film *Snow White and the Seven Dwarfs* showed that adapting fairy tales and children's bedtime stories for the cinema could be successful. Depression America needed make-believe and MGM Studios bought the rights to Baum's children's fantasy. On the silver screen, the story of gold came alive. The first movie to be shot in Technicolor, it would become one of the most successful films ever produced in the US and, at least for this non-American, is up there with Mickey Mouse, apple pie and *Scarface* as a great American cultural touchstone.

Over the following decades, countless American families watched the film each Christmas Day, singing along with Judy Garland to 'Over the Rainbow'. How many knew they were singing about the Gold Standard and the politics of money? You couldn't make it up.

17

MODERNIST MONEY

The stockbroker

In October 1913, James Joyce watched as a statue of Giuseppe
Verdi was unveiled in Trieste's Piazza San Giovanni, located
just a few streets away from the city's bustling stock exchange.[1]
Joyce, a lifelong opera buff and himself a talented tenor, had
spent the previous evening at an open-air production of *Aida*
to mark the centenary of the composer's birth. *Aida* had originally been commissioned by Ismail Pasha to mark the opening
of the Suez Canal. Set against the backdrop of ancient Egypt
– pyramids, temples, sphinxes and the glory of the Pharaonic
age – the opera premiered in Cairo in 1871 to enormous
acclaim.

In 1858, a few years after Darwin lost his shirt in collapsing
railway shares, Ismail Pasha was appointed khedive of Egypt
by the Ottoman sultan. Determined to modernise the country,
Ismail turned to the capital markets to finance infrastructure
that would drag the ancient nation into the nineteenth century.
His outstanding success was the construction of the Suez
Canal, which began in 1863. This audacious scheme, cutting
a large passage through the continent to link the Mediterranean

279

with the Red Sea, and thus Europe to Asia, slashed the journey times to India, China and Indonesia. The Suez Canal was as much a feat of finance as it was engineering. Without innovations in money, most specifically the popularity of stock markets as a way of financing mega-projects, it is unlikely that the idea of the canal would ever have been entertained, let alone realised. Issuing stocks to thousands of investors reduced the risk for any one company, while at the same time enlisting a new investor base into the project and, in turn, further projects. Financial engineering as much as mechanical engineering opened up the world.

Funded entirely by private capital, raised by a French registered company, the financial structure behind the canal was essentially a swap. The company raised money from investors through selling shares, and some of this money was swapped with the Egyptian government for the right to operate the canal and acquire revenues and fees from the operation. Egypt took control of 44 per cent of the company's shares, while the company retained 56 per cent. The company shouldered the risk and the financial perils of this endeavour, recouping its investment through charging ships a fee to use the canal. Although the canal remained officially Egyptian, the company was governed by French company law and based in Paris. Shareholders from all over Europe piled into the initial Suez share offering, which caught the public imagination.

Trieste, Joyce's adopted home, was central to the financing of the Suez Canal. Back in 1858, a self-made entrepreneur from the city, Pasquale Revoltella, had travelled to Paris to offer finance from wealthy Triestians to participate in the project. In acknowledgement of his contribution, Revoltella was nominated vice president of the Universal Company of the Suez Canal, and in 1861 he set out on a long journey to

Egypt to visit the site. He continued to work in support of the project and in 1864 he published an essay titled 'The Co-participation of Austria in World Trade', describing Trieste's pivotal role in the network of economic relationships between Europe and the rest of the world.

Revoltella was a typical example of the energetic merchants who built this thriving new city. The son of a butcher, he ascended through the ranks of Austrian society and was eventually made a baron in 1867. Trieste was a commercial city, the only port of the Austro-Hungarian Empire, and one of Europe's fastest-growing, most cosmopolitan and most lively mercantile centres. If there was a European city of money in the late nineteenth century, Trieste was it – which is quite a claim given the enormous financial innovation that was taking place elsewhere. In the thirty years from 1880 to 1910, half of the world's stock exchanges were set up. Cities rushed to build their own stock exchange, often constructed in neoclassical style, with columns, pediments and grand staircases leading up to these modern-day temples of finance. In Joyce's Trieste, the stock exchange building – which had been built in 1804, though the stock exchange was only instituted as a self-governing body in 1894 – was adorned with Doric columns and crowned with a statue of the Roman god Mercury, the god of money.

New districts were often built around the bourse, with fine avenues and squares, and these areas often had the most expensive real estate in the city. Inside the exchanges themselves, a new creature, the stockbroker, bought and sold a range of stocks and bonds from and to the expanding merchant class. All over the world, engineering projects – railroads, dams, bridges and canals – became the investment of choice for the new middle classes. For projects looking for investment, stock and bond markets were transformative, because investments that couldn't or wouldn't be taken on by one individual or company could be offered to many investors, spreading the risk.

During these years we see the emergence of a new type of magazine, the business paper. Global financial markets were generating huge amounts of news, data and analysis. *The Economist*, set up in the 1840s, published a list of stock and bond prices which ran to fifty pages of small print.[2] Journalism was becoming increasingly qualitative as savers tried to understand the forces that determine share price movements and to decipher mathematical shorthand to make some sense of the numbers. The finance bug was infectious. Karl Marx, the scourge of international capitalism, worked for many years for a financial newspaper, the *New York Daily Tribune*, lining his pockets with the proceeds of commerce while he excoriated finance in *Das Kapital*.[3]

Melting pot

The opening of the Suez Canal redrew the commercial and maritime map of the world and triggered a series of region-shifting developments. The journey to India from Europe, for instance, was cut by 5,000 miles and around ten days. Suez profoundly altered Europe's traditional navigation routes. The Adriatic became the new Atlantic, the channel of choice for goods and people travelling from Europe to Asia and beyond. One clear winner was Trieste, which, nestled in the crook of the Adriatic coast, became one of Europe's most dynamic port cities. Following the opening of the canal, tonnage handled by Trieste's port rocketed from 960,103 tons in 1870, to 2,158,524 in 1890, to more than 5 million tons by 1913. It would become Mitteleuropa's window to the world.

This bustling, diverse city was a product of money. Once a provincial backwater, overshadowed by its illustrious neighbour, Venice, it became a centre for continental commerce. The famous Austrian Südbahn (Southern Railway) connected Trieste to Vienna and the imperial hinterland. The Catholic Austrian monarchy, understanding that nationalism was a threat to its multinational empire, had passed the Patent of Toleration and the Edict of Tolerance in the eighteenth century, which allowed Orthodox Christians and Jews to fraternise and trade openly throughout the empire, paving the way for ambitious migrants to try their luck in Trieste. By the late nineteenth century this attitude to religious freedom meant that Trieste was a veritable melting pot of Italians, Austrians, Slovenes, Czechs, Croats, Poles, Armenians and Serbs. By the beginning of the twentieth century, it hosted the churches of Lutherans, Methodists, Swiss and Valdesian Protestants, Anglicans and Armenian Mechitarists in addition to large Catholic, Jewish, Greek and Serbian Orthodox communities. Its dialect, Triestino, absorbed bits of Armenian, English, Spanish, Sicilian, Turkish, Maltese, German, Hungarian, Croatian, Yiddish, Czech and Greek.[4] Marx ascribed Trieste's success relative to Venice's demise to its new cosmopolitanism:

How, then, came it to pass that Trieste, and not Venice, became the cradle of revived navigation in the Adriatic? Venice was a town of reminiscences; Trieste shared the privilege of the United States of having no past at all. Formed by a motley crew of Italian, German, English, French, Greek, Armenian and Jewish merchant-adventurers, it was not fettered by traditions like the City of the Lagunes.[5]

Money enabled this cosmopolitanism and at the centre of this bourgeois trading city was the figure of the port-merchant, a turn of the century version of medieval Datini. Commercial cities don't only attract traders and brokers; they attract artists, writers and thinkers too. It was here that James Joyce arrived from dreary Dublin in 1905. (In one of the many jobs he took during his time in Trieste, Joyce would teach English and business correspondence at the Revoltella School of Commerce, founded by the same Pasquale Revoltella, which Joyce referred to as the 'revolver university'.)

As he watched Verdi's opera in the autumn of 1913, Joyce was trying to get his books published. He'd been hawking *A Portrait of the Artist as a Young Man* and *Dubliners* around for years, and he was beginning to put together the spine of his masterpiece *Ulysses*. Things were starting to look up for the exiled Irishman. He had just been commissioned to give a paid lecture on *Hamlet* in Trieste's prestigious Società di Minerva library, named after the multi-tasking Roman goddess of, among other things, poetry and trade. Who said art and commerce don't go together?

On 15 December, a letter arrived from Ezra Pound. An inveterate talent spotter, Pound informed Joyce that his ears should be burning. Understanding that the artist needs encouragement on the sometimes impassable road to greatness, Pound informed the faltering Joyce that he had been talking to fellow Irishman and literary heavyweight W. B. Yeats. Together Yeats and Pound had convinced a modernist American literary magazine, *The Egoist*, to take some of Joyce's work and, more to the point, to pay him for the pleasure. Following frustrating years in the wilderness, ignored by the literati and their gatekeepers at a time when the European artistic and cultural scene was at its most expressive, James Joyce needed a break. Spurred on, he hurriedly redrafted the opening chapters of both *Portrait* and *Dubliners* and sent them by train to Pound in London. Within months, both books would be published. A star was born and the decks were cleared for his great work, a book about Dublin that was heavily influenced by multicultural, commercially savvy Trieste, featuring a protagonist who could easily have stepped off the streets of this melting pot on the Adriatic.

Schumpeterian progress

Like many Europeans, Joyce ended 1913 in an optimistic mood, looking forward with confidence to the year ahead. Europe was experiencing a commercial boom. European industrial production had doubled since the beginning of the century, and a myriad of investments were being financed by deep capital markets. More and more people were participating in the great adventure that is commerce, and a monetary web, financing cross-border trade, linked citizens and subjects of diverse countries as never before. Commercially, it looked like things could only get better.

Meanwhile, European writers, artists and thinkers were pushing boundaries, embracing a new movement, modernism. No longer content to ape what went before, the modernist movement was all about new ways of looking, doing and thinking about everything. Following the heavy hand of nineteenth-century morality, the new century burst with vibrancy. Nothing was off limits. All over the continent, thinkers and artists were creating, imagining and experimenting with the new. In mathematics, Einstein was working on his unified theory of relativity, while Picasso introduced the world to Cubism. Freud the dreamweaver, all the while keeping an eye on his rival Jung in Zürich, was the go-to man for the radical new field of psychoanalysis. The future beckoned.

The capital of Austria was the fulcrum of this movement. Confident, wealthy and expanding rapidly, absorbing ambitious immigrants, Vienna fizzed with promise. Home to Freud, Egon Schiele, Gustav Klimt and Ludwig Wittgenstein, the city was cultural and intellectual ground zero. If it was happening, it was happening in Vienna – politically, socially and financially. We see this pairing of commercial self-expression and artistic self-expression wherever we have vibrant cities. In medieval Florence, we had merchant banking and Renaissance art; in seventeenth-century Amsterdam, the Dutch masters and the golden age of Dutch commerce were intertwined. Innovation in art and innovation in commerce are both examples of Schumpeter's famous 'gales of creative destruction': new art forms replace the old in the same way as new commercial products replace old ones, paving the road to what we call progress. The engine of this process is the enquiring human mind.

In the early years of the twentieth century, the combination of scientific breakthroughs, access to money, mass migration and new technologies like electricity generated a creative frisson, an immense power, not unlike the nuclear energy that Einstein was exploring at the time. All kinds of products from tanks to transistors were being invented: in the opening years of the century, we see tea bags, instant coffee, air conditioning, cornflakes, the bra, vacuum cleaners and colour photography all being invented and commercialised. Those gales of creative destruction howled and the economy surged. One innovation triggered another and so on. Electromagnetic waves, discovered by Heinrich Hertz, would set the stage for radar, radio broadcasts and, later, television. In farming we saw the first tractors and synthetic fertilisers, pushing up yields. Combustion engines, electrical motors and the modern escalator were all unveiled. The Wright brothers secured their patent for the world's first commercially produced 'flying machine'. The age of aviation was just beginning.

The perfect indicators of this outpouring in commercial energy are patents, the legal protectors of innovation. The number of new patents granted per year in Germany increased from 8,784 in 1900 to 13,520 in 1913, an increase of around 50 per cent, while the total number of annual patents granted in Germany, France and Britain increased from 34,893 in 1905 to 46,086 by 1913 – an increase of around a third. The economy in Europe was evolving at an extraordinary rate. In the US, the pace of change was even faster: the number of patents applied for per year soared from 39,673 in 1900 to 68,117 by 1913.[6]

In the years preceding the war, Trieste was awash with ideas and money. The optimism of forty years of economic expansion made investors confident, leading to a boom in innovation and risktaking. Modernism in art and modernism in commerce moved simultaneously. Who better to blend the two impulses, the artistic one and the entrepreneurial one, than the man who would become the leading light of modernism, James Joyce himself? And where better to explore his entrepreneurial side than in the newest – most modern – art form of the day: the cinema?

A portrait of the artist as entrepreneur

Back in 1905, the year Joyce arrived there, the first permanent cinema opened in Trieste. By 1909, there were twenty-one cinemas and the port city had become a major film distribution hub for the Austro-Hungarian Empire. As is the case today, when a new technology hub emerges in a city or region, so too does speculative finance. Eva, Joyce's sister, who was visiting from Dublin that year, mentioned she thought it odd that Trieste had so many cinemas yet there wasn't one in Dublin, a far bigger city.[7] Joyce, himself a film enthusiast, saw his opportunity: he'd open the first cinema in Ireland and make his fortune. He had to find backers and, luckily for our young entrepreneur, Trieste was an ideal spot to raise money. Joyce quickly found a syndicate of potential financiers who had achieved success with a cinema called the Volta in Bucharest.

At the critical elevator pitch, Joyce whetted investors' appetites with his opening gambit: Dublin, a large European city, had no cinema and two more cities in the same country, Cork and Belfast, were also without a cinema. Ireland, with close to a million urban dwellers, was virgin trading soil ripe for far-sighted operators. For a man who was a better spender than saver, the contract Joyce negotiated reveals a canny financial operator. He convinced his partners to give him 10 per cent of the equity and profits, although he didn't invest a penny himself. James Joyce was now in business. Hands were shaken, the deal was done, Joyce was off.[8] A portrait of the artist as a young entrepreneur.

Why do we still find it hard to accept that these two roles – the artist and the entrepreneur – are not mutually exclusive? Commerce and art have always gone hand in hand, yet over a hundred years after Joyce's *Ulysses* introduced the world to a new sort of novel, the lazy idea of the indigent creative set against the uninspired businessperson, the ingenious bohemian versus the tedious bourgeois, remains as powerful as ever. But the mind that wrote *Ulysses* was also the mind that opened

Ireland's first cinema. While Joyce was haggling over the price of a projector back in Ireland, he was trying to get *Dubliners* published, writing those infamously explicit letters to Nora, and walking around Mary Street, imagining the plot of *Ulysses* and its characters, Blazes Boylan, Buck Mulligan, and Molly and Leopold Bloom.

With a material upside if things worked out, Joyce went about his business with freneticism, negotiating property terms with landlords, discussing design with painters and decorators, selecting films with distributors, talking to newspaper admen about publicity, buttering up journalists for flattering reviews, becoming expert in many fields from seating and upholstery to lights and technical projector operation. He learned about pricing structures for shows – cheaper for matinees, more expensive for the evening headliner. Joyce, the perennial bankrupt, proved to be a dab hand at cash flow management. In terms of publicity, something he took to naturally, Joyce generated enough hype to ram the first night, making the grand opening of the Volta cinema on 20 December 1909 a must-see event.

Any new venture in Dublin can count on half the city cheerleading your impending failure, particularly if you're a returned local made good, showing up the inactivity of the left-behinds. How many peers must have spat into their pints when they read the *Evening Telegraph*'s review of the Volta?

> Remarkably good . . . Admirably equipped . . . Large numbers of guests . . . No expense spared . . . Particularly successful . . . Excellent string orchestra . . . Mr Joyce has worked apparently indefatigably and deserves to be congratulated on the success. . .[9]

In January 1910, having established the brand, Joyce headed back to Trieste, leaving a manager to run the show in Ireland.

It should not surprise us that Joyce the artist was also Joyce the entrepreneur. Artists and entrepreneurs are blessed with similar outlooks; the type of minds that make art are also the type that create businesses. Sometimes artists don't see this similarity, schooled in an erroneous worldview that money is bad and poverty is noble, the artist expressive and free but the businessperson boring and conservative. In fact, both artist and entrepreneur see possibilities where others see limitations, bringing the previously unimagined into being. Both artist and entrepreneur have skin in the game, performing on the public stage of jeopardy. The creative – businessperson or artist – has strong opinions and is courageous enough to risk the ridicule of the crowd for their opinions to be heard. Success can only come *after* the effort has been made, making their entire existence inherently unstable. For both entrepreneur and artist, failure can be brutal and success is often a prelude to future disappointment. But they are driven by self-expression; it's in the DNA of these independent, sometimes unreasonable, often difficult sorts. Both the artist and the entrepreneur can suffocate when shackled by a boss, a wage or an insurance premium.

From a macroeconomic perspective, artists and entrepreneurs both create demand where no demand existed previously. The new products they offer create their own demand – and this is the key to all economic evolution. Unlike the critic, the artist and entrepreneur are eternally optimistic. They must believe in the future. The optimism of their will overcomes the pessimism of their intellect.[10] The artist and the entrepreneur, so often pitted against each other, are in fact on the same side. These people make money dance, driving the economy and culture, generating ideas, wealth and opportunity for others. As the young Irish entrepreneur John Collison, founder of the financial software company Stripe, put it in a social media post in 2022:

> As you become an adult you realize that things around you weren't always there; people made them happen. But only recently have I started to internalize how much tenacity 'everything' requires. That hotel, that park, that railway. The world is a museum of passion projects.[11]

Passionate people make passion projects happen. From a psychological perspective, the entrepreneur and the artist are driven by the same impulses to create the new; and from a sociological perspective, a society that rewards these people – who are often dissenters of one kind or another – is the society that will flourish.[12]

The creative society

Innovation – whether commercial or cultural – has a better chance of taking hold where it is encouraged, respected and lauded. As we've seen time and again from Florence and Mainz to Amsterdam and Trieste, the city or region that begins to tolerate more independence of thought is more likely to generate the innovative energy that propels society forward. In contrast, we can see that feudal, dogmatic or ideological societies that sneer at the notion of individual self-improvement tend to be sclerotic. Even China today, despite still being a one-party state, is more open and tolerant than the China of Mao's day, and as China eased up on harsh dogma, the economy expanded. We see this pattern repeated time and again. Less dogma, more growth.

It is not some inherent percentage of innovators that is important, but the attitude of the rest of society:[13] as long as the majority of people are supportive, they will embolden the innovators. The public mood is critical.[14] Liberal democracies, flawed as they may be, are the sort of societies that encourage the creative ecosystem to flourish. Based broadly on merit, these are places that offer the possibility of social advancement by means of your own smarts, rather than your hereditary title. Embracing diversity, tolerant societies allow dissenters to take chances and tend to experience a constant state of churn because they elevate questioning over dogma. In general, creativity, tolerance and commerce go together, which is what Joyce saw all around him when writing *Ulysses* in multi-ethnic Trieste, a thriving city in the centre of Europe.

Leopold Bloom, the hero of *Ulysses*, may have been at home in Joyce's Trieste, but by placing him in Dublin, Joyce created the ultimate outsider. Bloom, a Jew by his father's name, yet baptised three times – once Protestant, once Catholic and once for the craic – is an archetypal dissenter. Joyce, through Bloom, extols diversity – on the street, in the bar, shops and parks, at a funeral, down in Nighttown, and in the cabman's shelter. As Bloom strolls around Dublin, he bumps into rich and poor, Dubs and culchies, young and old, spoofers and savants, nationalists and unionists, whores and coppers, Christians and sinners, bohemians and bourgeoisie, artists and entrepreneurs. The modern city is depicted as somewhere where this synthesis can occur, where common ground can be found.

As Joyce celebrated the coming publication of his early works and looked forward to better times ahead, little did he or anyone else appreciate the fragility of this environment. Europe would soon go dark, and tolerance would be replaced with bigotry, peace with war, optimism with despair, and that free-wheeling, slightly chaotic spirit that generated such art and such wealth over the previous few decades would be snuffed out.

In 1913, the year Joyce was listening to Verdi in Trieste, a 23-year-old painter living in Vienna was turned down by the city's Academy of Fine Arts, and found himself eking out a living selling watercolours to tourists while dossing in a men's hostel in Meldemannstraße. Also in Vienna, less than 7 miles away, in a top-floor flat in Schönbrunner Schloßstraße, a Georgian revolutionary, travelling under the false name of Stavros Papadopoulos, was penning an essay on 'Marxism and the national question'.[15] These two men, Adolf Hitler and Josef Stalin, were both violently opposed to the tolerant, cosmopolitan, mercantile society of Joyce's Trieste. In time, they would crush both artistic and commercial self-expression, eradicate dissent and drag Europe towards the apocalypse. Both dictators used money – humankind's most potent technology – to help achieve their diabolical aims.

18

INTO THE ABYSS

Let them eat cake

In 1922, Einstein won the Nobel Prize in Physics, ushering in the nuclear age; the BBC made its first ever radio broadcast, marking the beginning of mass communication; Mussolini marched on Rome, signalling the arrival of fascism; and James Joyce published *Ulysses*, his modernist masterpiece, on the second day of the second month of the second year of the decade.

In September of that pivotal year, as the global influenza pandemic receded, a young journalist crossed the Rhine from the French city of Strasbourg to Kehl, the neighbouring German town. Based in Paris, he was writing for the *Toronto Star*. In his soon to be famous matter-of-fact style, Ernest Hemingway explained to his Canadian readers the reality of a society where money is destroyed. When Hemingway arrived in Strasbourg, just over the Rhine, he noticed that no one was selling German marks on the French side. No one wanted them. On the German side, he changed ten francs – less than one Canadian dollar – for 670 marks, which 'lasted me and Mrs Hemingway for a day of heavy spending and we still had marks left at the end'.¹

The writer tells of witnessing an elderly German gentleman who couldn't afford to buy an apple from a stall for only 12 marks – a minuscule sum to young Hemingway:

> The old man, whose life savings were probably, as most of the non-profiteer class are, invested in German pre-war and war bonds, could not afford a 12 mark expenditure. He is the type . . . whose incomes do not increase with the falling purchasing value of the mark and the krone.

Hemingway summed up the dilemma of the majority of Germans in 1922, who were dependent on wages or pensions and who had put their savings into government bonds. Their livelihood was being destroyed by hyperinflation. If, on the other hand, you could get your hands on foreign currency, even a German could live like a king, because everything was so cheap in Germany for foreigners. French citizens were absolutely forbidden from buying cheap manufactured goods in Germany lest it undermine the French economy, but they could eat and drink what they liked – the more the better – rubbing the indignity of military defeat into German noses. Hemingway noted that a five-course meal in Kehl's best hotel cost 150 marks, equal to only 15 Canadian cents. French children, having slipped over the border, gorged themselves on cakes, thanks to their valuable French currency. Hemingway observed, 'The miracle of exchange makes a swinish spectacle where the youth of the town of Strasbourg crowd into the German pastry shop to eat themselves sick.'[2]

Hemingway was witnessing a society destroying its money and, in so doing, breaking one of the fundamental bonds between the state and its citizens. Money, a most powerful instrument of the state, is part of the contract a state has with the citizen: you behave and we will behave; you save your money and we will protect it. Undermine the money and you undermine the state. The economy needs more than brilliant ideas; it needs structure and relative stability. Commercial societies, places that generate economic growth, need to be both free and protected at the same time. The protection of money – making sure currency means something, doesn't lose its value, can be saved, and lent out with a degree of certainty – is an essential part of the social contract. Money gives people autonomy and money is a tool of freedom, which is why autocrats always want to control it. That freedom must be guarded. Interfere with the money and you are interfering with the very freedom that propels the economy.

A prosperous society needs money to be managed carefully. Print too much of it and it loses its meaning, inflation takes off, savings are destroyed, and society lurches from crisis to crisis. Print too little and there isn't enough money to finance innovation, deflation takes hold, and great ideas and potential new companies are never formed because there isn't enough money to finance them. It is the responsibility of a liberal society to manage money in a fine balancing act between the giddiness of printing too much and the austerity of printing too little. That civic responsibility was abandoned, or more accurately was forced to be abandoned, in the opening years of the Weimar Republic.

As Germany descended into one of the most destructive episodes of monetary self-harm in history, Hemingway was on hand to tell the story. In the most successful economy in Europe, how come an elderly gentleman couldn't afford an apple? How did the immiseration of Germany happen?

A web of debts

In 1914, imperial Germany, confident of a quick victory, believing the 'home by Christmas' guff, decided to pay for the First World War by borrowing from its citizens. The Prussian army had beaten the Austrians in 1866 and the French in 1870, so why would 1914 be different? Confident in victory, Germany exchanged people's savings for IOUs, which offered generous interest rates to attract domestic money. As everyone expected to be paid back, for the average German, lending to their government was not only an act of national solidarity, but it was also prudent personal financial management. Right up to the end, the German people thought they were winning the war, with the working assumption that debts would be paid back with the purloined assets and gold of conquered peoples. It didn't turn out that way.

After the war, the new Weimar Republic was born, saddled with enormous war debts. But there was more. At Versailles there was little appetite for forgiveness. Britain and France wanted the new Germany to be punished for the crimes of old Germany. France's industrial northeast – an area the size of the Netherlands – had been destroyed in the fighting and France was adamant that Germany stump up. Meanwhile America wanted Germany to pay so that it could recoup the loans it had extended to the other Allies.

The war had profoundly changed the world's financial architecture. In 1914, Britain was the world's banker, controlling around $20 billion of foreign assets. London was the epicentre of global money, accounting for around two thirds of all trade in international capital.[3] Due to the unprecedented boom in global trade and investment during the Gold Standard era, all the major countries were indebted to each other. France had

overseas assets amounting to $9 billion, of which an extraor-
dinary $5 billion were tied up in imperial Russia alone.[4] The
communist Soviets defaulted on all Russia's old loans, leaving
the French, in particular, out of pocket. Other European
powers sold assets at fire sale prices to fund the war, borrowing
heavily from the one major player that stood aloof until close
to the end, America. The US emerged from the war as the
world's undisputed creditor. Not only was it owed billions,
but Americans snapped up European assets at bargain basement
prices as the war progressed. This global shift in the power
of money from London to New York would define the world's
monetary relations for the next century.

At the end of the war, the European Allied powers owed
$12 billion to the US, of which Britain owed $5 billion
and France $4 billion.[5] Britain itself was owed $11 billion
by various countries, including $3 billion by France – and
over $2.5 billion by Russia that it would never see again.[6]
The world was enmeshed with debts and counterdebts.
The early twentieth century's lender of last resort, America,
understanding that it had arrived in the dominant position
Alexander Hamilton had predicted when talking to
Talleyrand over a century earlier, was not about to squander
this opportunity.

From now on America, not Britain, would be the top dog
of global money and, as is typical when the once dominant
becomes supplicant, crestfallen Britain would extract its
pound of flesh. It did so by punishing the embryonic and
fragile Weimar Republic. Defeated Germany was on the hook
for everything.

Squeaking pips

During the British General Election campaign of 1918, Prime Minister Lloyd George promised to squeeze defeated Germany 'like a lemon until the pips squeak'. The Welshman was as good as his word. In 1914, one mark was worth 25 US cents. By 1920, it was worth only 1.5 cents. Despite political and social chaos following military defeat, most people thought that the collapse in the mark had run its course. There was an understandable and widespread belief that Germany, after a period of post-defeat turbulence, would snap out of it. Before the war, Germany was the richest, most innovative economy in Europe, leading the world in literature, science and philosophy; by the 1920s, Germany had produced more Nobel Prize winners than America and Britain combined.[7] Home of pre-war probity, discipline and order, it was inconceivable to most people that Germany wouldn't recover. The idea of mass pauperisation of German society was not entertained.

But Germany's situation had changed profoundly – politically, socially and monetarily. First, it had lost a war that, up until the very end, most Germans thought it was winning. Unlike the victorious French and Belgians, who had been partially occupied, no foreign troops had set foot on German soil. It was hard for Germans to accept that they had lost. This disbelief fuelled the 'stabbed in the back' conspiracy, which maintained that the solid nationalist German army wasn't defeated but betrayed by socialists, liberals and internal, cosmopolitan enemies like financiers and Jews.

In 1920, apart from the inherited war bonds, Germany faced enormous reparation bills that amounted to 100 per cent of German pre-war GDP (a renegotiation of the 300 per cent of GDP originally demanded). The final settlement required that Germany transfer 5 per cent of its GDP to foreign powers every year. Under such pressure, the German economy was buckling. In practical terms, paying reparations means the country must transfer real goods out of the economy, but the country doesn't get paid in hard currency for this output. Products were transferred to France and the invoices used to discount what was owed, so products manufactured in Germany that were supposed to be on German shelves were now in French shops. Empty shelves always put pressure on prices, guaranteeing queues or inflation, depending on whether or not the country decides to print money in response. There is an added complication. When produce is taken out of the economy, tax revenue falls because there is a loss of indirect tax, such as VAT levied on goods sold. Reparations had a knock-on effect on the budget deficit. Empty shelves and deteriorating public finances exacerbated the sense of panic that had set in after the unexpected defeat.

The German state was obliged to pay reparations in gold, and the consequent sale of marks put ongoing downward pressure on the currency. The government, hemmed in on all sides, was too fragile to raise taxes, so instead Berlin borrowed from its own central bank to pay its own producers for goods that would never be sold in Germany. As a result, Germany faced a shortage of goods in shops and, as the government was subsidising German manufacturers for goods that the French would never pay for, it also suffered from a massive build-up of government debt, added to a current account deficit and a constantly weakening currency, which pushed up the price of imports, fuelling inflation further.

Such a financial cocktail would have been explosive enough, but internal politics made things even worse. On the streets, the brittle Weimar government, trying to occupy the liberal centre, faced constant battles with Soviet-inspired communists on the left, who believed that the government was working for the Allies against the average working man, and old-school nationalists on the right, who believed that the government was working for the Allies against the German nation. Each extreme faction called on the weak Weimar government to make expensive commitments: education for workers on the one hand, war pensions for demobbed soldiers on the other. Reflecting its socially democratic DNA, the liberal Weimar government also committed itself to social reform, expanding spending on health and public housing. All this was putting pressure on the public finances. A precarious and perennially cash-strapped government couldn't renege on its international obligations, nor could it revoke its domestic political promises. To cover these national commitments, it began to print more and more money, while trying to ring-fence enough gold to pay the Allies. The fragile Weimar Republic juggled as best it could.

The more the currency jumped around, the more the people became jittery. In normal times, if faced with such skittishness, a central bank will smooth things over, using its own reserves to manage the currency – either selling gold to buy the currency in a predictable and stable fashion if it falls, or buying gold to sell the currency if it rises too quickly. This is called open market operations in the jargon. In plain English, it is about injecting sobriety into a wayward currency market. But Germany couldn't afford to spend its gold reserves, which it needed for reparations. Money flowed in and out of Germany, depending on rumour and counter-rumour. Bad news sent the currency plummeting up and down; mostly down.

In June 1922, news went from bad to worse when Walther Rathenau, the urbane industrialist and Jewish foreign minister, was assassinated by right-wingers. This sparked panic. Rathenau was respected in Berlin, Paris and London. Who would negotiate for Germany now? Within Germany, the state faced a conundrum. With armed militia on the streets, if the government cracked down on the various shadowy right-wing groups, would civil war follow? The mark fell precipitously. Without any viable alternative, and with the communists preaching revolution and breathing down its neck, the government continued to print money to pay workers to keep the proletariat on side. Hard as it is to imagine, in one year, 1922, the mark fell from 190 to 7,600 against the dollar and prices rose fortyfold. Speculators had a field day. For locals, everything was unaffordable. For foreigners, as Hemingway observed, Germany was the bargain basement of Europe.

The year of zeros

In early 1923, Germany failed to deliver 100,000 telephone poles to France that were, degradingly, being dug up by German workers from German towns. For France, this was the final straw. It was keen to use Germany's unwillingness to pay reparations in kind as an excuse to implement a plan that Paris had been working on since 1918. French and Belgian troops occupied the Ruhr, seizing Germany's industrial heartland. If the Germans wouldn't bring their reparations to Paris and Brussels, France and Belgium would take everything they could get their hands on. In the resulting panic, the currency fell further. On 11 January 1923, as the French and Belgians moved in to claim the telegraph poles, the mark, which at Christmas had been 27,000 to the dollar, was now at 50,000 to the dollar, and falling fast.

In the Ruhr, German workers went on general strike in response to the occupation, while some large German companies such as Krupp – a steel producer that during the war had made more shells than any other manufacturer – called for a mass campaign of civil disobedience.[8] The occupation was also resisted by secretive groups run by former soldiers, who sabotaged railway lines and killed several occupying soldiers. The French reacted. On 13 February a young German woman called Josephine Malakert was gang-raped by several French sailors, and throughout the spring of 1923 incidences of rape of German women increased. Local Germans were incensed; these cases highlighted the brutality of the Allied occupiers. Germany unified against the occupation, citing the abuse of its people in the hope that it might pressurise the international community – the Americans, in effect – to persuade the French to end the occupation.[9]

The Weimar government, sensing a much-needed national victory if it could resist until the French were urged to pull out, played for time. In solidarity, it printed money to pay the striking Ruhrland workers' salaries. The more the central bank printed, the more inflation rose, locking Germany into a battle between the willingness of its own people to sustain monetary chaos versus the ability of the Allies to remain united behind France's occupation. In what was ultimately a highly destructive game of chicken, the Germans were gambling that the Americans (and the British) would lean on the French before German society imploded under the madness of hyperinflation. The fate of Germany rested on who would blink first.[10]

By August 1923, a dollar was worth 620,000 marks and by November, one dollar was 630 billion marks. Neither side blinked. For France, occupation was part of the price it was extracting from Germany, even if in reality France received in the ten months of occupation less coal and coke from the region than it had received in the ten days before its troops invaded. For the Weimar Republic, financing passive resistance to the invaders was a price worth paying to secure a victory over the French and show the ordinary German people that Weimar wouldn't bow to its enemies. The cost of this showdown was German hyperinflation and the destruction of money.

During that turbulent summer, as inflation skyrocketed, Germans flocked to cinemas to watch the season's blockbuster, Fritz Lang's *Dr Mabuse, the Gambler*. With their money and savings disappearing, ordinary people were eager to get rid of cash as quickly as they could. They spent on bars, clubs, restaurants and cinemas – all were teeming. Berlin's famous nightlife boomed as money changed hands as quickly as it was printed. Hold onto money and you lost everything. Spend it and at least you had a good time. A new class of speculators emerged, buying and selling currency, and getting rich in the face of mass impoverishment. As one Berlin newspaper maintained, 'The extravagance of the newly rich, the rapid gambling on the stock exchange, the clubs, the addiction to pleasure, the speculation, the vast amount of smuggling, counterfeiting, is a portrait of our times.'[11]

Lang's blockbuster, a four-and-a-half-hour, two-part epic, captured the madness as the country descended into hyper-inflationary chaos. The movie's protagonist, the evil Dr Mabuse, is a malignant hypnotist with the magic power to drive share prices up and down and manipulate the stock market, exploiting people's minds and their pockets. To the average person in Weimar Germany, the movements of stocks and the currency were beyond comprehension. The character of Mabuse, a supernatural arch conspirator orchestrating it all, struck a chord with a damaged and confused population. People's money couldn't just disappear, surely? And yet it seemed that way to millions. Meanwhile, rich speculators were profiting. The more the currency fell, the more these people seemed to make, and the more the average family sank into destitution.

Someone was winning while the majority lost everything. The speculator – or *Raffke*, 'money grabber' – became a figure of both scorn and fascination. How did such people engineer the currency market? How come they always seemed to be one step ahead of the average citizen, lording it over everyone? The *Raffke* was everywhere, giving the two fingers to public opinion, appearing in the pages of *Berliner Illustrirte Zeitung*, Germany's first mass market magazine, which in the 1920s had a circulation of 1.8 million a week. '*Wir stehen ver-kehrt*' ('Things Are Topsy-Turvy'), a cabaret song of the time written by Carl Rössler, referred to the *Raffke* who 'can afford champagne, lobster, and women, just as he can commission paintings for his bathroom, even though he does not know whether a Botticelli is a cognac or a cheese'.[12]

In a world where prices were rising steeply and profiteers were making fortunes, the average citizen was discombobulated, and Mabuse served as the personification of greed and malice. In truth, speculation wasn't orchestrated; it was a survival mechanism for people who were trying to figure out ways of dealing with the hyperinflation. Far from being the preserve of a small, well-informed coterie, it is estimated that one million Germans were involved in the currency speculation game.

Although hyperinflation destroyed the social contract, different sectors of society were affected differently. Millions of hard-working, middle-class, tax-paying, government-trusting Germans saw their savings wiped out. Teachers, civil servants, policemen, doctors, clerks, white-collar functionaries, lawyers, academics, journalists – these professionals who had entered into a contract with the state and bought the supposedly cast-iron war bonds – were hung out to dry. The respectable middle and lower middle classes naturally felt that the new Weimar Republic had abandoned them.

In contrast, people who owned physical assets, such as landlords, farmers and industrialists, didn't suffer so much, as the value of their property adjusted upwards with inflation. And at the bottom, if you were a worker who had no savings, your position didn't change too drastically either: you had no savings to lose and fear of communism meant that workers' wages more or less kept up with inflation. (Wages were indexed, meaning the higher the rate of inflation, the more workers were paid. The effect, of course, was that wage increases pushed up inflation and inflation pushed up wages.)

Those at the top and at the bottom were least affected by the chaos, while those in the middle, the political ballast of the society, suffered most. After the hyperinflation, people would want somebody to blame – always a potent political imperative. One man was positioning himself and his party to benefit from this social catastrophe. In November 1923, just as hyperinflation was peaking, Adolf Hitler led a failed Munich *Bierkeller* putsch. Although a spectacularly ineffective rebellion, comical almost, the public stand against Weimar would allow Hitler to paint himself as the heroic father-figure, an inspired leader, who was ready to serve time in prison for his convictions. Hitler, having witnessed the 1923 chaos, when the contract between the state and the people was torn up, understood the opportunity presented when money dies. It was a lesson he would not forget.

A tale of two prison camps

On an August evening in 1943, Salomon 'Sally' Smolianoff, once a fine portrait painter as well as a Weimar Berlin night-club operator, found himself in the hell of Sachsenhausen concentration camp. Years before, using nightclubs to launder cash, Smolianoff – a refugee from Odessa – had found his true vocation: forgery. His painter's hands and exquisite attention to detail were generously rewarded in the counterfeiting game. In the 1920s, he had been arrested in Amsterdam for distributing fake English fifty-pound notes. After serving a short sentence he made it back to Berlin, just in time for the mid-1930s bonanza in the forgery business. As the true monstrosity of the Nazi regime became apparent, thousands scrambled to leave Germany. After the antisemitic violence of Kristallnacht in November 1938, that constant current swelled. Jewish people, desperate to flee, paid him handsomely and Salomon, Jewish himself, was at the centre of a black market in fake passports and exit visas.

As his opportunities for legitimate work dried up with every fresh antisemitic restriction, he honed his forgery craft. The forgeries had to be aesthetically perfect copies: forging documents, like printing money, is a game of cat and mouse between the legitimate printers and the enterprising counterfeiter. Official designers embedded security tricks within documents to protect against the fraudster. To be an expert forger, Smolianoff needed skill, guile and imagination. Having a delicate artistic hand wasn't enough; he needed to master engineering, engraving, metalwork, moulding and pantography to replicate intricate designs. The master forger is one part Leonardo, one part Gutenberg – half painter, half printer.

The law eventually caught up with Smolianoff again and he spent four years mining rocks in the slave labour camp of Mauthausen, surviving by drawing perfect (and flattering) portraits of his Nazi guards. As both a Jew and a convicted criminal, Salomon's chances of survival weren't great, but in 1943 he received a bizarre reprieve. He was moved from the Austrian camp to Sachsenhausen, near Berlin. His mission? To break the Bank of England.

As the sun was going down in the west, visible in June until after 10 p.m. across the flat north German plain, we can imagine the forger thumbing a linen and cloth mixture, trying desperately, because his life depended on it, to establish the components used in the English five-pound note. The setting sun may have reminded Smolianoff that there was a world somewhere beyond this Sachsenhausen hell.

Five hundred miles to the south, in another German prison camp, Stalag VII-A, Richard Radford watched that same sun set over the Bavarian hills. He counted his cigarettes and waited for the Red Cross package, praising his luck for having fought in a Canadian regiment. The Canadian Red Cross was the most benevolent among the Allied nations, and Radford imagined wholesome Ontarian housewives stuffing their parcels with spam, cake and jam. They'd never know how much their efforts boosted the prisoners.

What Radford and Smolianoff had in common was money. Radford was trying to create it; Smolianoff was trying to destroy it.

Made-up money

Radford, a young Cambridge-educated economist, had been taken prisoner in Libya in 1941 and would spend the rest of the war in a prison camp. In Stalag VII-A, Radford noticed something unusual. Here, in the most trying of circumstances, his peers had invented a form of common money.

The Red Cross supplied the prisoners with extra rations to supplement the regular camp meals. All prisoners were given a *compulsory* ration of cigarettes, as well as jam, butter, tea, treacle, honey, meat, corned beef, salmon, spam, chocolate, salt, pepper, soap, hash browns, powdered milk and tinned vegetables. With no actual money, the prisoners used cigarettes as a medium of exchange and a source of wealth that could be traded. The price of cigarettes became the foundational price of the prisoner of war (POW) system: the more cigarettes in circulation, the lower the value of cigarettes, and the higher the price of everything else.

Instinctively, the prisoners – British, Canadian, Yugoslav, Polish, French and Russian – understood the common language of money. A market economy, independent from the formal hierarchy of military rank, established itself without anyone pulling strings from above. An enterprising private might have more influence than a three-star general. Money delivered status and it overruled culture. Soviet communists, Indian Sikhs, British patricians and French farmers were brought together by money. At the same time, on a personal level, money gave the prisoners some small control over their world, some tiny way of exercising their own sovereignty and autonomy despite incarceration.

On his release at the end of the war, Radford wrote a compelling account about the emergence of the prisoners' economy, revealing how a monetary economy organically emerges, how currencies operate and what happens to a trading system as it evolves and becomes more complex. He was intrigued by the 'social organisation' that sprang up so readily as prisoners traded rations with each other. He wrote of his experience: 'The essential interest lies in the universality and the spontaneity of this economic life; it came into existence not by conscious imitation but as a response to the immediate needs and circumstances.'[13]

The POW economy experienced economic and credit cycles, just as in the real economy, with upswings, downturns, bouts of deflation and inflation. The Red Cross acted as a kind of POW central bank, issuing between twenty-five to fifty packs of cigarettes each month, controlling the 'money' supply. The value of that currency was determined by how much money the economy was demanding at a particular time, which is a function of human nature, as it is in the real world. When people are optimistic and want to spend, the demand for money will be buoyant and the amount of money in the system will generate more commerce. If, on the other hand, punters are a bit worried about the future, many might choose to hoard their money, waiting for an opportunity to spend in the future.

Unprompted, and in the most trying circumstances, thousands of humans from different cultures, speaking different languages, following different religious and moral codes, managed to create and abide by the universal code of money. What pertained in the POW camp pertains in society: people need money to organise their world. This is precisely why Hitler, having witnessed the pandemonium of Germany in 1923, ordered the greatest forgery the world had ever seen – and why the Jewish forger Sally Smolianoff found himself in Sachsenhausen watching the sun go down.

Hitler's money

Prisoner 93594, Sally Smolianoff, had a reputation that preceded him.[14] In a bizarre quirk of fate, one that saved his life, an SS officer called Hans Krueger, who had previously arrested Smolianoff as part of a criminal crackdown in Berlin, was put in charge of Hitler's mass forgery scheme. Krueger, the Nazi, knew he needed Smolianoff, the Jew. He found him languishing at Mauthausen and brought him to Sachsenhausen. Smolianoff now found himself the de facto leader of a motley crew of 142 Jewish specialists extracted from the concentration camps of the Third Reich. These men, who came from all over central Europe, had once been civilian printers, dyers, fine artists, engineers, engravers, metalworkers, mathematicians and photographers. They became the crack counterfeiting team tasked with breaking the Bank of England. The printworks in blocks 18 and 19 were shut off from the rest of the camp and no contact was allowed between the counterfeiters and the general camp population.

Smolianoff's life, and those of the rest of the team, depended on figuring out what material the English were using for their banknotes. Germany's bouts of hyperinflation in the early 1920s meant that German currency was printed on whatever paper could be sourced. When billions of worthless marks are being printed, who cares about the quality of the paper? But the Bank of England was a different story. Sterling, the global reserve currency for almost a century, wasn't printed on any old flimsy paper. Earlier forgers suspected it was printed on material made from a type of reed that only grew in the British colony of Malaya. There was something different about the texture of the English note.

After relentless testing and tearing up of real English

notes, the counterfeiters twigged that the English were using rags from old clothing that had been pulped. With this knowledge, their operation could begin. Initially, the secret workshop made limited amounts of five-pound notes. These prototypes needed to be tested, and where better to test the forgeries than the Bank of England itself?

A German 'industrialist' presented himself at a Swiss bank in Zürich claiming he had received some English notes on the black market and asked the bank to vouch for their legitimacy. The Swiss officials went to work with magnifying glasses and high-powered lamps. After careful examination, they declared the notes legitimate. The 'industrialist' doubled his bluff and – to be completely sure – asked the Swiss bankers if they'd telegram the Bank of England to double-check the serial numbers and dates of issue. The Bank of England affirmed that the notes were original. Krueger was elated – as was his boss, Heinrich Himmler, head of the SS. The counterfeiters' printing presses went into overdrive. The realisation of Hitler's plan to flood Britain with fake notes, forgeries so brilliant that not even the Bank of England could distinguish them from real ones, was mere months away.

The concentration camp forgers printed a total of £134,610,810, which amounted to four out of every ten pounds then in circulation. As outlined in the Introduction, the plan was for German bombers to drop the notes over Britain, but by 1943, the war situation had deteriorated for Germany, and the Luftwaffe could no longer provide the planes.

Undeterred, the SS had other plans. Germany at this stage was running out of hard currency. The Reichsmark, trading at forty to the pound officially, and much less on the black market, wasn't accepted for settling trades on the international market. Sterling was another story. As it was the global reserve currency, the SS could use the forged sterling to buy much-needed war materials and in the process line their own pockets. Sachsenhausen's brilliant forgeries infiltrated the global money supply via a network of middlemen who laundered the cash for Berlin. The dying months of the Nazi regime led to a black market in passports, visas and new identities, and a thriving market in stolen goods also emerged. Like various crypto-currencies today, the fake money found a dark market. The Sachsenhausen notes were deployed to bribe officials for fake documents given to Nazis fleeing Europe for Argentina.

Reports to the Bank of England that lots of sterling notes were being used by Nazis aroused suspicion; for example, the ransom for the kidnapped Mussolini was paid for in counterfeited sterling. At the end of the war, the Bank of England oversaw the destruction of these notes, but so worried was the Old Lady of Threadneedle Street about the quality of the forgeries that it retired all its old five-pound notes and introduced an entirely new batch.

Just think what might have happened had Hitler's money fallen from the heavens in 1943.

PART 5:

MONEY UNBOUND

19

WHO CONTROLS MONEY?

The beer hedger

In December 1992, a tailback of battered, second-hand Toyota Corollas, Ford Escorts and Fiat Mirafioris – the cars of a middle-income country – snaked its way from a supermarket car park in Northern Ireland all the way south to the border of the Irish Republic. On the northern side of the border, bemused British soldiers patrolling their watchtowers weren't sure what was going on. The Irish police, the Gardai, on the southern side, knew fine well what the story was – some of their colleagues were in the queue. It was Christmas, booze was cheaper in Northern Ireland than in the Republic of Ireland, Irish people like to drink and December is party time. Go figure, as our Irish American cousins say.

The queues were longer than usual. Traditionally, the booze arbitrage was exploited by people close to the border, where the short drive and minimal petrol expense are worth the hassle. That year, thousands more were desperate to spend their Irish punts. We were witnessing a run on the currency, triggered by rumours of an imminent devaluation. Spooked, people wanted to spend, and buying beer was a way for ordinary people to hedge exchange-rate risk. Beer hedging is practical: buy cheap British beer today with expensive Irish money before it too becomes cheap. There is no more damning vote of no confidence in a currency than your own people rushing for the exit. A currency collapse proceeds in stages: initially, it's the bankers, investors and speculators, probably with some inside knowledge, who become fidgety. By the time teachers, nurses, police officers and plumbers are trying to stock up on cheap booze, it's all over.

In the Ireland of 1992, we were observing a run on a relatively new type of money, a currency backed by nothing other than the promises of the state. By then, the whole world was using this type of money, which economists call fiat money (from the Latin, 'let it be done'). Everyone else just calls it money. The key difference between fiat money and money backed by a commodity (gold, for example) is that fiat money is legal tender made legal by the authority of the state alone. It is not unlike a police force that is made legal within a state by the state; no other police force can legally operate in that state. Canadian police, for example, can only operate in Canada – try to arrest someone in America wearing a Mounties uniform and see how far you get.

The legal tender or currency, issued by the state, is backed by the credibility of the state, its tax revenues and laws. In fact, it is so interwoven with these institutions that it is part of the state. You cannot opt out of the legal tender of a country; it is a condition of living there. As part of the social contract, the state undertakes to uphold the value of its legal tender, both internally in terms of inflation and externally in terms of the exchange rate. The stronger and more robust the state and its organs, the stronger and more credible the currency. People trust the currency because, in general, they trust the state. There are of course radicals on the extreme left and extreme right who do not trust the state, but as a general rule, whatever they say on social media, most citizens – when push comes to shove – have confidence in their own state. If you doubt this, who do you call when someone breaks into your home: a private vigilante gang or the state police force?

Let's briefly tell the story of how the world abandoned gold and embraced a new form of money, the one we all use today.

Saigon or gold?

In the story of money, it has taken a long time for widely accepted fiat money to appear. Over the preceding chapters, we've come across various currency arrangements where money's value is grounded by something real. Thousands of years ago, the value of the Sumerian shekel was determined by a handful of grain and everyone understood the value of that grain. The Lydians used gold, whose value stemmed from its ornamental cachet. The Greeks preferred silver to gold and the Romans used a combination of both. In Dante's Florence, they created their fabled gold florin, which Maestro Adamo the counterfeiter was condemned for corrupting.

In East Asia, the Chinese introduced paper money (largely backed by commodities like metal and silk) because it was easier to use in larger denominations than coins. Fast-forward a few hundred years and we see John Law's land-backed currency idea, which was an inventive way of weaning perennially gold-starved France off the tyranny of precious metal. In the end, his currency was based on an extravagant debt-for-equity swap that failed, undermined French finance and contributed to the later French Revolution. Following the disastrous experiments of Talleyrand's assignats and George Washington's Continentals, throughout the nineteenth century, money backed merely by a government's promise was a hard sell. Political revolutionaries rarely make good bankers. During the nineteenth century, an era of great scientific discovery, innovation with currency stalled. In a victory for tradition, the century of Darwin and Pasteur was the era of gold, not too dissimilar from 2,000 years earlier.

By the end of the century, American Populists were fighting the 1896 election over whether money should be tied to scarce gold or plentiful silver. The Gold Standard was abandoned during the First World War as countries printed money and borrowed to fund the war effort. After the war, experiments with paper money ran aground, destroyed by reparations and the overhang of war debts. By the mid-1920s European hyperinflation led the world to commit once again to the discipline of gold. Ultimately, that reconstituted Gold Standard system was undone by an inability to print money when the world slumped and slouched towards the Great Depression. The Gold Standard staggered on until the mid-1930s when Roosevelt abandoned it altogether.

During the Second World War, the US state took control of the levers of the economy. With America and the dollar pre-eminent in 1946, the US decided, once again, to peg the dollar to gold, making the dollar the anchor for the global financial system, in a set-up that could be described as a quasi-gold standard. This arrangement worked well as long as the American government was happy with the monetary constraints gold imposed on it. However, by the early 1970s, the American budget deficit was stretched by the Vietnam War. Adherence to the quasi-gold standard hampered American efforts to finance the war, and the US was faced with a choice: Saigon or gold. President Richard Nixon, keen to expand the military budget, abandoned the strictures of gold – the second time in forty years that the Americans, expediently, dropped the Gold Standard. The Federal Reserve was now responsible for both printing and maintaining the value of the dollar. The Americans replaced the fixed for the variable, the immutable for the flexible, and ultimately placed the value of money in the hands of intelligent humans who can respond and adapt to the evolving economy in a way that a fixed metal supply cannot. Where America led, the world followed. By the mid-1970s, most countries had adopted this fiat regime.

Fiat money is the most significant innovation in money since the Lydians minted their first coin. For the first sustained period, countries, and of course their citizens, were truly free from the brace of precious metal. Given that this book has focused on the transformative impact of money on our lives, it will come as no surprise that this era of fiat money coincided with the most vigorous expansion the world economy has ever seen. Give people money and, in economic terms, magic happens.

In a growing economy, limiting the money supply to something fixed such as gold has an automatically deflationary effect. Fixing the money supply, like fixing any supply, benefits those who already have it and penalises those who don't. As people's incomes rise, the demand for money goes up and so too (unless supply responds) does its price. When the price of money goes up, it means the price of everything else goes down relative to money. This implies that people, you and me, will have to sell more of everything to get a fixed amount of money. When you think about it, what are most of us selling? We are selling our time and our talent. We are selling our time in exchange for a wage. If we are all chasing a fixed amount of money, we have to sell more of our time to get it. In the real world that means taking a pay cut. If people's wages start to fall, prices will fall accordingly. It won't be too long before people postpone spending today and hoard their money, hoping for yet more bargains – lower prices – tomorrow.

As is so often the case, abandoning a bad idea can often be more difficult than adopting a good one. The Gold Standard or quasi-gold standard was one of these bad ideas that clung on for far too long. The fiat system comes with modest inflation targets because a little bit of inflation is less challenging than deflation. Deflation is built into a fixed commodity-based money, while moderate inflation is built into a fiat system because the money supply, not being fixed, can expand continuously as the economy grows and the demand for money grows too. Experience had shown governments that it is harder to kickstart a moribund deflationary economy than to slow down a bustling inflationary one. In a sense, manageable small-scale inflation does for debt what confession does for sin: a little bit of forgiveness, every now and then. If you borrow, inflation makes it easier to pay back debt, offering, let's say, a more lenient, Catholic option. Deflation in a currency linked to gold punishes debtors mercilessly, and can, in contrast, be seen as a more fundamentalist, day-of-reckoning approach to debt.

A jockey riding two horses

A flexible currency reveals the health of an economy. If it is falling, something fundamental is going wrong or expected to go wrong with the economy at large. When a currency's credibility comes into question, and a gap opens up between the value the state puts on the currency and the value the average punter believes it has, there tends to be movement of money out of the country. The currency acts like a lie detector. As we have seen, there is no limit on how much a central bank can print. Nor is there any limit on how little it

might print. It is a balancing act, hemmed in by a few param-
eters but anchored by the promise to keep the rate of inflation
stable and low. If the central bank wants less money knocking
around, it will raise the rate of interest and people will borrow
less and save more, exerting a moderating influence on the
amount of money in circulation.

In 1992, I witnessed from the inside what happens when
people lose faith in a currency. The experience of working in
a central bank has guided my thinking on money, monetary
policy and monetary economics ever since. The first lesson I
learned from that crisis is that, when it comes to money,
people are smarter than central bankers think they are. You
can't fool them for long.

By the early 1990s, most of Europe's fiat currencies were
tied to the German currency, the deutschmark. Post-war West
Germany was the exemplar of how to manage a fiat currency:
maintain the value of money, and yet ensure that there is still
enough around to keep the economy ticking over. Following
the German experience with hyperinflation in the 1920s, the
new Federal Republic of Germany vowed never again to break
the bond between the central bank and the people. For post-war
West Germans, stable money and a stable society were seen as
two sides of the same coin. As a result, West Germany had the
best record on inflation in Europe. Adopting an 'if you can't
beat them you might as well join them' approach, after much
soul-searching and a run on the French franc in 1982, most of
the western European countries elected to tie their exchange
rate to the deutschmark. Once a country's exchange rate was
fixed against West Germany's, it could not print money at a
faster rate than the Germans did. If you did print at a faster
rate than the Germans, there would be more of your currency
floating about and its price would therefore fall. If the price of

your currency fell, your central bank would have to raise interest rates to attract more money to push up your currency and maintain the fixed exchange rate.

In this way, by tying the exchange rate to West Germany's, both the external and internal value of the country's money is maintained. Do this long enough and people believe that your money is indeed as good as the Germans', and you are rewarded with lower interest rates. The aim of the game was lower interest rates predicated on the assumption that German interest rates would always remain relatively low because German inflation would also remain relatively low. Nobody expected the Berlin Wall to fall on 11 November 1989. The reunification of the country drove German interest rates upwards because Germany, for the first time since the end of the war, began to borrow heavily. In addition, the Bundesbank raised interest rates to offset the inflationary consequences of the political decision to convert the East German ostmark 1:1 with the deutschmark, despite its 'true' value being only a fraction of this. Because all European currencies were pegged to the deutschmark, higher German interest rates pushed up the interest rates of all other countries, prompting crises across western Europe.

At the time, the UK was suffering from the aftershock of the late-1980s housing market collapse. British balance sheets were fragile and couldn't handle higher interest rates. On 16 September 1992, sterling devalued and crashed out chaotically from the German-centred exchange rate system in an event known as Black Wednesday. Without the requirement any longer to maintain the link with Germany, British interest rates could fall along with the value of the currency. A falling currency is how a fiat system deals with instability. Contrast this with a Gold Standard where the currency cannot fall and all the adjustment for an economic shock such as a housing bust must be absorbed through unemployment, defaults and bankruptcies. Fiat money is flexible money and this flexibility, in contrast to the clumsiness of commodity-based money, means that recessions will tend to be shallower and shorter, which is what Britain needed in the early 1990s.

But Britain's move made little Ireland's position extremely difficult. When it comes to money, small countries are rule takers not rule makers, so their policies must take into account what larger neighbours might be doing. Typically, these bigger neighbours have no idea how many sleepless nights their unilateral decisions are creating in the immediate region. Monetary policy in small countries is tricky – balancing money flowing in and out of the country, managing local interest rates and the exchange rate, while all the time making sure inflation remains stable. With Ireland's historic economic links to the UK, and its strategic political desire to be closer to the continent, Ireland became like a jockey riding two horses: the British horse and the German horse. As long as the two horses were travelling in the same direction, the jockey's position was just about tenable, but when the horses started to move away from each other, the jockey's nether regions became very uncomfortable, potentially excruciating. Expecting a copycat devaluation, money flowed out of Ireland, irrespective of what any Irish authority pleaded.

Rather than accept the inevitable, the Irish central bank decided to fight by spending all the country's reserves buying punts that no one wanted. The central bank also increased interest rates to an incredible 101 per cent to staunch the outflow of money. Rates of interest like this guaranteed a recession, making a devaluation even more likely. The ordinary people twigged what was going on, panicked and, staying ahead of the authorities, jumped in their cars and headed across the border to buy their cheap Guinness for Christmas! A month later, in January 1993, Ireland devalued its currency.

If the first lesson I learned from this currency crisis is that the people are smarter than the central bankers think they are, the second lesson is that money is international – it finds its way around borders. Countries want their money to be sovereign, but money is ephemeral, it moves. In the Irish case, we have a constitutional border on the island, but money ignores it, and this ability to permeate is a fundamental aspect of money, rarely appreciated even by those who are in charge of it. One further result of the crisis was a small seed of niggling doubt in my mind: if these central bankers – my bosses – appeared at sea when faced with a currency challenge, what else might they be misdiagnosing?

The high priests of money

Less than two decades after that currency crisis, Ireland, along with much of the Western world, experienced a devastating banking crash. The same gang was in charge of the nation's money. Within the space of sixteen years, they had managed to preside over two massive monetary crises, suggesting that their grasp of exactly what money is and how it works might not be that solid. The Irish central bankers were not alone; they were part of a greater club, a global priesthood. Could the entire worldwide clerisy be wrong about money?

As a young economist, first in the central bank and later in investment banking, I didn't quite appreciate that the world was entering a new relationship with money. We were entering the age of the technocrats – modern-day high priests or Brahmins. As in older caste-based societies, the Brahmin class is the sage caste, those who interpret the rules and set the laws.

When a central bank is bestowed with the extraordinary ability to create money, the people who run these places also wield enormous power. Within the central bank, a sort of monetary tabernacle, the Brahmins perform the rituals whereby money is fashioned. The central banks operate under government charter: they print the currency and it is given legitimacy by the fact that the government decrees this currency is the money we pay taxes in. This ability to pay taxes is key because, without this attribute, the notes in your pocket would be just paper.

Unlike politicians, who are voted in or out, the technocrats are not accountable to the electorate. Take, for example, the European Central Bank. It is entirely independent yet utterly political. Because money drives the economy and the economy drives the political cycle, money is – by definition – political. Today, the professional competence of central bankers underpins the world's financial architecture. In an intellectual game of cat-and-mouse with the press and the financial markets, the central bank Brahmins disguise and obfuscate; the pronouncements of central bankers have often been described as Delphic, after the ancient Greek oracle that predicted the future in riddles. There is also a strong element of moral judgement in their opinions. For example, economies can be described as delinquent or out of control, with reputations and credibility at stake. With their gospel of free capital movements, central bankers ensure that flows of money around the world make the global economy more integrated than ever. As money travels unhindered across continents, events in one part of the world have an immediate impact on other regions. It is impossible to imagine globalisation without fiat money flowing effortlessly around the globe.

The era of fiat money has produced the most extraordinary prosperity, coinciding with both a material decline in global inequality and a unique period of technological innovation. The Chinese economy, for example, would not have burgeoned had it been stymied by an absence of money. Imagine if the global economy of 7 billion people was trying to grow under a monetary system tethered to a piece of metal. Since the 1970s, we've seen a dramatic increase in global literacy from 61 per cent to 83 per cent for women and from 77 per cent to 90 per cent for men. For countries defined as low-income, the percentage of girls not in school dropped from 72 per cent in the last year of the quasi-gold standard to 23 per cent by 2016. The equivalent figures for boys are 56 per cent and 18 per cent.[1]

With education, women are more likely to control their own fertility and, since the end of gold, the average number of children per mother in low-income countries has fallen from 5 to 2.4. Under the global fiat regime, higher economic growth rates and fewer children has resulted in a surge in income per head. In the 1970s, 40 per cent of the world's population lived under the World Bank's poverty line; today it is 10 per cent. Average human life expectancy has risen from the late fifties to the early seventies, while infant mortality has plummeted. The contrast in quality of life for hundreds of millions of people between the old world of metal-based money and the new world of fiat money has been extraordinary. Obviously, correlation is not causation and a myriad of reasons might explain these changes – from technology to medicine, sanitation, education drives and public policy – but these advances have occurred under the umbrella of global fiat money. We have been in this fiat money regime for over fifty years and things have been improving. This is what progress looks like.

Currency vs finance

Fiat money is one of the world's most liberating and marvellous technologies, giving more people access to money than ever before, and allowing economies to take off. But fiat money is also a great illusion and, being based on trust, it is a source of fragility as well as strength. At the centre of this system are the central bankers, the Brahmins who deploy the media, think tanks and policy gatherings to convert others to their philosophy of money. They claim to control money – but do they really?

Ever since the time of Kushim and the Sumerians, there have been two types of money: money in the form of grain, for instance, which we can call commodity money, and a more ephemeral type of money in the form of a contract, which we can call finance. In finance, I owe you, you owe me, we write the amounts down on a slate and on an appointed day we clear the contract and start again. It is only at the point of clearing the contract that actual currency – commodity money – is required. The Lydians introduced their gold coins as much to clear these contracts as to trade day to day. They introduced smaller coins to trade, and kept their valuable gold coins to square outstanding debts and credit at the end of the contract period. They also established laws to govern commercial contracts, creating a web of obligations, commitments and counter-commitments, governed by rules.

Over the thousands of years we have been observing money, we see this dual nature evolve: money as currency, anchored by something like gold or the guarantee of a state; and money as finance, created by commercial banks and governed by commercial law. Creating credit is what your barman does when he opens a tab. You drink happily all evening and the bill is settled at the end of the night. Bank credit operates like this, but on a much grander scale. Most of the innovations we have seen in money are innovations in the world of credit – or the area broadly known as finance. Refined and expanded by the Florentine merchant bankers with their double-entry balance sheets, by the time we get to the Dutch and mercantile Amsterdam, commercial lending is increasing dramatically and it is finance, rather than currency anchored by metal, that fuels the trading economy.

Today, currency – such as the cash in your pocket – amounts to around 10 per cent of all the money supply; finance in all its various manifestations – your mortgage, for instance – makes up the rest. The pre-eminence of finance in the story of modern money has significant implications. When you go to the bank and ask for a loan for a car, the bank creates the money out of nothing, and puts it into your account. The new money didn't exist yesterday; today it does. It has been created not by the central bank, but by a commercial bank. This money, or credit, is the lubricant of finance, governed by contracts. Finance is not determined by the central bank, although the central bank would like to control it. Finance is an energy that can propel the economy and society, sometimes off its axis, whether that means a boom or a bust. The central bank knows that it is on the hook for the mistakes of finance, so it tries to set up a series of guardrails, such as a requirement for lenders to keep deposits with the central bank, to keep finance on side. But finance is an unruly version of money, not easily disciplined.

Could it be that the traditional economic view of the relationship between the central bank and the commercial banks is the wrong way around?

Push or pull?

When talking about the fiat regime, economists have typically contended that the central bank creates the money, prints it and gives it to the commercial banks – and from there the commercial banks leverage this amount, pushing money into the economy. This interpretation seems logical, and it places the central bank at the centre of the system, determining how much money is in circulation. It's a reassuring story, because someone is in charge. It is the story economists learn in university. Let's call it the push story. The amount of money the economy requires is determined by the all-knowing high priests, using complex economic models. That amount of money is pushed from the central bank to the commercial banks and then pushed into the economy. And when you read about the US Federal Reserve in the media, you are reassured that you are reading about an institution that has its hand on the monetary tiller.

But having worked as an economist, both in a central bank and large commercial banks, I'm not sure that's how the system operates. It may work like that in textbooks, but in reality the world functions differently. Having seen various crises where the central bank is not only not in charge, but doesn't appear to have a clue what is going on, I believe money works the opposite way. Let's call this other story the pull story, where the central bank is not pushing money into the economy, but is being pulled by the economy and the economy's appetite for money, which is whetted and served by commercial banks.

The commercial banks are like franchisees; operating under licence from the central bank, they create money in response to demand. An innovation in money that we met way back in Florence, double-entry bookkeeping, is key to understanding how banks create money – every asset has a corresponding liability. You want to buy a house and go to the bank for a mortgage. The bank doesn't ask for permission to create that money; it generates new money after its own credit committee decides whether or not you are good for the loan. This is a loan to you and it pays the seller of the house. On the bank's balance sheet, there is a liability: the newly created deposit, which you transfer to the seller of the house. And there is also a newly created asset: the loan to you, collateralised by the deeds of the house, on which you pay interest. After this bit of alchemy, there is still only one house, which you now own, but the seller of the house now owns a deposit created by the loan the bank has made to you. The magic of bank leverage is that you get the house, the seller gets the cash, and the bank has both a new asset (the loan to you) and a new liability (the deposit now owned by the seller of the house).

The bank can do this over and over again. Indeed, as the profitability of the bank is based on income from its assets, there is an incentive for the profit-maximising bank to keep lending. Additionally, if the bonus of the boss is linked to the bank's share price, there will always be a management incentive to lend as much as possible, even if this becomes reckless, which is why some might conclude the easiest way to rob a bank is to run it – banks go bad from the inside out.

Currency, meanwhile, is money created by the central bank. It comes in physical form – the notes and coins we keep in our wallets and tills on the high street – and in electronic form, used by the commercial banks to settle payments between one another. How is this electronic currency created? As the dollar is the world's reserve currency, we'll use the Federal Reserve as our central bank example, but the fiat system works the same way all over the globe.

When the US government borrows money, it issues IOUs called treasuries, which are typically sold to commercial banks and the financial markets. The central bank can also buy treasuries in the open market. When it does so, it creates a deposit for commercial banks at the Fed. These deposits are known as central bank reserves, and they consist of electronic currency. These electronic cash reserves are created *only* by the central bank, and are held *only* by commercial banks, and they are used to settle transactions between the latter. They can act as a constraint on commercial bank lending and borrowing: the more reserves a commercial bank has at the Fed, the more lending and borrowing it can execute. Banks can also convert these reserves into physical currency, fresh dollars, from the Fed to stuff in the ATMs. Meanwhile, they must hold onto a certain amount of reserves at the Fed in case of an emergency – although, as we will see, it's rarely enough when things go wrong.

In the fiat system, the government is the issuer of the original treasuries and the central bank is the printer of money, and because both are public institutions, it's a case of the left hand of the government lending to the right hand of the government, using the commercial banks as facilitator. But those commercial banks are not part of the state. The central bank tries to oversee the commercial banks, and it does this by obliging them to provide collateral in the form of treasuries. The Fed also requires banks to hold treasuries as part of their capital. These stipulations create a demand for treasuries. Without treasuries, commercial banks and other financial institutions cannot play the money game. Once US treasuries become the premier collateral accepted by the Federal Reserve, they acquire a value over and above the willingness of the market to lend to the American government. They become the entry point – a sort of 'pay to play' asset.

The most valuable secret in the world

The system is internally sealed: the government issues treasuries, which are bought by the commercial banks and the central bank, giving the government money, and giving the financial system collateral. The commercial banking system then acquires the permission to create new money. This is why the most important price in the US financial system is the price of US government treasuries, or the bond yield for short. The most important treasury bonds are the 10-year bond, which is used as a benchmark for pricing many financial assets, and the 30-year bond, which in America is the reference rate for mortgages. The 'yield' or interest rate on the 10-year and 30-year treasuries is the short-term interest rate plus a risk premium, so the long-term rate is typically higher than the short-term rate. The short-term rate is set by the central bank and anchors the entire system. Legions of financial journalists and market analysts try to decipher the utterances of the high priests of money, to try to guess where the long bond rates might go. The central bankers are guessing what direction the economy and the money supply might take and the financial markets are speculating on that guesswork. Not exactly reassuring, is it?

As you can see, the traditional economic view of the fiat regime, the one that suggests the central bank decides the appropriate amount of money for the economy and pushes this quantum of cash into commercial banks for them to disseminate, has the system back to front. It's good for textbooks but doesn't explain the real world. In reality, the commercial banks pull the central bank around the place. And there is one more aspect of how money is created that the Federal Reserve doesn't want you to know about. It is the most valuable secret in the world.

The large commercial banks that create money have another trick up their sleeves, and it's called the Eurodollar market. Eurodollars are dollars that are created offshore, far from the grasp of the Federal Reserve. Despite their name, they have nothing to do with the euro. Eurodollars originated following the Second World War when the Marshall Plan led to lots of dollars circulating in Europe. These were deposited in banks that were not regulated by the US authorities – either foreign banks or offshore branches of US banks. These offshore banks had to lend these dollars out to make interest, and over time, the banks began to create Eurodollar loans, largely for transactions on the financial markets.

The Eurodollar market became a sort of parallel capital market, which continued to grow as banks made more loans, creating more deposits that in turn created more loans. As capital markets grew exponentially in London and various other offshore financial jurisdictions, so too did this Eurodollar market. Remember, these Eurodollars trade as dollars but, because they are produced offshore, they are not governed by the Federal Reserve's regulatory requirements. Lobbying by the big US banks domiciled outside the US led to a situation where the Fed, in essence, looked the other way as these international banks created more offshore dollars. Today, Eurodollars are the dominant currency for international financial markets. There are 12.8 trillion Eurodollars circulating around the globe. The American money supply is only just over $20 trillion. So, on top of the regulated amount of US dollars in the world, a further 64 per cent of that amount is flowing around, over which the Federal Reserve has no control. In short, the US doesn't really control its own currency.[2]

In contrast to the textbook understanding of fiat currency, the central bank doesn't limit the amount of credit the commercial banks create. The central bankers might try to influence the amount of money in circulation by putting conditions on the banks, requesting more collateral; they might try to manipulate the price by adjusting the interest rate; they might even take to the media to admonish banks or opine on the state of the world. But can they control finance and its role in the economy? Not really! They can control the price of money (the rate of interest) but not the quantity of money or where it is deployed or created. This means that, at best, they have a guiding influence on the amount of money in the system, and the time it takes for the rate of interest to influence the economy can vary. It is in this interim period that things can go wrong, and when things do go wrong, it is the central bankers who are left carrying the can.

The Eurodollar secret – a $12 trillion secret – is one that the high priests don't want you to know about. Rather than pushing money into the economy, the central bank is in reality pulled by finance and its form of bank-created money – credit. The inconsistency between the official push story and the unofficial pull story, pretending they have competence when in reality they don't, undermines the high priests of money and so often renders them after-the-event explainers rather than masters of money's destiny. When you ask yourself why we have recurrent banking and financial crises, this is the answer – the people in charge are not in charge. And behind all the central banking pomp and ceremony, which is dressed up as theory, almost catechism, there are mortal humans dealing with that most incendiary of substances: money. Bear in mind when you are looking for a mortgage that the price of it is determined by the credit cycle, that most unstable element of money, which is less governed by rational economics and more a function of the madness of crowds.

2 0

THE PSYCHOLOGY OF MONEY

Fox News

On St Patrick's Day, 2008, I walked into the Fox News TV studio smack in New York's Midtown. Festooned in green, the Big Apple was Irish. At Fifth Avenue's parade, the boys of the NYPD choir were actually singing 'Galway Bay'. That afternoon, all hell had broken loose. Bear Stearns, one of Wall Street's oldest and biggest banks, had gone bust. No one was talking about anything else. Meanwhile, I was there to talk about a book I'd just published. Seconds before we go on air, Liz Claman, the presenter, looks at me, shaking her head of fiery red hair, and says, 'Hey! You must know about banking and money – it says here in my notes you are a former bank economist. Screw Ireland, let's talk Bear Stearns.' And with that, the red light goes on, dazed employees are coming out of Bear Stearns on the screen behind me, I'm live on Fox Business and Claman's first question is, 'Well, David McWilliams, how did we get here?'

Well, Liz, as was the case with Ireland, it all started and ended with houses. The Irish economy is a miniature version of the US economy, but as we are in America, let's talk America.

We are in an asset price meltdown. It's half economics and half human nature. A volatile cocktail! If the Fed keeps interest rates too low for too long, people borrow more money against their asset, say their home. The more valuable their asset, the more bankers will lend them. And the easiest way to manipulate any asset price is to pump it up with leverage – borrowed money. This is a chicken and egg dilemma. Is the asset price going up because there is more leverage or is there more leverage because the asset price is going up? Leverage bloats and distorts prices, pushing them upwards and outwards. The idea of prices moving upwards is fairly comprehensible, but what do I mean by outwards? I mean that the higher prices go, the more people hear about them. As the price of certain assets rises – for example, condominiums in the US – more people desire them, wanting to get into a rising market.

Americans took on more debt, as we would expect. Naturally, as demand for real estate rises, so too does supply. Seeing the profits being made in the condo market, builders who were going to build commercial offices retool their sites to erect condos because they follow the money. More condos are supplied, boosted by glossy brochures depicting young singles with great teeth, luxuriant hair and yoga mats. Property porn of this type seduces yet more buyers. In time, the quality and location of new condominiums will deteriorate. All the condos on the first row from the beach are gone, so the second, third, fourth and fifth rows are built.

The banks are now financing both sides of the trade, providing loans to both the developer-builder and the buyer-speculator. As loans go up, bank profits head ever skywards. Profits push up banks' credit ratings, which reduce their cost of borrowing. Emboldened, they issue IOUs to other banks and finance houses, who buy the IOUs, giving the issuing banks money that they can immediately give out via yet more loans. Over time, the type of people who borrow begins to change. Lending at such an accelerated rate means that, in no time, the banks run out of credit-worthy customers. Undaunted, banks entertain borrowers whose incomes might not be as robust as they would normally require. But things are going well and if bank A doesn't lend out, bank B will, so why not?

These new less than financially bulletproof borrowers acquired the name subprime borrowers. Traditionally, banks wouldn't lend to these people in a month of Sundays, but in a boom they become subprime clients.

The crowd

The average punter doesn't join the dots. We see a number going up and that number, if we own the asset, is making us rich. In contrast, if we don't own that asset, the number going up makes us feel we are missing out compared to our increasingly rich neighbour. This is something that economists tend to misunderstand. US house prices were moving upwards and that's all people could see. The increase in prices both excites and terrifies us, leading to an altered collective state of mind.

As we noted in Chapter 10 in relation to Dutch Tulipmania – and can be seen in recurring contemporary financial crises where economists, despite purporting to understand money, fail to predict what is going on – traditional economics profoundly misunderstands this psychology. It fails to grasp the trippiness of money.

If you study economics in university, you will be told that the price in economics is the place where supply equals demand. This fabricated notion of equilibrium has been hatched by economists to make sure their models work. A moment's thinking about the real world concludes that such an illusion could only be maintained by people who don't get out enough. The economy we experience every day and live in is not a model; it is an adapting complex system that is spontaneous and unpredictable. In real life, price motivates us, enthuses us, and – to use the language of the street – rising prices give us the financial horn. When we are thinking with the horn rather than the brain, our decision making is rarely at its most discriminating.

Although we saw similar psychological dynamics in the Tulipmania story, the modern economy has far more credit and opportunities to create credit, so the boom becomes even more effervescent and the busts considerably more dramatic. In addition, the presence of leverage, which was absent in Tulipmania, means that many more people can be involved in the speculative upswing and more balance sheets can be destroyed in a slump – and, because the debts incurred have to be paid back, the consequent recession can endure a great deal longer.

Typically, there are two types of investor: the momentum investor and the value investor. The value investor is the one the finance classes talk about: a person who looks at the numbers and ratios, finds fair value based on some metric of objective worth and plays according to a set of rules, looking at profits, earnings per share, dividends, deviations from means and value relative to other stocks or assets. Value investors benchmark their investments against risk factors. Based on their calculations, they make a considered, unemotional decision. Although reasonably common in business school textbooks, in reality, this type of person is part of a small minority.

The majority of us are momentum investors. We don't want to miss out and so we go along for the ride. If something is going up in price, we want to own it too. As prices rise, we get sucked in. Optimism infects us. On paper, everyone in the market is getting rich. The banks extend leverage. Rising asset prices distort one side of the balance sheet, but they also do something weird to the other side. The bank that lends money does so based on a ratio – the amount of the loan is under-pinned by an amount of collateral. This is termed margin financing. It's the best way to borrow when prices are rising. Imagine the price of a condo is $900,000, which the bank takes as collateral for a $1,000,000 loan. This means the borrower needs to come up with $100,000 in cash. If the price of the condo rises 10 per cent to $1,000,000, the collateral now covers all the risk of the loan. The borrower, buoyed up by the paper gain, goes back to the bank wanting more leverage to buy another apartment off plan in a new waterfront development, the one featuring those singles with great teeth and yoga mats. The bank checks its records and sees the borrower has more than enough equity at the new higher value of condos, and 'prudentially' offers the borrower yet more credit.

The exhilaration phase

In this climate of optimism, every condo owner becomes a converter, a sort of money missionary, recruiting others into the game. Rarely seeking any direct financial gain from enlisting others, they are simply tripping on money, and want to share their good fortune. At this stage, many cautious people who don't easily part with money are coaxed over, experiencing a financial 'Come to Jesus' moment. The upswing is not limited to personal balance sheets. The government's balance sheet and corporate balance sheets also benefit. All three come together in what we usually call an economic boom.

In the case of the government's balance sheet, credit bleeds into the greater political, budgetary and fiscal cycle. All this new money, created by the banking system to feed the property boom, drives up consumer spending. Credit card limits are raised. People feel richer because their wealth has increased on paper. This spending drives VAT and indirect tax takes, boosting government revenue, reducing the budget deficit and creating the space for tax cuts in the coming budgets. In addition, as the construction industry pays taxes and it is operating at full tilt, another source of government revenue rises. And, because construction is labour intensive, unemployment falls as more people find jobs not just directly in the construction industry but in the nexus of property construction, banking and advertising – all of which are boosted by the original credit surge. Once taxes are cut, another injection of money is administered as people have more to spend. Prices keep heading skywards.

On the corporate balance sheet, buoyant sales are driving revenues. As inflation remains muted (as it did in America largely due to the downward pressure on consumer prices from cheap goods from China), low interest rates trigger a bout of financial engineering. Companies that can't grow quickly enough turn to debt-financed mergers to acquire more of a share in these growing markets. The lower interest rates mean the cost of failure is low, so companies invest in start-ups that might never have had any hope of success had interest rates been higher. We can see how, if interest rates are held down for too long, cheap money finances fragile companies or weak ideas that are only sustained by the overall monetary effervescence. Old companies that have remained solvent due to interest rates being too low, so-called zombie companies, go bust when interest rates rise. But so too do new companies, phantom companies – those start-ups burning through investors' money but without profit. These zombie and phantom companies will be the first to implode when interest rates rise again.

It was against this effervescent background in the noughties that millionaire property developers were treated with messianic respect in the pages of the financial press. As overleveraged banks won awards, their chief executives appeared in Davos opining on climate change. People were buzzing and nothing could wreck the mood. With governments running budget surpluses for the first time in years, people complained about not being able to get a restaurant table on Wednesday nights while the *New York Post* recorded the marriage of a celebrity chef to the daughter of a property magnate in Martha's Vineyard.

In every credit-driven upswing there are three types of borrower with three different underlying balance sheets. The first type of borrower is the hedge borrower.[1] This person has enough income to be able to pay both the monthly interest payments on the loan and the annual principal on the capital. A second type of borrower is the speculative borrower. This player can only afford to pay the interest on the debt and will need to roll over her capital payments, hoping to sell the asset at the end for a large profit and only then pay off the capital. The third type of borrower is the Ponzi borrower, who can neither pay his interest nor his capital from his income and needs prices to keep rising to pay back anything. He is in the market to 'flip' the condo onto the next person coming in. Fundamentally, the market, at these ridiculously high prices, makes no financial sense. The edifice is maintained only by mass delusion. It is at this point that we hear stories about new paradigms, newfangled theories about valuations, prices and money. This is the moment of peak risk and yet it is the moment when most amateurs get into the game.

The downturn

Some savvy investors take their profits, aware that no one ever lost money by selling too early. There is a rarely an overt sell signal, or if there is one, it is only appreciated in hindsight. These shrewd investors get out near the top, selling to those coming in at the bottom. The market now depends on fresh players at the bottom of the pyramid. Following the savvy players, a few more decide it's time to sell. For the first time since before the optimistic phase, prices wobble a bit.

We are entering the denial phase. Those who have been making easy money dismiss the correction in prices as a blip on the upwards trajectory. In fact, many of the true believers use this fall in prices as an opportunity to buy yet more, claiming to see bargains. Prices might rally as a result of the already committed committing more. But something has changed; that feeling has altered. Seasoned players call this late-stage upswing after the market has turned a 'bull trap', meaning it gives the impression of a new upward movement, when in fact the spell has already been broken. There seemed to be an infinite number of buyers only last week, but sellers are now finding buyers have disappeared.

The rumour mill begins to work in the opposite direction. Buyers evaporate, more sellers emerge and prices start to fall. Panic sets in. People try to sell their condos, but the market is flooded. We call this the 'paradox of aggregation' in economics, which means what is good for the individual is not always good for the collective. In this case, the banks, watching their own balance sheets, see that the collateral they were basing their lending on has fallen in value. The banks then contact individual borrowers to tell them they need more cash to cover the margin. When the bank advises one condo owner to sell, that's OK, but the paradox of aggregation kicks in when all the banks ask all their clients to sell to raise cash. When everyone is selling, who is buying? The market is flooded with condos. Buyers see prices falling and, if any buyers are left, they deduce the bargain will come tomorrow when prices fall yet further. Think of a football match. The game gets exciting and the guy in front of you stands up to get a better view. This only works for him as long as no one else stands up. But his standing up signals to the rest of us to stand up to get a similarly better view and soon the entire stadium is standing when we have paid to sit and no one gets a better view. In the same way, if I sell and I am the only seller, my balance sheet will improve because I get a good price for my condo, but if everyone is selling, we all get lower values for our condos and everyone's balance sheet deteriorates.

Fear abounds and prices continue tumbling, leading to widespread depression as the herd grasps its mistake. The banks realise that their balance sheets are umbilically tied to the collapsing market as more and more borrowers hand back the keys, unable to pay their debt. Our Ponzi borrower is the first to give up. His position was always the most precarious and, once prices start falling, his strategy of selling to a 'greater fool' tomorrow is goosed. He has neither income nor wealth and walks away, chased by lawyers and debt collectors. As prices continue downwards, the speculative borrower, who could only pay her interest, starts to sink. Her income, like everyone else's, is based on the broader economy, and when the condo craze collapses, so too does extra credit in the economy. Banks start to call in loans. This is what a credit crunch looks like. Money today becomes far more valuable than promises of money tomorrow.

At this stage, it begins to dawn on people that the money they have in the bank, which most of us believe is there for safekeeping, is in fact a loan that we make to the bank in return for interest. The bank uses this loan to create more loans and, as long as those loans are all performing, no one asks any questions. Money goes in and money goes out. But what happens when loans stop performing, when people default and the banks face a cascade of bad loans?

The banks had lent out hand over fist and for each new loan they were required to square their balance sheet with deposits. The more deposits the banks had, the more they could lend. But as they continued to lend, they ran out of deposits and were compelled to raise money elsewhere. In that mania phase, when deposits were exhausted, the banks borrowed from other banks. Sometimes they borrowed in the very short term, issuing IOUs that rolled over or needed to be refinanced every year. In a credit crunch, the banks have a mismatch between their assets (the loans they lent out) and their liabilities (the deposits and other short-term paper that must be paid back). You will notice that, in a credit crunch, banks will offer higher rates on deposits because they want to keep their deposits from leaving. If deposits flee a bank, the bank has a major problem because banks borrow in the short term and lend in the long term. For example, when they lend for a condo, it's usually a thirty-year mortgage, so they can't get that money back in full for thirty years. In contrast, their depositors have the right to demand their money immediately. The fundamental rule of banking is to make sure loans are performing and depositors are at ease.

Money, banking and finance are all about trust. If we trust the banks, we rarely concern ourselves about whether our money on deposit is secure or not. We expect it to be there and, as a consequence, if we are lucky enough to have savings, we never bother to take them out of the bank. But what if people begin to question the solvency of the bank? Share prices on the way down are an alarm, warning that there may be something going on in the bank that the executives would rather hide. That something is bankruptcy. As bad debts rise, and borrowers sink under the weight of a collapsing market, the banks' share prices fall. Sellers queue up to flog bank shares, but there are no buyers, and the share price collapses.

Worried depositors take their money out. Usually, this begins gradually with large corporate depositors. Once it starts, it can accelerate quickly, which is why a bank run is called a run, not a stroll or an amble. Just as a surge in asset prices is driven by rumour and gossip, so too is a bank run. Typically, a bank will go to the interbank loan market and try to raise funds. But who is going to lend money to an entity that looks like it is going bust? This is the predicament in which Bear Stearns had found itself in 2008. The specific details of what securities or derivatives it was dealing in are less important than the process outlined here. When Bear Stearns went to the interbank market, no banks were prepared to lend to it. When it tried to sell a chunk of itself to other banks to shore up its balance sheet, no deal could be done. The Federal Reserve, traditionally the lender of last resort, tried to backstop the bank in early March but by St Patrick's Day the game was up, because the extent of its overall losses was not clear.

On Fox News, Liz Claman probably wished she'd never asked the question.

The intended consequence of policy

In the weeks and months that followed the 2008 St Patrick's Day Massacre, one bank after another would go bust. In a crisis, you don't just run out of money, you run out of time. Had the banks been able to buy time, they might have tempered the panic, but in a crisis time becomes incredibly scarce. Selling continued, balance sheets imploded and, in the dash for cash, good assets were sold to pay for the losses on dodgy assets. One collapsing bank share price infected and dragged down others and by September that year, six months later, the 2008 global financial crisis was upon us.

This story underlines many of the properties of money that we have explored. Money is a store of wealth that motivates and excites us. It amplifies human behaviour, bringing into focus attributes such as enthusiasm, hope and optimism, as well as greed, envy and pride. This is the essential plutophyte aspect of money – money changes human behaviour and human behaviour changes money. Money allows us to travel in time: by borrowing we are taking tomorrow's income to pay for today, while by speculating we are painting a picture of the future for ourselves expressed in money and potential profit. And even when things fall apart, and we promise ourselves never again, we never learn. The seeds of the next cycle are the ruins of the last, as yet again value investors pick up the fallen asset cheaply, become enthusiastic, and off we go.

In the decade after 2008, global recession compelled the Brahmins in the central banks to cut the rate of interest dramatically and print money with flamboyant enthusiasm. Their aim was to refloat the balance sheets of America's consumers and its banking system. The type of recession that followed the 2008 crash is termed a balance sheet recession:

on one side of people's balance sheets were assets, largely houses, and on the other were the debts they incurred to buy those houses and other assets. After the crash, the asset prices collapsed but the debt remained the same.

Quantitative easing was a new policy introduced by the Fed in 2009, named so to distinguish it from the more traditional price easing. Usually, if the central bank wants to get the economy moving, it will cut interest rates. This will set the price of credit and, as credit is cheaper, people will borrow more and save less, and banks will lend, driving spending upwards. But in 2009, interest rates couldn't get the economy moving because it was stuck in what Keynes described as a 'liquidity trap'. This is when people have too much existing debt and they won't borrow, no matter how low the interest rates, while the banks have too much bad debt and won't lend either. Depending on interest rates to propel the economy is as useful as pushing on a string, as Keynes remarked. In such a situation the central bank has to flood the economy with money and force the banks to lend.

Technically, the Brahmins don't actually print money to carry out quantitative easing. The Fed contacts the banks and offers to buy, let's say, $10 billion of the treasuries that the banks have on their balance sheets, meaning that something that was illiquid, a bond, is made liquid by the central bank and is immediately converted into new dollars. The banks can then do what they want with this money. At a stroke, the Federal Reserve has created $10 billion that didn't exist before. In this case, it is pushing money as opposed to being pulled by money.

On top of this, the Fed did one more thing. It had to make sure the banks would lend this new money rather than sit on it or buy some other asset that was ideal for saving. Traditionally, the asset of choice for savers was the US government's 10-year bond, which yielded a decent return. The Fed decided to buy up these bonds, taking them out of the market, and choking off this savings refuge for the banks. The banks had no choice but to lend the new money, and this money went to their favourite customers. Who are they, typically? The already wealthy. Lower interest rates drive up asset prices and, when asset prices rise, who benefits most, the rich or the poor? The rich, of course, because they own stuff – that's why they are rich. The small minority of people who depend on assets, rents and dividends for their income benefit significantly more than the vast majority of us who rely on wages. Soaring wealth inequality was not the unintended consequence of quantitative easing – it was the objective.

More and more people found themselves locked out of the wealth party, and their stake in society diminished. These people might not have a stake but they do have a vote; they vote for the person or idea that appears to address their plight. Movements with simple slogans, offering comfort in this unequal world, begin to look attractive. Donald Trump and Brexit are, among other things, the political offspring of quantitative easing – both nativist movements chime with the 'left behinds' and are fuelled by wealth inequality. Populism was birthed in the central banks, created by the very elite that populism considers the enemy.

As inequality in the West rose, and the banks were seen to be bailed out while austerity was imposed on ordinary people, respect for money's institutions and the ability of the central bankers to deliver was undermined. With trust in the global financial system at a low ebb, and established monetary policy exacerbating wealth inequality, might there be a new form of money on the horizon, a new promise?

THE EVOLUTION OF MONEY

Private vs public

On Friday, 13 October 2023, in Dublin's St Patrick's Cathedral, I sat below the pulpit where, from 1713 to 1745, Dean Jonathan Swift delivered his sermons. The American writer Michael Lewis was there to discuss a new form of money, cryptocurrency, focusing specifically on his blockbuster *Going Infinite*, which documents the rise and fall of the so-called JP Morgan of Crypto, Sam Bankman-Fried, who was hailed as the future of money, fêted by journalists, celebrities and politicians alike.[1]

His company, FTX, was valued in the billions of dollars and all sorts of seasoned investors vied for a piece of the action. In the end, like tulips, highly leveraged condos, and a whole host of assets that have soared and fallen back to earth, the entire thing turned out to be nothing more than a massive bubble, inflated by hot air and historically low interest rates. Quantitative easing following the 2008 crisis created a lending bonanza and, with short-term interest rates at zero, banks were forced to lend for much longer periods and to much riskier ventures so they could acquire a yield. With this 'free' money, banks started taking riskier bets. We were witnessing a giant experiment that had never been tried before. The Brahmins of economics might have played around with this idea in textbooks and on blackboards, but in reality, zero interest rates had never existed. From a macroeconomic perspective, zero interest rates make sense for a short time, as eventually the balance sheet will right itself. But keep rates too low for too long and all sorts of strange schemes get financed, few questions asked. FTX was one such venture.

Lewis, charitable and empathetic to the last, regarded Bankman-Fried, with whom he had spent many hours, as less a duplicitous criminal and more an extravagantly incompetent personality, emotionally unsuited to running a sweet shop, let alone a company that held billions of dollars of customers' deposits in trust. The jury at Bankman-Fried's 2023 criminal trial in New York didn't see him in such a generous light, however, and the judge found him guilty of stealing other people's money.

It seemed apt to be discussing yet another monetary boom and bust in this particular place of worship. In 1720, when Britain and Ireland were suffering the economic and political fallout from the collapse in the South Sea Company's shares, Jonathan Swift – who, along with Isaac Newton, got caught up in the scam – penned his satirical poem *The Bubble*. Lambasting the directors of a speculative company who suckered innocents into their wheeze, he wrote:

> The nation then too late will find,
> Computing all their cost and trouble,
> Directors' promises but wind,
> South Sea, at best, a mighty bubble.

Bankman-Fried was to the 2020s what these operators were to the 1720s; when it comes to money, speculation, human nature and the credit cycle, what held 300 years ago still holds today. Will we ever learn? Bankman-Fried and his supporters weren't just playing with a new asset in a far-off land; they were part of a new movement, captivated by advances in technology that purported to control a completely new type of money, cryptocurrency.

Crypto may be a new type of money, but the battle over who controls and creates money has been waged for millennia by emperors, rulers and monarchs against each other and against the merchants and the banking class who pioneered and disseminated finance. Over the past 500 years, this struggle has ebbed and flowed, but in the twenty-first century the monetary world has arrived at a synthesis – a truce, if you like – between the push of central bank control and the pull of commercial banking. The state, via the central bank, which is answerable to the government, issues the currency. The commercial banks create credit, orchestrating finance under the watch of central bank regulators. As we saw in Chapter 19, the push theory favoured by economics textbooks is largely wrong. Fiat money is more about the pull of commercial banks, but despite their power and size, they can still be taxed and regulated. Washington can choose to put manners on Wall Street. In this way, money remains within the competence of the state – it is public. Could you imagine the state giving that power away?

Time and again over the millennia, a cast of characters as diverse as the coin-debasing Emperor Nero, Dante's counterfeiter Maestro Adamo and even Adolf Hitler have tried to control money by manipulating it. All these were efforts aimed at privatising public money and the latest example in this illustrious list is crypto. Dressed up though it may be in the rhetoric of liberation for the average person, crypto is a form of private money. Be under no illusion, the rich will benefit most from private money – after all, they will own it. A major battle in the years to come will be between private money issued by private entities and public money issued by the organs of the state in the name of the citizen.

Crypto vertigo

Much of the cryptocurrency hype feels like little more than digital counterfeiting for the TikTok age. That is not to say that money will not adjust to and take on new forms in our data-driven era, but a few tech-savvy bros issuing tokens and calling these coupons 'currency' is not the future of money. More or less an elaborate scam, crypto capitalised on an era when public trust in democratic institutions and markets reached a new low. The promise of crypto was a new democratic, egalitarian and honest form of money, and its manifesto involved a kind of revolutionary appeal – smashing the establishment's hold on finance, and opening up the world of money beyond Wall Street. At least, that was the spin.

Rather than being issued by allegedly corrupt governments, cryptocurrencies such as bitcoin are governed by incorruptible algorithms, underpinned by a new technology called blockchain, made possible by the ongoing global data revolution. Blockchain is a clearing house for all trades in cryptocurrencies and is designed to eliminate the banking system's role in clearing transactions. Bitcoin has an inbuilt self-destruct algorithm, and the number of bitcoins that can be mined is finite. In total there are 19.6 million bitcoins available. Over 93 per cent have already been mined and the rest continue to be extracted by so-called bitcoin miners. Guess who is making all the money from bitcoin: the exchanges, which take a clip every time it is traded, and the people who already hold bitcoin and have acquired it at far lower prices than prevail today.

Although bitcoin's status as crypto is sometimes disputed by its advocates, it is generally considered to be part of the crypto family. Its finite supply distinguishes it from other forms, issued by various crypto companies, which are little more than home-made mints. Guess who will make all the loot on this second type of cryptocurrency: the people who issue it, naturally, as has been the case throughout history. This second type of crypto, embodied by Sam Bankman-Fried and FTX, has no limits on how much can be issued, as long as the hype continues. But we know what happens when the tide goes out. If a private, unregulated company issues tokens, and calls these tokens money, the risk of being the last buyer should be reasonably obvious. At least with bitcoin there is a fixed amount of the currency available and when it is gone, it's all gone.

Some argue that even if cryptocurrencies end up as mere collectibles from the internet age, like digital Pokémon cards, blockchain is still a game-changing technology. But what problem is it solving? The idea that there is some large, inefficient global payments system whose wastefulness can be solved by blockchain appears to be, if not baseless, not as much of a problem as claimed. There are already plenty of digital payment systems processing billions of online transactions priced in regular money, particularly dollars. Is it necessary to add the extra dimension of a new money into an exchange where old money is working? Blockchain technology – essentially a digital version of an old-fashioned tallystick – remains an extremely slow, energy-intensive ledger, which appears to be insufficiently scalable to deal with the trillions of dollars of transactions that are made every hour using existing technologies. Compared to the plain old credit card or the global banking settlement systems – problematic as some may be and susceptible to occasional hacks as they sporadically are – blockchain remains in its infancy.

The most widely owned and best known of all the digital currencies, bitcoin, has an obvious problem: the claim that 'bitcoin is money' is patently not true. As we've seen, history suggests that one of the key characteristics necessary for money to be truly useful is that its value must be stable. This means money must be managed. For everyday transactions, bitcoin is unusable in practical terms because its price jumps all over the place. This instability in price comes down to basic traditional economics: the price moves up and down precisely because the supply of bitcoin is fixed. As we saw with gold, a fixed supply of anything doesn't allow dynamic adjustments in response to changes in demand.

As bitcoin becomes popular and more people buy it, its price rises too quickly. This militates against it being used for transactions. Bitcoin promoters sometimes portray a spike in its price as evidence that it *is* money, when in fact the opposite is the case. Why spend bitcoin when it's going up in value against everything else? Due to its fixed supply, it can't act as a stable medium of exchange and thus it ends up being hoarded for capital gain; rather than functioning as money, it becomes an asset of sorts. The unscalable and brittle technology coupled with basic supply and demand realities imply that crypto-assets are incapable of fulfilling even the three essential roles of money as: 1) a unit of account, 2) a medium of exchange and 3) a store of value. Crypto-assets don't merit the name crypto-currencies because they are not currencies. They are tokens that represent some value for someone – and they constitute a perfect vehicle for naked speculation. The property that renders crypto ideal for speculation and gambling is its vola-tility. Who would ever punt on a boring, stable asset? But this is the very same property that renders it dysfunctional as a means of payment and therefore as money.

An asset?

A little bit of thinking about speculation and investment raises another red flag. Are crypto tokens even assets? An asset should have a flow of income paying you for your investment. Unlike a bond or an equity, cryptocurrencies generate no cash flow or income. Cryptocurrency entails no legal claim on anything. When you buy a share, you are buying a bit of a real company. When you buy a bond, you are also buying a claim on the assets underlying the bond, be it a company or a state. Unlike these other investments, crypto doesn't contribute to any capital formation. When you buy the shares of a company, the understanding is that your money goes to the company and might be used to buy equipment or finance the expansion into a new market, from which you hope to profit. The prospect of this investment will be dependent on, among other things, underlying economic activity.

Trading on sentiment alone, crypto is by contrast the ulti-mate speculative punt, a tradable gambling contract. The 'market' for these tokens is a zero-sum game in which any one participant's gain has to be another's loss. Trading crypto-currency has nothing to do with the broader economy; it is gambling – and offers the same excitement and addiction. But unlike gambling, crypto markets are unregulated. They are offshore, opaque and subject to a high degree of insider ma-nipulation, as we will continue to see in fraud trials like Bankman-Fried's. The state issuer of money is answerable to the people, unlike the crypto fantasy where the issuer can be a private company – a digital printing press with an imaginative marketing department.

There are other types of crypto, the so-called stable coins, that are tokens backed by holdings of fiat money. This makes them nothing more than money market funds dressed up as something else. Whatever form they take, the fact remains that digital tokens issued by a private company that tries to pass them off as money are a heist. There is a kind of digital currency that is expected to be launched imminently by central banks, but this is effectively nothing more than paper money in another guise, still issued by an organ of the state.

For society in general, crypto results in a net wealth transfer from typically poorer punters – including those angry X- and Reddit-obsessed crypto bros – to sophisticated private cartels that operate the offshore exchanges, backed incongruously by the very Wall Street firms that crypto was supposed to crush. In aggregate, crypto, at least for now, fails as both an investment and as money. The underlying technology, now nearly twenty years old – the same age as the iPhone – has found little, if any, application beyond criminal activity and gambling. And if, like gold before it, a cryptocurrency's quantity is fixed, it will be beneficial only to the people who already own it. The more its price goes up, the wealthier they become. It doesn't matter if it is digital gold, as proponents of crypto like to say, or real gold – the drawbacks of a fixed supply are evident.

Bitcoin was supposed to be used to buy stuff – that old 'money as a medium of exchange' thing – but this never transpired. Instead, it has come to be seen as a store of wealth that many millions of people believe in. As its price rises, more people will be attracted to it, despite it having no fundamental value or income accruing to it. We know that the best way to keep an asset inflated is to have more and more people with a stake in it. In time, there will be a significant group of people with an interest in maintaining its value, talking it up. After all, their wealth is tied up in bitcoin. They will lean on regulators to bolster it, protect it, disseminate it and ultimately drive up or at least maintain its price. The best way to do this is through extended distribution channels. To protect their own wealth, the bitcoiners have enlisted Wall Street to market bitcoin to the masses via exchange trade funds, a mechanism that allows investors to buy and sell bitcoin in greater numbers, and more transparently. Bitcoiners have got into bed with the very firms they once lambasted as corrupt, venal and destructive. The original alternative protest investment has become mainstream.

Allying with Wall Street and lobbying regulators is a long way from the original impetus for bitcoin, which was at first a bet on the complete collapse of the Western political order and the end of fiat money. The early adopters of bitcoin were part of a doomsday cult, who believed that fiat regimes were about to collapse in a bout of hyperinflation that would devalue all major currencies, and from which bitcoin would emerge as the great saviour. These Armageddonist tendencies mean bitcoin's more extreme promoters have tended to cheerlead political forces that might undermine the West, so finding them on social media applauding regimes such as Putin's Russia, inimical to Western power, is not a surprise.

Don't get me wrong – I am not offering financial advice. People can do what they want with their money, including buying bitcoin. My point is that bitcoin is not money in any definition of money that I understand. Bitcoin is a financial lobby group more than a new form of money. And, like most lobby groups, the game is to force its agenda on the authorities to enhance the interests of its owners, those who stand to benefit most from its fixed supply.

In January 2024, after extensive lobbying, the US Securities and Exchange Commission approved bitcoin funds for the first time, allowing them to be traded in the mainstream market without investors having to go through the process of acquiring bitcoin themselves. When very rich people – in this case, the early adopters who bought bitcoin for pennies and have therefore become astronomically wealthy – lobby the state to legitimise something that was explicitly intended to be illegitimate, and seek to enlist and enrich Wall Street in the process, alarm bells should ring. When this is pursued in a fashion that opens up avenues to sell bitcoin to small investors, who will be excited by the higher prices that result from the government's approval of the funds, those bells should ring louder and clearer.

Over the years we have seen that money is a technology designed to solve a problem. I'm scratching my head as to what problem bitcoin in particular and crypto in general actually solve. Despite the small foothold bitcoin has gained in the mainstream US investment market, crypto looks set to remain on the fringes, a source of obsession for its supporters and aficionados, but not very useful or practical in reality. Bitcoin is to money what Esperanto is to language.

The most critical problem for cryptocurrencies is that they are private and money, when it is functional and properly managed, is always public. For all its faults, the fiat system is still a state-run system. Even the most powerful commercial banks are under state supervision and could be more so if it were deemed necessary, just as it would technically be possible to bring the Eurodollar market within the American state's remit. There is no world in which I can envisage the state giving up the power to issue money in its own jurisdiction, because to do so would be to give the private sector control over the most potent substance in the state's armoury. Unless the state withers away, replaced by something else, it is impossible to imagine circumstances where money is not the domain of the state or adjuncts of the state. It is simply too powerful a tool to give away. And it is too dangerous in the wrong hands.

Modern monetary theory

Around the same time that crypto enthusiasts were first imagining a world of private money, some academic economists deep inside university departments were suggesting that the future of money would be public. Advocates of modern monetary theory (MMT), such as the US monetary economist Stephanie Kelton, argue that the traditional way of looking at government spending – and the constraints on government spending – is wrong. The traditional view holds that taxes are raised first, then the government spends the money that has been collected through taxation. MMT contends that this is back to front and that, in reality, the state prints money first and taxes are paid subsequently. So, it's a spend first, tax later world rather than a tax first, spend later one. This would mean that the political obsession with balancing the books – where politicians compare the state finances to a household with a fixed budget – is built on false assumptions. Proponents of MMT argue that the state, because it issues money, can never run out of it.

The consequence of this type of thinking is that national budget deficits don't really matter, or at least they don't matter in the way we tend to think they do. We often hear commentators and economists talk about the need to set debt ceilings, as if once the national debt hits some arbitrary number, the country will run out of money. MMT suggests that this can't happen in countries that issue their own currency: the only constraint on the amount of money the government can print is inflation, which advocates of MMT argue is determined by the resources of the economy. They say that when prices start to rise, the government should raise taxes to take the steam out of consumer demand and, in this way, the economy will cool down, as will inflationary pressure.

For a large economy like the US, which issues the global reserve currency, the implication of MMT is that the government has discretion over how much money it creates and where it chooses to spend it. Indeed, the monetary experience during the Covid pandemic, where various governments issued cheques to populations forced to stay at home, is seen by the MMT disciples as evidence that a government can simply print money and give it to the people without the need for the banking system in the middle.

I have some sympathy for the idea that governments might have more budgetary space in which to operate than previously thought, and I also understand that many of the voices arguing against government spending and intervention are ideologically driven, but I am not so sure that the future of money will pan out as the MMT academics hope. There are a number of practical difficulties facing MMT. In the Eurozone, for instance, countries do not issue their own currency, but instead use a common currency – the euro – issued by the European Central Bank. The governments of the individual countries in the group are therefore not able to create and spend money in the way that MMT proponents describe.

Even countries that issue their own currency, such as the UK, will have practical budgetary constraints set by the financial markets' perception of the nation's monetary discipline. In 2022, the Liz Truss government's ill-fated attempt to boost the UK growth rate by increasing borrowing and cutting taxes led to a run on the currency and the gilt market. Investors dumped UK assets, fearing inflation. Even though, theoretically, the UK can issue as much sterling as it wants, in practice it is hemmed in by the realities of the international financial markets, and their view of policy probity.

The main obstacle for proponents of exclusively private money such as bitcoin, or exclusively public money as endorsed by some of the MMT economists, is that both options, while theoretically interesting, are impractical. Crypto, as we have seen, is not a serious means of exchange, while the hard constraints of inflation and the bond market are real and render MMT far less radical than it sounds.

Back to Africa

Over the course of this book we have seen incremental innovations in money emerging to suit the demands of the economy. Like language, money is a living thing, and like the adoption of a new word, phrase or idiom, each innovation made money more useful; the more useful it was, the more used it became. We are seeing an example of this trial-and-error process of monetary innovation playing out right now in Africa.

To achieve its potential, money must be usable and acceptable to the widest possible audience; it must be abundant and diffuse rather than scarce and concentrated. If money can be dispensed into the hands of more people, and is accepted as a stable medium of exchange for people who were previously locked out of the monetary world, the impact can be immediate and the consequences remarkable.

While social media and Wall Street were heralding crypto

and its celebrity evangelists were hyping it up in Superbowl ads, a far more compelling form of money was emerging – organically – in an unlikely region. In much of Africa, a major impediment to development is a lack of credit and banking, two innovations that make money more effective – credit because it allows people to invest in the future, and banking because it is the platform where people save and borrow. Many, particularly rural, Africans rarely see a bank in their day-to-day lives, but they do have mobile phones. In 2007, the same year bitcoin arrived, a more ingenious currency called M-Pesa was being introduced, with little fanfare or investment. It would turn out to be useful as money, solving a problem – unlike crypto, which remains a solution looking for a problem.

M-Pesa ('M' is for mobile and *pesa* is Swahili for money) turns mobile phone credit into money. It is a bottom-up adaptation that responded to a real demand and solved a real problem, and it became widely adopted. On street corners in Kenya, you'll see hawkers selling 'pay as you go' mobile phone airtime. They are agents of an incipient monetary and social transformation. Using basic text messaging technology, M-Pesa allows Kenyans to deposit money on their phones, buy and sell using the debit and credit functions on their phones, transfer money via their phones and borrow and save through phone credit. Safaricom, the country's leading mobile phone provider, undertook to cash mobile phone minutes for the local currency, shillings. This move allowed mobile phone minutes to become currency, with commercial banks facilitating the exchange. In rural Kenya, small loans are extended to tide farmers over from harvest to harvest, not unlike the 'putting out' system we described in the early medieval period. The 'money' loaned is phone credit, whose value is understood by everyone. Once poorer people accessed this basic banking tool, phone-based money took off.

M-Pesa has reduced the cost of banking and increased access to money. Without a functioning banking system, before M-Pesa, the way to send money home to the Kenyan countryside was to give a bag of cash to a bus driver who would charge up to 30 per cent of its value to deliver it to a remote village. Often, the money simply disappeared. With M-Pesa, the money is transferred via phone credit and the phone credit is then used to buy supplies in the local shop. No bus driver, no risk. Today, there are 50,000 registered agents acting as tiny banks all over Kenya, and 70 per cent of the population use M-Pesa while 30 per cent of the country's GDP is generated via M-Pesa.[2]

Money evolves because the economy evolves. Take the difference between crypto and M-Pesa. The former attracted billions of dollars of investment, oceans of newspaper coverage, ceaseless advertising campaigns, and ultimately the support of Wall Street's wallet, and yet it has failed to live up to the hype. In contrast, M-Pesa – which was conceived in response to poverty, not affluence – is thriving and could be the model for money in much of Africa. Crypto has struggled because it failed the evolutionary test that all economic innovations must pass. What problem did it solve? None. Was it the best design to fit the challenge or requirement at the time? No. Was M-Pesa, that cobbled together, organic solution, the best design to fix the Kenyan dilemma at the time? Yes.

Recently, as I walked through the front gates of Trinity College Dublin, where I first studied monetary economics many years ago, I considered the evolution of money. With a pleasing sense of circularity, I was on my way to teach the same subject I had become fascinated by as a student. In the intervening three decades, the progress of money has been relentless, even in the remotest parts of the world; a working woman in Kenya can now instantly send money home to her mother in the countryside using her mobile phone.

Today, our advanced civilisation has electric cars, smartphones, vaccines, coffee machines, dance clubs, thriving cities, abstract art, pop music, social networks, nuclear weapons, recreational drugs, contraceptive pills, cosmetic orthodontics, precision engineering, artificial intelligence, takeaway tandooris and global supply chains – and 8 billion of us manage to live on this crowded planet. Such feats of organisation, productivity, innovation and collective brainpower are not enabled by ideology or religion or even force, but by money. Money acts as the central nervous system of that highly complicated, always adapting organism we call the global economy. A Promethean tool, money has propelled and continues to propel humankind, and it is woven inextricably into the fabric of our civilisation. Money is a defining technology of humanity, and over the past five millennia, we *Homo sapiens* have become plutophytes – a species adapted by and constantly changing with money.

M-Pesa is the embodiment of money's evolution, spontaneously adapting and thriving in response to its environment. Money has always developed organically and it will continue to do so. Who would have predicted that only a few years after they were widely adopted, mobile phones would become banks and phone credit would become money? In recent years, M-Pesa has been embraced in the Democratic Republic of Congo by people living in the same river basin where our investigations began thousands of years ago with the Ishango Bone. The evolution of money, like the evolution of humanity, constantly surprises.

ACKNOWLEDGEMENTS

Writing a book like this, essentially a popular economic history of money, is a huge feat of organisation, and I'm not a very organised person, so by definition I couldn't have done this on my own. To get everything down on the page, you must amass countless facts and figures, becoming familiar with the completely unfamiliar, and then turn these disjointed ideas into an overall story that makes some kind of logical sense. It's not enough to join the dots; the aim is to tell the story in a lively way that appeals to a real reader, not just the obsessive author. And I'm not one of those solitary writers; I'm a chatty one who likes to bounce ideas off others, who gets distracted and who forgets as much as he retains. I'm what you might call a social writer, and I need people around me. God love them – they've suffered for my craft! And for that, I am eternally grateful.

This book is in truth a joint effort with my wife and soulmate, Sian Smyth, who guided me through the project, pushing me back on track when I swerved off on more than a few tangents and, sometimes bluntly, telling me when my ideas were going nowhere. Lots of late nights, early mornings and long afternoons; writing, rewriting and red pen through oceans of print. It wouldn't be this book without her.

I'm grateful to my agent Marianne Gunn O'Connor for getting the idea commissioned in the first place and managing what turned out to be a longer, trickier affair than initially anticipated. I've been extremely fortunate to have a brilliant editorial team at Simon & Schuster, led by Assallah Tahir. With his ever-helpful comments, attention to detail and fine turn of phrase, Alex Eccles helped shape this book – I'm not sure he ever wants to hear the term 'monetary economics' again. Jack Ramm was drafted in early when the book was a sprawling mass of ideas; he cut and slashed it into a more coherent story – not an easy task. I'm thankful for the keen eyes of copy editor Tamsin Shelton and proofreader Jonathan Wadman. My two researchers par excellence, Alice Marcoux and Eliza Notaro, deserve huge thanks for their digging and filtering, always undertaken with wide smiles and great humour.

Opinions and errors are my own, but if there are any real howlers, you can blame the following people. I'm only messing. Economics is an endlessly fascinating subject, but there's so much to know that it always surprises, and this book is blessed to have been read by a few special economists who kept me sane and were generous with their time and knowledge. Particular thanks is owed to Brendan Greeley of Princeton University, whose encyclopaedic knowledge of the history of money was indispensable. My professor of monetary economics when I was an undergrad, Antoin Murphy, shared his learning on Talleyrand, Hamilton and Law with me on socially distant pandemic walks along Dún Laoghaire pier. He's a world expert on John Law, so I couldn't have been in better hands as I tried to navigate money in the eighteenth century.

Every November, I host an economics and stand-up comedy

festival, and the Kilkenomics travelling circus of economists – Mark Blyth, Marla Dukharan, Martín Lousteau, Peter Antonioni, Ronan Lyons – and historian Peter Frankopan all nudged me along, as did the monetary specialists Eric Lonergan and Paul McCulley, who read some of the later chapters. Their comments were invaluable. Special mention goes to Deirdre McCloskey, author of the magnificent *Bourgeois* trilogy, for her insights on Joyce, the Enlightenment and liberalism.

On the modernist period, I called on Declan Kiberd and an expert on James Joyce's years in Trieste, John McCourt. On money in Weimar Germany, Mark Jones was one of my guides. Angus Mitchell put me straight on Roger Casement, while Corinna Salvadori Lonergan schooled me in Dante. Lynda Mulvin's artistic suggestions were enormously helpful, and I am indebted to Nassim Nicholas Taleb for his comments.

My thanks also to friends who offered general advice as well as reading parts of early drafts, including Terence Ward and Idanna Pucci, who welcomed me in Florence, took me on a historical tour of the city and showed me the Pucci archives. Thanks to Conor McPherson for reading some early material and to Kathryn Osborne and Owen Medler for also perusing those early drafts. To Gula, the sage of Zlarin, for prompting me to explore the impact of the bicycle on society. A special thank you goes to Bono, who one evening in 2019, after lots of chat about the economy, said, 'You know what, David, you should write a book on money.'

As I said, I'm a social writer, so lots of the ideas in this book were inflicted on anyone who might listen, and in this regard, one of the greatest listeners I know is my podcast partner John Davis, who's heard it all before. The podcast allowed me to flesh out notions before committing them to paper. Cheers, John.

Finally, it all comes back to the kitchen table and, as this was partly a pandemic book, huge thanks go to my children – well, adults now – Lucy and Cal for keeping us all laughing throughout the lockdown, and for benchmarking progress on any other efforts, be they musical or college-related, against Dad's book, which was 'taking ages'. Thanks also to my mother, Alice, for never asking if that thing is finished yet.

ENDNOTES

INTRODUCTION

1 This quote was unearthed by economists Michael V. White and Kurth Schuler in 'Retrospectives: Who Said "Debauch the Currency": Keynes or Lenin?', *Journal of Economic Perspectives*, vol. 23, no. 2, Spring 2009, pp. 213–22.

2 Lawrence Malkin, *Krueger's Men: The Secret Nazi Counterfeit Plot and the Prisoners of Block 19*, New York: Little, Brown, 2006, p. 177.

3 Ibid., p. 62.

4 James C. Scott, *Against the Grain: A Deep History of the Earliest States*, New Haven: Yale University Press, 2017, Chapter 1.

1 MONEY IN THE BEGINNING

1 For a more detailed analysis about the possible function of the Ishango Bone, see Chapter 2 of George Gheverghese Joseph, *The Crest of the Peacock: Non-European Roots of Mathematics*, Princeton: Princeton University Press, 1991.

2 Scott, p. 38.

3 Jared Diamond, *Guns, Germs and Steel: A Short History of Everybody for the Last 13,000 Years*, London: Vintage, 1998, pp. 111–12.

4 Scott, p. 38.

5 Scott, pp. 3, 43, 46; Diamond, pp. 111, 142.

6 Robin Dunbar, *Human Evolution: Our Brains and Behavior*, New York: Oxford University Press, 2016.

7 David Graeber, *Debt: The First 5,000 Years*, London: Melville House, 2014, p. 39.

2   BY THE RIVERS OF BABYLON

1   It is also possible that Kushim was not an individual – Kushim might have referred to an institution or group of administrators. For more on Kushim, see Yuval Noah Harari, *Sapiens: A Brief History of Humankind*, London: Vintage, 2014, pp. 138–40.

2   Edward Chancellor, *The Price of Time: The Real Story of Interest*, London: Allen Lane, 2022, p. 10.

3   Graeber, p. 216.

4   Ibid., p. 39.

5   Ibid., p. 214.

6   Reuven Yaron, *The Laws of Eshnunna*, Jerusalem: Magnes Press, 1988, p. 20.

7   Aziz Emmanuel al-Zebari, 'Shekels: An Ancient Currency', Ishtar TV (11 August 2011).

8   English Standard Version Bible, Proverbs 11;1.

9   William N. Goetzmann, *Money Changes Everything: How Finance Made Civilization Possible*, Princeton: Princeton University Press, 2016, pp. 37–40.

10 For a more detailed analysis of the Drehem tablet, see the fascinating account in Chapter 2 of Goetzmann.

3   FROM CONTRACTS TO COINS

1   This famous myth is brilliantly retold by Stephen Fry, *Mythos: The Greek Myths Retold*, London: Michael Joseph, 2017, pp. 384–95.

2   Peter L. Bernstein, *The Power of Gold: The History of an Obsession*, New York: John Wiley & Sons, Inc., 2000, p. 27.

3   Ibid., p. 28.

4   Ibid.

5   For more on this, see Jack Weatherford, *The History of Money: From Sandstone to Cyberspace*, New York: Crown Publications, 1997, pp. 30–31.

6   Karl Polanyi, *The Great Transformation*, New York: Farrar & Rinehart, 1944, Chapter 4.

7   For more on the social impact of universal value, see Felix Martin, *Money: The Unauthorised Biography*, London: Vintage, 2015, Chapter 3.

8   Herodotus, *The Histories*, New York: Barnes & Noble Classics, 2004, Book I.94.

9   Ibid.

10 Bernstein, p. 30.

11 This time frame is generally accepted among scholars according to Susanne Berndt-Ersöz, 'The Chronology and Historical Context of Midas', *Historia: Zeitschrift für Alte Geschichte*, vol. 57, no. 1, 2008, pp. 1–37.

12 Bronze Age experts might argue that the Phoenicians have equal claim to being the first commercial empire.

13 For more on this, see Bernstein, Chapter 2.

4 MONEY AND THE GREEK MIND

1 Diogenes Laertius, *Lives of the Eminent Philosophers*, Oxford: Oxford University Press, 2018, Book 2, pp. 47–8.

2 Ivana Marková, *The Dialogical Mind: Common Sense and Ethics*, Cambridge: Cambridge University Press, 2016; William Keith Chambers Guthrie, *A History of Greek Philosophy: Volume 2, The Presocratic Tradition from Parmenides to Democritus*, Cambridge: Cambridge University Press, 1965; Robert L. Fowler, '*Mythos* and *Logos*', *Journal of Hellenic Studies*, vol. 131, 2011, pp. 45–66.

3 For a lively discussion on the difference between Homer and Xenophon, see Weatherford, Chapter 2.

4 Goetzmann, p. 73.

5 James Watson, 'The Origin of Metic Status at Athens', *Cambridge Classical Journal*, vol. 56, 2010, p. 262.

6 James M. Redfield, 'The Development of the Market in Archaic Greece' in A. J. H. Latham and B. L. Anderson (eds), *The Market in History* (Routledge Revivals), London: Routledge, 1986, pp. 45–6.

7 Goetzmann, p. 96.

8 Ibid., p. 87.

9 Weatherford, p. 38 fleshes out this point convincingly.

10 Xenophon, *Oeconomicus*, III.x.

11 Ibid., III.xiv.

12 Diogenes Laertius, Book 9: 50–53.

13 See more on the origins of the word democracy in Raphael Sealey, 'The Origins of "Demokratia"', *California Studies in Classical Antiquity*, vol. 6, 1973, pp. 253–95.

14 Alain Bresson, *The Making of the Ancient Greek Economy: Institutions, Markets, and Growth in the City-States*, Princeton: Princeton University Press, 2016, Part IV.

15 Quoted in ibid., p. 109.

16 Socrates, in Plato, *Phaedo*, 109b.

17 Athenaios, *Deipnosophistai* 14.640b–c, quoted in Ben Wilson, *Metropolis: A History of the City, Humankind's Greatest Invention*, London: Jonathan Cape, 2020, Chapter 3.

18 For more on Socrates and the agora, see Wilson, Chapter 3.

19 Bresson, p. 104.

20 François de Callataÿ, 'Money and Its Ideas: State Control and Military

Expenses' in Stefan Krmnicek (ed.), *A Cultural History of Money in Antiquity*, London: Bloomsbury Academic, 2019.

21 Ibid.

22 Ibid., p. 60.

5 THE EMPIRE OF CREDIT

1 Robert I. Curtis, 'Archaeological Evidence for Economic Life at Pompeii: A Survey', *Classical Outlook*, vol. 57, no. 5, 1980, pp. 98–102.

2 Ibid.

3 Pliny the Elder, *Historia Naturae*, 12.41. 'At the very lowest computation, India, the Seres, and the Arabian Peninsula, withdraw from our empire one hundred millions of sesterces every year – so dearly do we pay for our luxury and our women. How large a portion, too, I should like to know, of all these perfumes, really comes to the gods of heaven, and the deities of the shades below?'

4 Miko Flohr and Andrew Wilson, 'The Economy of Pompeii' in Miko Flohr and Andrew Wilson (eds), *The Economy of Pompeii* (Oxford Studies on the Roman Economy), Oxford: Oxford University Press, 2017, p. 452.

5 Duncan E. MacRae, 'Mercury and Materialism: Images of Mercury and the Tabernae of Pompeii' in John F. Miller and Jenny Strauss Clay (eds), *Tracking Hermes, Pursuing Mercury*, Oxford: Oxford University Press, 2019, p. 403.

6 Written on the tombstone of former slave Tiberius Claudius Secundus, quoted in Brian K. Harvey, *Daily Life in Ancient Rome: A Sourcebook*, Indianapolis: Focus, p. 256.

7 Marcus Tullius Cicero, *De Officiis*, 1.151.

8 Quoted in Edward Chancellor, *Devil Take the Hindmost: A History of Financial Speculation*, New York: Farrar, Straus and Giroux, 1999, p. 5.

9 More on this in Chapter 20.

10 Goetzmann, p. 132.

11 For more on this, see Walter Scheidel, *Escape from Rome: The Failure of Empire and the Road to Prosperity*, Princeton: Princeton University Press, 2019.

6 TWILIGHT OF THE FEUDAL ECONOMY

1 For more detail on this, see Peter Spufford, *Money and Its Use in Medieval Europe*, Cambridge: Cambridge University Press, 1988.

2 Ibid., pp. 9–14.

3 Bernstein, Chapter 3.

4 Bernstein, p. 86.

5 Recent studies using Danish data indicate that the introduction of the plough

'accounts for more than 40 percent of the increase in urbanisation experienced in the High Middle Ages in Denmark in particular and 15.7% in Europe more generally': Thomas Barnebeck Andersen, Peter Sandholt Jensen and Christian Volmar Skovsgaard, 'The Heavy Plough and the Agricultural Revolution in Medieval Europe', *EHES Working Papers in Economic History*, no. 70, 2014.

6   Spufford, Chapter 5.
7   For more on these developments, see ibid.
8   Ibid.

7 SARACEN MAGIC

1   Bartel L. van der Waerden, *A History of Algebra: From al-Khwārizmī to Emmy Noether*, Berlin: Springer, 2013, first published 1985.
2   Robert Kaplan, *The Nothing That Is: A Natural History of Zero*, Oxford: Oxford University Press, 1999.
3   Timothy James Smit, 'Commerce and Coexistence: Muslims in the Economy and Society of Norman Sicily', PhD dissertation submitted to the Faculty of the Graduate School of the University of Minnesota, 2009, Chapter 1.
4   For more on Fibonacci, see Goetzmann, Chapter 13, and Niall Ferguson, *The Ascent of Money: A Financial History of the World*, London: Penguin Press, 2008, Chapter 1.

8 DARKNESS INTO LIGHT

1   For more on Dante, there is plenty of material out there but I recommend Ian Thomson's brilliant, lively and informative account with some fine illustrations and literary references: *Dante's Divine Comedy: A Journey Without End*, London: Apollo, 2018.
2   Christopher Hibbert, *Florence: The Biography of a City*, London: Penguin, 1993, pp. 50–51.
3   Ibid.
4   For more on early European innovation, see David S. Landes, *The Wealth and Poverty of Nations: Why Some Are So Rich and Some So Poor*, New York: Abacus Press, 1998, pp. 45–59.
5   Thomson, p. 59.
6   Hibbert, pp. 50–51.
7   The currency wasn't entirely free-floating. The Florentines tried to manage the value of the florin to keep it stable. These days, such activities are known as central bank open market operations, whereby the central bank of the country with the powerful currency sells its own currency to moderate its

value. Despite the Florentines' efforts, relentless demand for the florin pushed its value up over time.

8 Iris Origo, *The Merchant of Prato: Daily Life in a Medieval Italian City*, London: Penguin, 2017, p. 69.

9 If you would like to read more about horizontal and vertical hierarchies, I recommend Niall Ferguson's *The Square and the Tower: History's Hidden Networks*, London: Allen Lane, 2017.

9 GOD'S PRINTER

1 Quoted in 'Pope Pius II's Scotland Visit in 1435 Explored', *The National*. The quote originates from Pope Pius II's 13-volume autobiography, the 'Commentaries'.

2 Neil MacGregor, *Germany: Memories of a Nation*, London: Allen Lane, 2014, Chapter 16.

3 Ibid., p. 290.

4 For more on Gutenberg's press, see Fran Rees, *Johannes Gutenberg: Inventor of the Printing Press*, Minneapolis: Compass Point, 2006.

5 Ibid.

6 Jeremiah Dittmar, 'Information Technology and Economic Change: The Impact of The Printing Press', *Quarterly Journal of Economics*, vol. 126, no. 3, 2011, pp. 1133–72.

7 Ibid.

8 Brendan Greeley, *The Almighty Dollar*, Penguin Random House, forthcoming.

9 Jared Rubin, 'Printing and Protestants: An Empirical Test of the Role of Printing in the Reformation', *Review of Economics and Statistics*, vol. 96, issue 2, 2014, pp. 270–86.

10 Ibid.

11 Camilla Townsend, *Fifth Sun: A New History of the Aztecs*, New York: Oxford University Press, 2019, p. 98.

12 Bernstein, p. 135.

10 INVISIBLE MONEY

1 Daniel Brook, *A History of Future Cities*, New York: W. W. Norton & Co., 2013, Chapter 1.

2 Simon Sebag Montefiore, *The Romanovs: 1613–1918*, London: Weidenfeld & Nicolson, 2017.

3 Chancellor, *Devil Take the Hindmost*, pp. 14–20.

4 Peter M. Garber, *Famous First Bubbles: The Fundamentals of Early Manias*, Cambridge, MA and London: MIT Press, 2001, p. 83.

5 Ibid.

11 THE FATHER OF MONETARY ECONOMICS

1 Joseph Schumpeter, *History of Economic Analysis*, London: Routledge, 1997, pp. 295–6, first published 1954.
2 Antoin E. Murphy, *John Law: Economic Theorist and Policy-Maker*, Oxford: Clarendon Press, 1997, p. 33.
3 Antoin E. Murphy (ed.), *John Law's 'Essay on a Land Bank'*, Dublin: Aeon, 1994.
4 Martin, p. 172.
5 Suzanne Vesta Kooloos, 'Magic Lanterns and Raree Shows: Metaphors of Financial Speculation during the Bubbles of 1720', *Early Popular Visual Culture*, vol. 20, no. 4, 2022, pp. 368–87.
6 Murphy, *John Law*, p. 303.

12 THE BISHOP OF MONEY

1 For more on Talleyrand, read Duff Cooper, *Talleyrand*, London: Vintage, 2010, first published 1932.
2 Andrew Dickson White, *Fiat Money Inflation in France*, New York: D. Appleton-Century Company, 1933, p. 59.
3 Alexandre Tuetey, *Publications relatives à la Révolution française. Répertoire général des sources manuscrites de l'histoire de Paris pendant la Révolution française*, 11 volumes, Paris: Commission des travaux historiques de la Ville de Paris, 1890–1914, vol. IV, Preface.
4 Bruce Berkowitz, *Playfair: The True Story of the British Secret Agent Who Changed How We See the World*, Fairfax, VA: George Mason University Press, 2018, Preface.

13 MONEY AND THE AMERICAN REPUBLIC

1 For more on Talleyrand's time in the US, see Hans Huth and Wilma Pugh (ed. & trans.), *Talleyrand in America as a Financial Promoter, 1794–96: Unpublished Letters and Memoirs*, New York: Da Capo Press, 1971, first published 1942.
2 Ron Chernow, *Alexander Hamilton*, New York: Penguin Press, 2004, p. 466.
3 Cooper, p. 270.
4 Chernow, p. 720.
5 Ibid., Chapter 11.
6 Ibid., Chapter 26.
7 Robert Nisbet, 'Many Tocquevilles', *American Scholar*, vol. 46, no. 1, 1977, pp. 59–75.
8 Ferguson, *The Ascent of Money*, p. 20.

9 Weatherford, p. 119.

10 Alexander Hamilton, *Report Relative to a Provision for the Support of Public Credit*, Treasury Department, 9 January 1790.

11 Chernow, Chapter 15.

12 Chernow, p. 466.

13 For more on the legacy of Hamilton, see Robert Scylla, Robert E. Wright and David J. Cowen, 'Alexander Hamilton, Central Banker: Crisis Management during the US Financial Panic of 1792', *Business History Review*, vol. 83, no. 1, A Special Issue on Scandals and Panics, 2009, pp. 61–86.

14 Alexis de Tocqueville, *Selected Letters on Politics and Society*, Berkeley: University of California Press, 1985, p. 39.

14 EMPIRICISM AND THE EVOLUTIONARY ECONOMY

1 Joseph Roth, *Weights and Measures*, London: Penguin Books, 2017.

2 The idea of decimalisation had been championed by the Russians as early as the 1550s. However, as Russia was seen as backward, enlightened American patriots couldn't be seen to be borrowing from Moscow or deploying the Russian term kopeks.

3 Jean-Baptiste Lamarck proposed – before Darwin – the idea that species evolved, but Darwin came up with the theory of natural selection and the idea that we all have a common ancestor.

4 Alfred Marshall, *Principles of Economics*, London: Macmillan, 1890, p. xiv.

5 For more on the perils of the overconfident forecaster, read Nassim Nicholas Taleb's *The Black Swan: The Impact of the Highly Improbable* (London: Allen Lane, 2007), and *Antifragile: Things That Gain from Disorder* (London: Penguin, 2012). Both books are classics packed with humorous anecdotes and a large dollop of wisdom.

15 MONEY ON TRIAL

1 Charles C. Mann, *1493: Uncovering the New World Columbus Created*, New York: Vintage, 2011, Chapter 7.

2 U.S. Patent Activity, Calendar Years 1790 to the Present, Table of Annual U.S. Patent Activity since 1970, n.d., https://www.uspto.gov/web/offices/ac/ido/oeip/taf/h_counts.htm, accessed 20 January 2024.

3 Albert Fishlow, 'Lessons from the Past: Capital Markets During the 19th Century and the Interwar Period', *International Organization*, vol. 39, no. 3, 1985, pp. 383–439.

4 Adam Hochschild, *King Leopold's Ghost: A Story of Greed, Terror and Heroism in Colonial Africa*, London: Macmillan, 1999, p. 92.

5 Félicien Cattier, *Étude sur la situation de l'État indépendant du Congo*, Brussels: Larcier, 1906, p. 193; Robert Harms, 'The World Abir Made: The Maringa-Lopori Basin, 1885–1903', *African Economic History*, no. 12, 1983, pp. 125–39.

6 Harms.

7 Ibid.

8 Hochschild, p. 199.

9 Ward to Morel, 1903, quoted on p. 103 of William Roger Louis, 'Roger Casement and the Congo', *The Journal of African History*, vol. 5, no. 1, 1964, pp. 99–120.

10 Ibid., p. 109.

11 Ibid., p. 114.

12 Ibid, p. 115.

13 Brian Inglis, *Roger Casement*, London: Hodder & Stoughton, 1973, p. 346.

14 Vladimir Ilyich Lenin, *Imperialism, The Highest Stage of Capitalism*, London: Wellred Books, 2019, first published 1916.

16 YELLOW BRICK ROAD

1 For more on the rise of American populism, see Thomas Frank, *The People, No: A Brief History of Anti-Populism*, New York: Metropolitan Books, 2020.

2 Weatherford, pp. 172–3.

3 R. H. Hooker, 'Farm Prices of Wheat and Maize in America, 1870–99', *Journal of the Royal Statistical Society*, vol. 63, no. 4, 1900, pp. 648–57.

4 Politically, a similar dynamic unfolded in the early twenty-first century. After the 2008 global financial crisis, a catastrophe caused almost exclusively by the overlending of bankers, many Western governments reacted with austerity, squeezing the living standards of those at the bottom who had nothing to do with the mess made by those at the top, leading to an explosion of populist and nativist political parties, ideas and movements. Centrist governments pitted the 'left behinds' against the 'out of touch', with populist results.

5 For more on this Populist movement, see Frank.

17 MODERNIST MONEY

1 For more on Joyce in Trieste, see *The Years of Bloom: James Joyce in Trieste, 1904–1920* by John McCourt, to whom I am indebted for his insights, particularly about Joyce's link to Baron Revoltella and Marx in Trieste. Dublin: Lilliput Press, 2000.

2 For more on early financial journalism, see Goetzmann, Chapter 23.

3 Ibid., p. 410.

4 For more on the mixed ethnicity of Trieste, see McCourt.

5 Karl Marx, 'The Maritime Commerce of Austria', https://marxengels. public-archive.net/en/ME0988en.html, accessed 20 January 2024.

6 U.S. Patent Activity, https://www.uspto.gov/web/offices/ac/ido/oeip/ taf/h_counts.htm, accessed 20 January 2024.

7 Richard Ellmann, *James Joyce*, New York: Oxford University Press, 1959, p. 300.

8 McCourt, p. 142.

9 Ellmann, p. 303.

10 To mangle Gramsci!

11 John Collison, @collision, Twitter, 25 May 2022.

12 For more on the link between bourgeois societies and economic vitality, see Deirdre McCloskey, *Bourgeois Dignity: Why Economics Can't Explain the Modern World*, Chicago: University of Chicago Press, 2010.

13 As Deirdre McCloskey has observed in *Bourgeois Equality: How Ideas, Not Capital or Institutions, Enriched the World* (Chicago: University of Chicago Press, 2017), it is a mistake to simply count the number of innovators in a given society, and this mistake has misdirected the academic study of entrepreneurship away from sociology and towards psychology.

14 As McCloskey argues in *Bourgeois Dignity* and further demonstrates in *Bourgeois Equality*, 'values like acceptance, dignity, hope and even love drive commercial activity'.

15 For a brilliant exploration of pre-war Vienna, see Florian Illies, *1913: The Year Before the Storm*, London: Clerkenwell Press, 2014.

18 INTO THE ABYSS

1 Adam Fergusson, *When Money Dies: The Nightmare of the Weimar Hyperinflation*, London: William Kimber & Co, 1975, p. 87.

2 Ibid., p. 88.

3 Liaquat Ahamed, *Lords of Finance: The Bankers Who Broke the World*, London: William Heinemann, 2009, p. 130.

4 Ibid.

5 Ibid.

6 Ibid.

7 For more on the German Genius, see Peter Watson, *The German Genius: Europe's Third Renaissance, the Second Scientific Revolution, and the Twentieth Century*, New York: HarperCollins, 2010.

8 For an excellent read on this period of German history, see Mark Jones, *1923: The Forgotten Crisis in the Year of Hitler's Coup*, London: Basic Books, 2023.

9 Ibid.
10 This is very well explained by Mark Jones in *1923*.
11 Quoted in J. Hoberman, 'An Evil Doctor Who Casts a Spell on Subjects and Viewers Alike', *New York Times*, 6 May 2020.
12 Gerald D. Feldman, *The Great Disorder: Politics, Economics, and Society in the German Inflation, 1914–1924*, New York: Oxford University Press, 1997.
13 Richard Radford, 'The Economic Organisation of a POW Camp', *Economica*, November 1945.
14 For more on this counterfeiting operation, see Malkin.

19 WHO CONTROLS MONEY?

1 Oded Galor, *The Journey of Humanity: The Origins of Wealth and Inequality*, London: Vintage, 2023, Chapter 7.
2 Iñaki Aldasoro and Torsten Ehlers, 'The Geography of Dollar Funding of Non-US Banks', *BIS Quarterly Review*, December 2018.

20 THE PSYCHOLOGY OF MONEY

1 These terms, hedge, speculative and Ponzi borrower, were coined by the economist Hyman Minsky.

21 THE EVOLUTION OF MONEY

1 Michael Lewis, *Going Infinite: The Rise and Fall of a New Tycoon*, New York: W. W. Norton & Co., 2023.
2 Matt Cooke, 'Driven by Purpose: 15 Years of M-Pesa's Evolution', McKinsey & Company, 29 June 2022.

A NOTE ON FURTHER READING

Dear Reader,

If you've got this far it means I've struck some sort of chord. Thanks so much for your time and your attention; I hope you've enjoyed the ride. The topic of money's central role in the development of our civilisation has fascinated me for many years, and any authority I might claim to have stems from working in the field of monetary economics and reading the work of experts. Much of what I read shaped the main arguments of this book, and sometimes my reading led me down little tributaries that could be equally as fascinating. Here I'll give you some notes on my sources, which you will hopefully find helpful if you want to research further into any of the subjects I've covered. And if not, who knows, you might simply find yourself with a spare moment, rummaging enjoyably through one of the following books.

I'll set the reading material out in chronological order, chapter by chapter, but before that, I should say that one book that influenced my thinking throughout the enterprise was *The Origin of Wealth: The Radical Remaking of Economics and What It Means for Business and Society* by **Eric D.**

Beinhocker, which looks at the economy as a complex system and sees wealth creation as an evolutionary process. This line of discussion crystallised what I'd been thinking for many years – that the economy is a dynamic, never static, always-on system. More importantly for our purposes, it got me thinking about money as a social technology that played a key role in the evolution of human society. If you are looking for an eye-opener, Beinhocker is well worth a few hours of your concentration.

Chapter 1 owes much of its flavour to *Against the Grain: A Deep History of the Earliest States* by **James C. Scott**, a wonderful book that outlines, among other things, the central role of fire as a technology in human development. This framework helped my thinking about money as a similarly critical technology. More than that, it gave me a sense of the great sweep of ancient history – prehistoric history, if you will – and the role of economics before economics was invented. No perspective on ancient money, debt and contracts is complete without reading **David Graeber**'s *Debt: The First 5,000 Years*, whose sections on debt in Druidic Ireland fascinated me. While not making it into the end text, this scholarly work was essential in my early reading for the sense it gave me of deep economic history.

My main companion in Chapter 2 was *Money Changes Everything: How Finance Made Civilization Possible* by **William N. Goetzmann**. Detailed, dense and delightful, Goetzmann's book was with me throughout the project generally, and his sections on Sumerian money are outstanding. Understanding the critical role of the rate of interest allowed me to dig a bit deeper in this chapter and my essential guide was the excellent *The Price of Time: The Real Story of Interest* by **Edward Chancellor**. Like everything Chancellor writes, this book is a pleasure from start to finish, and it gets us thinking about the rate of interest in ways that I'm sure most of us rarely do.

Once I got to the Lydians and Greeks in Chapters 3 and 4, **Peter L. Bernstein**'s wonderful *The Power of Gold: The History of an Obsession*, so brilliantly written and such fun to browse, was enormously incisive. Another book that steered me through the economics of Midas, Xenophon and co. is a real gem written by American anthropologist **Jack Weatherford**, *The History of Money*. For the non-economist, this is a gripping read, as it wrestles the story of money from my economist tribe's narrow focus and broadens it, giving it anthropological heft. Meanwhile, money's essential urbanness was reinforced to me by *Metropolis: A History of the City, Humankind's Greatest Invention* by **Ben Wilson.** If urbanism is your thing, this is one for you. Regarding the Romans and credit crises, my views were sharpened by *Manias, Panics, and Crashes: A History of Financial Crises* by **Charles P. Kindleberger**, a classic, pure and simple. In fact, on the issues of money, debt and cycles, anything by Kindleberger will reward. On the end of the Roman Empire, *Escape from Rome: The Failure of Empire and the Road to Prosperity* by **Walter Scheidel** is a brilliant source, as is his *The Great Leveler: Violence and the History of Inequality from the Stone Age to the Twenty-First Century*, on the persistence of inequality.

When I moved ahead to the medieval era and the pivotal introduction of Hindu/Arabic numerals and zero into Europe, a little gem of a book helped me enormously. *Zero: The Biography of a Dangerous Idea* by **Charles Seife** tells the story of how zero unlocked the power of mathematics in early-fourteenth-century Europe, after centuries in the relative darkness of Greek and then Roman rudimentary counting. For Dante's Florence, as well as **The Divine Comedy** itself, a wonderful friend was **Ian Thomson**'s **Dante's Divine Comedy: A Journey Without End**, a beautifully concise study of the literature, life, politics and intrigue of Florence in the late thirteenth and early fourteenth centuries. It you want to go deeper into the life of the emerging merchant class of the period, **The Merchant of Prato: Daily Life in a Medieval Italian City** by **Iris Origo** is an indispensable guide, and to get a feel for the pre-Renaissance world, **The Swerve: How the World Became Modern** by **Stephen Greenblatt** is obligatory. Niall Ferguson's **The Square and the Tower: Networks, Hierarchies and the Struggle for Global Power** on the power of networks wasn't ever far away in these chapters on the networks of the merchants, and it was particularly useful in examining the impact of Gutenberg's printing press.

As we move into the section called 'Revolutionary Money', my thinking has been influenced by the writings of **Deirdre McCloskey** and in particular her vital trilogy on bourgeois values. The first book in the series, **Bourgeois Dignity: Why Economics Can't Explain the Modern World**, opened my mind to an entirely new way of looking at the intersection between economics, culture and, believe it or not, social manners, and gave me a plausible basis from which to examine the role of money from the seventeenth century onwards. I'm also greatly indebted to the work of my old monetary economics professor and the biographer of John Law, Professor **Antoin E. Murphy** of Trinity College Dublin. His thoughts are particularly well laid out in **John Law: Economic Theorist and Policy-Maker**. Antoin's guidance on Chapters 11, 12 and 13 on Law, Talleyrand and Hamilton was indispensable.

For Chapter 14 on Darwin and the evolutionary economy,

my inspirations were **Beinhocker**'s *The Origin of Wealth* and *The Secret of Our Success: How Culture is Driving Human Evolution, Domesticating Our Species, and Making Us Smarter* by the evolutionary biologist **Joseph Henrich**. Henrich outlines how culture evolves and this triggered my thinking about money being a cultural concept as well as a financial notion. Chapter 15 was the product of lots of foraging from all over the place, but when things seemed a bit overwhelming – as they can during the writing of a big book – daily strolls down the road to the statue of Roger Casement in Dún Laoghaire invigorated me. If inanimate art has a role in kickstarting the efforts of the writer, this is a great example. Next time you are out this way, south of Dublin city, Casement's statue is worth a visit. 'Yellow Brick Road' and my thoughts about the role of money in the 1896 American presidential election were greatly enhanced by *The People, No: A Brief History of Anti-Populism* by **Thomas Frank**. Its description of nineteenth-century populism rescues this mass liberation movement from the current shorthand that regards populism as in some way atavistic. Frank reframes this movement and our understanding of the power of money and currency.

Chapter 17 features **James Joyce**. *Ulysses* was a joy to discover properly. I say properly because many Dubliners pretend to have read it, and this project forced me to actually do so, with bountiful rewards. Also essential reading for this chapter was **Declan Kiberd**'s *Ulysses and Us: The Art of Everyday Living*, as was **Richard Ellmann**'s biography **James Joyce**, and for details on Trieste, **John McCourt**'s *The Years of Bloom: James Joyce in Trieste, 1904–1920* was invaluable; it kept me focused on central Europe, its culture, its economy and its money. I read **Adam Fergusson**'s *When*

Money Dies: The Nightmare of the Weimar Hyperinflation a long time ago and came back to it for Chapter 18. This book and **Mark Jones'** *1923: The Forgotten Crisis in the Year of Hitler's Coup* offer wonderful background on the monetary chaos of Weimar, while Hitler's great forgery is brilliantly documented in **The Devil's Workshop: A Memoir of the Nazi Counterfeiting Operation** by **Adolf Burger**.

All through the months of writing, two books that share the title of this one, *Money* by **Eric Lonergan** and *Money: The Unauthorised Biography* by **Felix Martin**, were constantly open, and are now full of scribbled notes in their margins. Both will pay your time back in spades.

The full reading list is far more comprehensive than this inventory, but I hope drawing your attention to a few of these books that helped me will also help you.

PICTURE CREDITS

1. Royal Belgian Institute of Natural Sciences, Brussels; © 2015 GrandPalaisRmn (musée du Louvre)/Mathieu Rabeau
2. INTERFOTO/Alamy Stock Photo; ARTGEN/Alamy Stock Photo
3. Iberfoto/Bridgeman Images; Historic Collection/Alamy Stock Photo; public domain
4. Ahvenas/Atlas Obscura; The History Collection/Alamy Stock Photo
5. Robert Kawka/Alamy Stock Image; Ghigo Roli/Bridgeman Images
6. Bridgeman Images; The Picture Art Collection/Alamy Stock Photo; Raffaello Bencini/Bridgeman Images
7. North Wind Picture Archives/Alamy Stock Photo
8. The Unique Maps Co.; Art Media/Print Collector/Getty Images; Trustees of the British Museum
9. Imago/Kharbine Tapabor; Heritage Image Partnership Ltd/Alamy Stock Photo
10. Zoom Historical/Alamy Stock Image; Steve Stock/Alamy Stock Image; Everett Collection/Shutterstock
11. World History Archive/Alamy; Painters/Alamy Stock Photo
12. Punch; Pictorial Press Ltd/Alamy Stock Photo
13. ARCHIVIO GBB/Alamy Stock Photo; Penta Spring Limited/Alamy Stock Photo
14. World History Archive/Alamy Stock Photo; Albert Harlingue/Roger Viollet via Getty Images
15. © 2024 The Andy Warhol Foundation for the Visual Arts, Inc./Licensed by DACS, London/Photo © Christie's Images/Bridgeman Images; Martin Lubikowski
16. instagram.com/kimkardashian; Bloomberg/Getty Images

INDEX

abstraction/abstract thinking 4, 9, 15–16, 26, 32, 35, 48, 66, 123–4, 134, 168, 238
accountancy 30–1, 35, 99, 210, 243
Adamo, Maestro 120, 319, 353
Africa 10, 15–16, 60, 63, 96, 102, 126, 137, 159–60, 165, 167, 168, 244–8, 251–8, 276, 363–6
agora (Greek marketplace) 51–2
al-Khwarizmi 97
Alexander the Great 45, 53, 106, 217
Alexandria 71, 97, 115, 121
algebra 97, 98, 108, 109
algorithms 354–5
Alighieri, Dante 11, 112, 113, 119, 120, 124, 134, 319, 369; *The Divine Comedy* 112, 113, 120, 122–3, 141
Amazon rainforest 247, 253
American Revolution (1765–83) 10, 191, 196, 205–6, 208–22, 230, 231, 232. *See also* USA
Americas, Columbus discovers 153–5, 167–8
Amsterdam 159–60, 162, 164–7, 171, 173, 174, 175–6, 180, 194, 286, 291, 307, 330
Anglo-Belgian India Rubber and Exploration Company (ABIR) 252–4
animal spirits 180, 243
annuity 137, 139–40, 147, 163
antoninianus 76–7
Aquinas, Thomas 123

Arabs 102, 107, 131, 219; Arabic mathematics/numerals ('Saracen magic') 96–101, 104–8, 111
Aristotle 49, 99, 171
Artaxerxes II, King 44
Arte della Lana (wool weavers' guild) 130
artisan 38, 47, 64, 66, 83, 91, 92, 93, 94, 116, 139, 140, 146, 148–9, 151, 160, 175
assets 22, 27, 66, 71, 152, 181, 190, 197
    asset-backed security 202
    banks and 331–2, 333, 334, 338, 339, 346
    credit cycle and 267–8, 270
    cryptocurrency and 351, 353, 356–61
    First World War and 297–8
    Global Financial Crisis (2008) and 338, 339, 341, 343, 346, 347, 348–50
    gossip and 171–2
    paper money and 196
    Weimar Republic and 306
assignat 200–2, 204, 206, 207, 211, 319
Atatürk, Kemal 104
Athens 44, 46–7, 49–53, 54, 59, 114–15
Atlantic Ocean 137, 153, 159, 268, 269, 282
Augustus, Emperor 58, 75, 232
Austrian Empire 229–30
Aztec Empire 154–5

Babylonians 32, 34, 100, 195
Baghdad 28, 101

balance sheets 11, 22, 70, 71, 97, 98,
    110–12, 126, 197, 253, 272, 324,
    329–32, 341–2, 343, 345, 346, 347,
    348–9, 352
Bank of England 3, 164, 167, 176, 182,
    221, 273, 308, 311, 312, 313
Bank of Louisiana 270
banks/banking
    banking industry, evolution of 243–4
    central banks see central banks
    crashes see individual crash name
    credit markets and 267–8
    Dutch Empire and 161, 163, 164–7,
        175–6, 178
    Florence, emergence of in 110, 117,
        122, 123, 124, 129–34, 142–3,
        144, 286, 329
    interbank loan market 347
    Law/revolutionary France and 180–5,
        187–8, 190, 194, 195, 197, 207
    merchant banker 109–10, 115, 131–4,
        136, 144, 329
    middle class and 250
    offshore banks 335
    Roman 61, 70, 71, 72, 77
    USA and 221, 222, 223, 273, 274, 277
    See also individual type of bank
Bankman-Fried, Sam 351–3, 355, 357
bankruptcy 71, 72, 119, 146, 152, 175,
    182, 220, 223, 271, 289, 325, 347
Barings 273
barley 22, 23–4, 26, 27, 28
barter 36, 83, 154
base numbers 29–30
Baum, L. Frank: The Wizard of Oz 263–5,
    269, 277–8
Bear Stearns, collapse of (2008) 11, 337,
    347
beeswax 97–8
Bejaia 97–8, 108
Belgian Congo 245–8, 251–8, 259
Berlin Conference on Africa (1884–1885)
    251
Bernanke, Ben 72
bicycle 244, 246–50, 251, 369
bill of exchange 131
billets d'état 184
bitcoin 354–6, 358–60, 363, 364
Black Death 96, 115, 116, 121–2, 133
black market 203, 307, 312–13

blockchain 354–6
Boccaccio, Giovanni 114; Decameron 115
Boer War (1899–1902) 258
Bonaparte, Napoleon 2, 37, 41, 192–3,
    198, 206, 209, 210, 231
bonds
    American Civil War and 270, 271
    American Revolution and 221, 223
    assignat 200–2, 204, 206, 207, 211,
        319
    bond markets 155, 193–4, 221, 281–2,
        363
    bond yield 334
    cryptocurrencies and 357, 363
    First World War/Weimar Republic and
        295, 299, 306
    Holland and 165–6, 168–70, 176, 194
    junk bond 136
    municipal bonds 140, 147
    perpetual bond 168–70, 176, 194
    quantitative easing and 349–50
    treasury bonds 332–4, 349–50
    West Germany and 323
bookkeeping 10, 98
    double-entry 110–12, 126, 329–30
boom-bust cycles 172, 175
bottom-up economy 36–7, 41, 54, 364
Brahmins, central bank 326–7, 329, 348–9,
    352
brain size 20
Britain 179, 204
    Barings bailout 273–4
    Black Wednesday 324–5
    central bank see Bank of England
    colonialism 251–2, 53, 255–8
    dirty tricks employed to destroy
        foreign currency 205–6
    First World War and see First World
        War
    General Election (1918) 299
    Glorious Revolution 176
    India and 239–41
    industrial revolution and 193–4
    Second World War and see Second
        World War
    South Sea Bubble 188, 189, 191, 193,
        234, 352
British East India Company 253
Bryan, William Jennings 264, 269, 275,
    277

budget deficit 202, 274, 275, 300, 320, 342, 361–2
bull trap 344
Bundesbank 324
Burke, Edmund 231
Burr, Aaron 210, 225
business papers 282
Byzantine Empire 82–5, 90, 102, 104, 105, 106–7

California gold rush 266, 270, 276
Calonne, Charles Alexandre de 197–8
Calvinists 153, 160, 167, 194
candles 97–8, 139
capital
    central bankers and 327, 333
    cryptocurrency and 357
    Eurodollar market and 335
    evolutionary economy and 241–2
    Florentine bankers and 122, 129, 130
    French Revolution and 196, 201
    globalisation and 261
    Holland and 168–9, 171, 173, 176
    industrial revolution and 193, 194
    Mississippi Company and 184, 186
    origins of market for 31, 32
    perpetual bond and 168–9
    printing press and 146, 147, 148
    Romans and 61, 66, 70
    Suez Canal and 279
    USA and 221, 223
    venture capital 252
capitalism 2, 61, 68, 148, 166, 212, 223, 261, 282
Carmack, George 276
carried interest 67–8
Casement, Roger 11, 246, 254, 255–62
cathedrals 85–6, 97, 107, 110, 151, 351
Catholic Church 4, 93, 94, 108–9, 115, 119, 123, 124, 130, 132–3, 136, 137, 138, 139, 141–2, 149, 150, 151, 152, 162, 193, 195, 197–8, 199, 283, 292, 322
central bank 4, 22, 72, 164, 174, 178, 182, 190, 207, 221–3, 267–8, 277, 300, 301, 303, 310, 322–36, 348, 349, 350, 353, 358, 362. *See also individual central bank name*
Central Bank of Ireland 4
cheque 30, 130, 362

China 18, 21, 39, 149, 153, 163–4, 180–1, 280, 291, 319, 327–8, 342
Christianity 55–6, 63, 85, 90, 98, 99–101, 102, 104, 107, 137, 144, 153, 283, 292
Church, Angelica 206
Cicero: *De Officiis* 65
cinema 245, 263–5, 269, 277–8, 287–90, 304
City of London 117, 167, 251
Claman, Liz 337, 347
Clarion Cycle Club 249
Clarion, The 249
Claudine dynasty 64
Clearchus 44
Cleisthenes 49
Cleveland, Grover 274
clock 94, 95
coinage
    Christianity and 56
    Coinage Act, US (1792) 211–12, 230
    credit and 72–4
    crypto *see* cryptocurrency
    debasing 74–8, 120, 152, 207, 353
    Florence/florin 114–15, 117–18, 120–3, 129, 133, 134, 163, 164, 319
    Germany, Middle Ages 89–91, 95, 137, 150
    introduction of Lydian gold 11, 32, 34–43, 45, 46, 47–8, 50, 51, 53–4, 55, 56, 155, 321, 329
    Roman 60, 62, 66, 72, 73–7, 83, 353
    Sicily and 97, 106
    silver dollar 219–20, 266, 273
    See also individual coin name
Colbert, Jean 194
collective intelligence 84
Collison, John 291
colonialism 6, 155, 165, 248, 251, 253, 259, 260–2
Columbus, Christopher 137, 153, 167
commercial banks 4, 329–35, 353, 360, 364
commercial law 133, 329
commodities 35, 47, 78, 122, 261, 267, 319
commodity money 329
Compagnie d'Occident (Company of the West) 184–5
Conan Doyle, Arthur 257, 259

Congo Free State 252–9, 261, 262
Congo Reform Association 257–8
Congo River 15, 246, 247, 251
Congress of Vienna (1814) 193
Connecticut Compromise 214
Conrad, Joseph: *Heart of Darkness* 245–6
Constitution, US 213–15, 218
Constitutional Convention (1787),
    Philadelphia 214
Continental currency 205, 211, 213, 220,
    319
contracts 23, 30, 32, 34, 61, 67, 68, 126,
    133, 139, 173, 186, 201, 329, 330
cooking 16–17
copper 27, 35, 54, 75, 83, 120, 122, 163,
    164, 180, 292
Cortés, Hernán 153–4
counterfeiting/forgery 1–3, 11, 34, 41,
    120–3, 205, 211, 260, 304, 307–13,
    319, 353, 354
counting, origins of 10, 15–16
Coxey, James 274
creativity 6, 66, 161, 194, 243, 286, 288,
    290, 291–3
credit 4, 10, 15, 22
    balance sheets and 342
    credit card 342, 356
    credit crises/credit crunch 69–75, 150,
        273–4, 277, 346
    credit cycle 69–73, 267–8, 310, 336,
        353
    credit ratings 338–9
    Florentine economy and 130–4,
        329–30
    letter of credit 130–1, 133
    M-Pesa and *see* M-Pesa
    Roman Empire and 61–2, 66–75,
        77–8, 83, 84
Croesus, King 37, 40–1
Crusades 94, 101–2, 105, 107, 144
cryptocurrency 11, 313, 351–65
cuneiform 26, 29, 31
currency
    cryptocurrency 11, 313, 351–65
    debasing 1, 74–8, 120, 152, 207, 353
    decimalised 230
    devaluation 133, 268, 317–18, 324,
        325–6, 359
    electronic 332–3
    faith in 322–6

fiat 178, 318, 319, 321, 325, 327–9,
    353, 358, 359
finance and 328–30
gold and *see* gold
inflation and *see* inflation
open market operations 301
reserve currency 118, 121, 122, 311,
    332, 362
See also individual currency name
Cyrus the Younger 44

Dark Ages 81–95
Darwin, Charles 11, 233–9, 242–3, 279,
    320
Datini, Francesco di Marco 124–6, 131,
    132–3, 284
debt
    ceilings 361–2
    French national 182, 184, 184, 186,
        187, 190, 197, 199–200, 201, 202,
        203, 319
    Germany/Weimar and 297–8, 300
    Global Financial Crisis (2008) and 338,
        340, 342, 343, 345–6, 347, 349
    Gutenberg and 135–6
    Mesopotamia and 22, 24, 27, 29, 30,
        34, 35
    MMT and 361–2
    Roman Empire and 61, 70, 71, 72, 73–4
    USA national 220–3, 268, 272, 273,
        320, 338
decimalisation 229–33
default 54, 74, 135, 139, 140, 169, 200,
    221, 236, 273, 298, 325, 346
deflation 74, 263, 264, 267, 276, 296,
    310, 321, 322
Delhi, Old 5, 240–1
democracy 10, 49–51, 53, 114, 115, 118,
    119, 161, 167, 214, 231, 269, 273,
    292, 301, 354
Democratic Republic of Congo 366
Democratic Party 274, 275, 276;
    Democratic National Convention
    (1896) 269–70, 275, 277
denarius 74, 76
deutschmark 207, 323, 324
devaluation 133, 268, 317–18, 324,
    325–6, 359
digital currency 356, 358. *See also*
    cryptocurrency

Diocletian, Emperor 77
Diogenes 44
Dionysus 33, 34
Disney, Walt 277
dix 270
dollar, United States 9, 41, 74, 121, 122,
    196, 207, 208, 210, 302–4
    birth of 211–12, 215, 217–20, 221
    decimalised currency 230
    digital payment systems and 355–6
    dix and 270
    Eurodollar market and *see* Eurodollar
        market
    Gold Standard and 266–76, 320–1
    reserve currency 332–3
domestication 8, 16, 19, 21, 240
Dr Mabuse, the Gambler 304
drachma 28, 47, 50
Drehem tablet 31
Dublin 11, 89, 125, 246, 260, 262, 284–5,
    288–9, 292, 351–2, 365
Dunbar, Robin 20
Dundas, Henry 205–6
Dunlop Industries 247–8
Dunlop, John Boyd 246–8, 250–2, 257,
    262
Dutch Republic 10, 121, 137, 155, 163,
    178, 181, 184, 185, 194, 221, 252,
    253, 261, 286, 329–30
    Dutch East India Company (VOC) and
        166, 171, 176, 184, 253
    economic miracle in 164–71, 176, 182
    Peter the Great and 159–62
    Tulipmania (*Tulpenwoerde*) 173–6, 339, 340

Ebusus 60
economics
    basis of 45, 46
    classical economics 172–3, 339–40
    economy, concept of 237–9
    economists 4–6, 11
    monetary economics 164, 177–8, 195,
        323, 365–6, 368
    network economics 126–7, 133
    word 45
Economist, The 282
Edict of Tolerance 283
Egoist, The 284–5
Egypt 53, 60, 71, 84, 96, 101, 105, 279,
    280–1

Einstein, Albert 285, 286, 294
electromagnetic waves 286–7
electronic currency 332–3
electrum/white gold 34, 39
empiricism 100, 111, 232, 238
Enlightenment 134, 198
entrepreneur 116, 130, 135, 150, 183,
    186, 240, 241, 242, 244, 280, 287–91,
    292
equilibrium 173, 340
Eubulus 51–2
euro 28, 41, 217, 334, 362
Eurodollar market 334–6, 360
European Central Bank 327, 362
evolution, theory of 11, 17, 19–20, 163,
    234, 237, 238–9, 241–3, 244, 365,
    366
    evolutionary economy 241–3
exchange rate 137, 164, 318, 323–5
exchange value 48

farming/agriculture 7–8, 18, 20, 22, 27,
    47, 81, 85–92, 94, 96, 104, 129, 138,
    139, 154, 201–2, 203, 215–16, 236,
    263–4, 271, 272–5, 277, 287, 306,
    309, 364
Federalist Papers, The 215
feudal system 9, 81, 85–6, 111, 114, 115,
    129, 134, 167, 291
fiat money 178, 318, 319, 321, 325,
    327–9, 353, 358, 359
Fibonacci 11, 96–8, 108, 109, 110–12,
    123, 124, 125, 126
finance 129, 132, 133, 134, 138, 169, 175,
    212, 220, 261, 282
Fiorelli, Giuseppe 59
fire 8, 11–12, 16–18, 22
First World War (1914–18) 261, 276–7,
    297–301, 320
Florence 10, 110–34, 144, 146, 164,
    167–9, 252, 286, 291, 319, 329–30,
    331
florin 114–15, 117–18, 120–3, 129, 133,
    134, 163, 164, 319
follaro 97, 106
Force Publique 254–5
foreign investment 251
forgery 1–3, 11, 34, 41, 120–3, 205, 211,
    260, 304, 307–13, 319, 353, 354
Fox, Charles James 209

Fox News 11, 337, 347
fractional reserve banking 131, 143
franc 323
France 18, 29, 83, 137, 143, 167, 169,
    179, 180
    assignat and 200–2, 204, 206, 207, 211,
        319
    decimalisation in 231–2
    French Revolution (1789) 10, 191,
        192, 193, 195–208, 209, 213, 216,
        231–2, 319–20
    Law and financial innovation in
        177–91, 193, 194, 196–7, 207, 319
    Talleyrand and financial innovation in
        see Talleyrand-Périgord, bishop
        Charles-Maurice de
free time 88, 160–1
French Louisiana 184
Freud, Sigmund 285, 286
FTX 351, 352, 355
Fugger banking family 150

'gales of creative destruction' 243, 286
Gallienus, Emperor 75–7
gambling 52, 170, 173, 177, 183, 243,
    303, 304, 357–8
General Bank 182–3, 185
Genoa 97, 101, 118, 126, 131
George I, King 189
Germany 137
    Berlin Wall, fall of (11 November
        1989) 324
    coinage in 88–90, 94–5, 219
    Luther/Reformation and see Luther,
        Martin
    patents in 287
    printing press and see printing press
    reunification of (1990) 324
    wars and see individual war name
    Weimar Republic 1, 205, 294–307
    West Germany 323–4
glasses, optical 116, 144, 145
global financial crises
    (1892) 273–4
    (2008) 71, 72, 267–8, 337–50
globalisation 115, 248, 250, 260, 261, 327
Godolphin, Lord 180, 182
gold 27
    America/USA and 218, 219, 220, 222,
        263–78, 297, 320–2, 324–5, 328

crypto and 358
fiat money and 178, 180, 181, 182,
    183, 189, 190, 201, 207, 319
florin and 114–15, 117–18, 120, 121,
    132, 134, 135, 319
Gold Standard 263–9, 272, 273–8,
    297, 320–2, 324–5, 328
Lydian gold coins, introduction of
    33–41, 47, 83, 163, 319, 329
New World and 153, 155
Roman 60, 62, 66, 70–1, 73–5
Weimar Republic and 300, 301
Goslar 88–9
gossip 17, 52, 57, 91, 171–2, 184, 347
Gould, Jay 272
Gournay, Vincent de 198
grains 19, 28
Great Depression (1929–39) 70–1, 276–7,
    320
Greece 10, 11–12, 23, 28, 81, 99, 100,
    102, 104, 105–7, 327
Greek Empire, finance and 44–56, 63, 84,
    126, 163, 319
    Lydian gold and 34–5, 37–8, 40, 43,
        84
greenbacks 270
guilds 92, 113–14, 115, 116–17, 119, 121,
    128, 130, 151
guilder 121, 165, 171, 174, 178
Gutenberg, Johannes 11, 135–43, 144–51,
    162, 242, 308
Gyges, King 40

Hamilton, Alexander 11, 206–8, 209–25,
    230, 266, 273, 298, 368
hard thinking 46, 48
hedge borrower 344
hedge exchange-rate risk 317–18
Hemingway, Ernest 294–6, 302
Henry VIII, King 152, 199
Herodotus 37–8, 41, 49
Hertz, Heinrich 286–7
Himmler, Heinrich 312
Hindu-Arabic numerals 98, 99, 102, 104,
    111
Hippocrates of Kos 49
Hijri calendar, Islamic 107
Hitler, Adolf 1–3, 293, 306–7, 310,
    311–13, 353
Holland. See Dutch Republic

Holy Roman Empire 114, 127, 149
Homer 45, 46
Houblon, John 167
housing market 171, 173, 174, 267–8,
  301, 324–5, 331–2, 337–9, 349
Huguenots 167
Hundred Years' War (1337–1453) 137
hunter-gatherers 8, 16, 17, 19, 20, 21
hyperinflation 1, 75–8, 196, 203, 207, 220,
  222, 295, 303, 304, 305–6, 311, 320,
  323, 359

Ibn al-Hawwàs, Emir of Agrigento and
  Castrogiovanni 102–3
Ibn Thumna, Emir of Syracuse and Catania
  102–3
income
  controls 203
  per head 87, 222, 328
India 39, 60, 99, 101, 137, 252, 280, 282,
  309
  Hindu-Arabic numerals 98, 99, 102,
    104, 111
  independence (1947) 260
  Indian Mutiny (1857) 239–40
indulgence, letter of 141–3, 150, 152
Industrial Revolution 148, 193, 222,
  232–3, 237–8, 248
inequality 56, 267, 327–8, 350
inflation 2, 3, 77–8, 182, 189, 196, 203–4,
  271, 296, 300, 306, 310, 318, 322–5,
  342, 351, 359, 362–3. *See also*
  hyperinflation
innovation. *See individual innovation name*
insurance 61, 188, 193–4, 290
interbank loan market 347
interest rates 5–6, 23, 24, 25, 69, 70, 77,
  108–9, 123, 139–40, 171, 194,
  199–200, 250, 268, 273, 297, 324–5,
  334–6, 338, 342–3, 349–52
International Monetary Fund 207
investment 24–5, 31
  assignat and *see assignat*
  commercial class of investor 244
  Dutch Empire and 165–6, 171, 172,
    173–6
  Florence and 122, 130
  foreign investment out of Europe,
    colonialism and 251–3
  investment banking 3, 326

Law and 185–6, 190, 193–4
  momentum investor 172, 340–1
  printing press and 147
  public company and 252–3
  Roman 66–7, 71
  SPACs 188–9
  value investor 172, 340–1, 348
Ireland 89, 91, 103, 173, 224, 234, 236–7,
  259–62, 288–90, 317–18, 324–6,
  337–8
Ishango Bone 15–16, 27, 246, 366
Ishnuna Code of Law 27–8
Islam 82, 84, 98, 106–7
Ismail Pasha, khedive of Egypt 279
'issuer' of money 41, 122, 163, 333,
  357–8

Jay, John 215
Jefferson, Thomas 210, 212–13, 224
Jesus 11, 20, 31, 57, 90
Jews 62, 102, 104, 105, 106, 167, 229,
  269, 283, 292, 299, 302, 307, 308,
  310, 311
jizya model 105
Joyce, Eva 288
Joyce, James 11, 45, 113, 279–81, 284–5,
  287–90, 292–3, 294, 298–300, 369
'just price' 123

Kelton, Stephanie 361
Kenya 364–6
Keynes, John Maynard 190, 243, 277, 349
Krueger, Hans 311, 312
Kushim 11, 23–6, 29, 32, 36, 129, 329

Lapo, Ser 125
'laissez-faire, laissez-passer' ('freedom to
  produce and freedom to trade') 198
Lascaux cave paintings 18
Latin 104, 106, 117, 151, 230, 318
Laurion 47
Law, John 177–91, 193, 194, 196–7, 207,
  319
League of Florentine Bankers 117
ledger 29, 110, 111, 125, 355
lender of last resort 72, 222, 298, 347
Lenin, Vladimir 1–2, 3, 5, 106, 195, 261
Leonardo of Pisa/Fibonacci 11, 96–8, 108,
  109, 110–12, 123, 124, 125, 126; *Liber
  Abaci*, the Book of Calculations 108

Leopold II, King 246, 251–2, 254, 255, 256, 258
Levi, Primo: *If This Is a Man* 113
Lewis, Michael: *Going Infinite* 351–2
liabilities 331–2, 346
liquidity 71, 72, 121, 122, 139, 140, 222, 349
literacy 48, 147, 148, 162, 328
loans 23, 25, 30, 61, 70, 72, 121, 131–7, 139, 140, 168, 173, 207, 270, 271, 273, 297, 298, 330, 331–2, 335, 338–9, 341, 343, 346–7, 364–5
Loi du Maximum Général 204
London 1, 63, 83, 91, 115, 117, 121, 167, 175–6, 178–80, 188, 191, 194, 203, 206, 211, 218, 240, 246, 251, 252, 255, 256–8, 259–60, 273, 285, 297, 298, 302, 335
Louis XIV, King 182, 194
Louis XVI, King 197, 206
Love-Letters Between a certain late Nobleman and the famous Mr. Wilson discovering the true History of the Rise and surprising Grandeur of that celebrated Beau 179
Luther, Martin 149–53, 176
Lydian Empire 34, 35, 36–43, 46, 47, 50, 83, 84, 126, 155, 163, 319, 321, 329

M-Pesa 364–6
MacDonald, Major General Hector 256
Machiavelli, Niccolò 112, 118
Madison, James 212, 214–15
Mainz 135, 136, 142, 146, 147, 150, 242, 291
Mainz, Archbishop of 136, 142, 150
Malakert, Josephine 303
Malaya 258, 311
Malthus, Thomas 87, 235–7
margin financing 170, 341
Maringa-Lopori basin 252, 253
mark, German 299, 302
market economy 37, 56, 91, 309
markets 51–2, 55, 58, 60, 61, 89, 92, 94, 96, 129, 147, 151
Marshall, Alfred 238–9
Marshall Plan 271, 334
Marx, Karl 123, 283; *Das Kapital* 282
Marxism 195, 261, 293
mass card 142
mathematics 3, 8, 97–101, 104, 106, 108,

110–12, 124, 125, 126, 134, 154, 180, 282, 285, 311
Mauss, Marcel 103
MBAs 30, 111–12
McKinley, William 275
Medici family 117, 133
mental arithmetic 97
merchant 6, 22, 27, 47, 66, 67
  Arab 96–8, 104, 106
  Dutch Republic and 164, 165–8, 170, 173–4, 175, 176, 329–30
  Florence and 110–12, 114, 115, 116, 117–20, 123–38, 144, 168–9, 252, 286, 329
  merchant banker 109–10, 115, 131–4, 136, 144, 329
  Middle Ages and 92–3, 96–8, 104, 106, 108–10, 112, 114, 115, 116, 117–20, 123–38, 141, 144, 147–8, 155, 159, 161, 163, 164
  printing and 147–8
  Roman 77–8
  Trieste and 281, 283, 284
Mercury (god) 60–2, 281
Mesopotamia 10, 23, 27, 29, 30, 31, 36, 129
Messina, Sicily 96, 105, 108
metric system 232
Midas 33–4
Middle Ages 10, 79–155
middle classes 191, 202, 243–4, 248–9, 250–1, 271, 281, 306
migration 52, 90–1, 168, 224, 234, 236–7, 266, 269, 272, 283, 286
mint 3, 37, 53, 72, 75, 89, 128, 132, 134, 142, 218, 219, 355
Mirabeau, Comte de 200
Mississippi Company 185–91
Moctezuma II, Emperor of the Aztecs 154
modern monetary theory (MMT) 361–3
modernism 11, 212, 284, 285, 287, 294, 369
moneta di piccoli 118
monetary policy 265, 323, 325, 350
moneychanging 39–40, 61, 96, 117, 129
moneylenders 20, 61, 70, 109, 114, 123, 129, 137, 139, 152
money supply 53, 70, 74, 181, 182, 275, 310, 313, 321, 322, 330, 334, 335
monoculture 242

Morel, E. D. 255, 257, 258
mortgage 5–6, 138–9, 174, 330, 331, 334, 336, 346
Muslims 102, 104–7, 144
Mussolini, Benito 294, 313

Napoleonic Wars (1803–15) 231
national goods (*les biens nationaux*) 200
natural selection, theory of 234, 235, 237, 238
Nehru, Jawaharlal 260
Nero, Emperor 11, 75, 353
network economics 126–7, 133
New Exchange 170
New Orleans 270
New World 111, 137, 155, 182–5
New York 11, 212, 215, 225, 282, 298, 337, 343, 352
Newnham College 249
Newton, Isaac 234, 352
Nixon, Richard 320–1
Nobel Prize 294, 299
Normans 93, 94, 96, 97, 101–7
North, Colonel John Thomas 252
Norton, Rictor 179
numerals 29–30, 96–101, 104–8, 111

Odessa 268, 307
olive oil 42, 47
open market operations 301
opportunity cost 25, 109
Origo, Iris: *The Merchant of Prato* 124–5
Ottoman Empire 104, 137, 144, 160, 173, 279

Pacioli, Luca 110, 126
Palermo, Sicily 105–7
pamphlets 147–8, 151, 152, 153, 162, 179, 191, 215, 225, 257, 273
pandemics 19, 276, 294, 362, 368, 369–70
Pankhurst family 249
paper money 155, 163–4, 176, 180–3, 186, 190, 196–7, 203, 205, 213, 220, 265, 270, 319, 320, 358
paradox of aggregation 344–5
patents 135, 247, 250, 283, 287
pawnbroking 117, 129, 138, 163–4, 180–1
Peloponnesian War (431–404 BC) 44, 53
Persia 34, 39, 105, 106

Persian Empire 40, 44, 45, 46, 47, 49, 84, 100–1
personal liberty 169–70
personal responsibility 50
Peter the Great, Tsar of Russia 11, 159–62, 164, 168, 170, 175, 243
Pharae 54
Philippe Duc d'Orléans 182
Phocylides of Miletus 51
Phoenicians 84, 102
Phrygia 33
Pienza 144
Pitt the Younger, William 205
Pius II, Pope 143–5
Pius VII, Pope 206
Playfair, William 205–6
Pliny the Elder 60
Pliny the Younger 58, 60
plough 7, 82, 86–9, 93, 94–5, 101, 102, 131, 182
pneumatic rubber tyre 246–8, 254, 257
polis 50–1
political, money as 327
Polybius 67
Pompeii 57–61
Ponzi borrower 343, 344, 345
Pope 249–50
population size 19–20, 21, 46, 87–8, 93, 95, 101–2, 114, 169, 195, 214, 233–7, 254, 266
populism 263–4, 350
Populist Party 263, 273–7, 320, 350
port-merchant 284
Portugal 137, 159, 167
positive checks 235–7
Potosí mine, Peru 219
Pound, Ezra 284
poverty 55, 138, 153, 242, 271, 290, 328, 365
precision, notion of 111
prices
    asset price meltdown 338–450
    bottom-up economy and 36
    bubbles *see individual bubble name*
    classical economics and 172–3
    controls 77, 203–4
    credit and 73
    gold and 267–8, 271, 272, 276, 321–2
    just price 123–4
    law of one price 42

Mesopotamia and 23–8
MMT and 362
reserve currency and 122
printing, invention of 135–55, 162–4, 242, 358
prisoners' economy 309–10
productivity 28, 87, 89, 94, 116, 117, 147–8, 232, 366
Prometheus 11, 23
property developers 343
property rights 29
Protagoras of Samos 49
Protestantism 151–3, 159
Proxenus 44
public share company 252–3
publicani 66
publicly traded company 250–1
Pucci Palace, Florence 110
pull story 331, 336
Punic Wars (264–146 BC) 53, 102
push story 331, 336
putting out system 129, 364–5

quantitative easing 72, 190, 349–50, 351
Quesnay, François 198

Radford, Richard 308–10
railway companies 234, 243, 246, 272, 279, 283, 303
Rathenau, Walther 302
reals 219
recession 74, 325, 340, 348–9
reciprocity 36, 47–8
reckoning schools 111–12, 124
Red Cross 308, 309, 310
Reformation 10, 134, 162–3, 242
refugees 159, 167, 237, 307
Renaissance 10, 98, 113, 114, 118, 124, 128, 134, 154, 168, 286
rents 36, 85, 139, 233, 267, 350
reparations 298–302, 320
Republican Party, US 213, 224, 271, 273, 274, 275, 276
reserve currency 118, 121, 122, 311, 332, 362
Revoltella, Pasquale 280–1, 284; 'The Co-participation of Austria in World Trade' 281
Reynolds, Maria 224–5
Robespierre, Maximilien de 203, 204, 210

Roger I, Grand Count of Sicily 102, 103–4
Roger II, Grand Count of Sicily 104, 105, 106–7
Roman Empire 10, 40, 53, 54, 83, 84, 86, 87, 88, 97, 102, 107, 136, 148, 149, 151, 163, 191, 232, 234, 252, 261, 319
credit and 57–78
fall of 77–8
Roman numerals 104
Rome 59–60, 62–3, 65, 66, 67–9, 71–8, 92, 104, 109, 114, 118, 150, 294
Roosevelt, Franklin Delano 274, 277, 320
Roth, Joseph: Weights and Measures 229–30
Royal Bank 185–6
Royal Belgian Institute of Natural Sciences 15
rubber 246–58, 261, 262
Ruhr, French occupation of (1923–5) 302–3
Russia 1, 2, 3, 68, 83, 91, 159–62, 169, 182, 196, 229, 268, 298, 309, 359

Sachsenhausen concentration camp 3, 307, 308, 310, 311, 313
Safaricom 364
Sardis 38, 39, 40
Sasanian Empire 76
savings 91, 147, 153, 168, 169, 186–7, 191, 244, 250–1, 267, 295, 296, 297, 304, 306, 347, 349–50
Schumpeter, Joseph 178, 243, 286
Scott, James C. 16
Second World War (1939–45) 1, 2–3, 308–13, 320, 334
Sejanus 69
Sephardic Jews 102, 167
Seven Great Guilds, or Arti Maggiori 117
shares 31, 61, 64, 66–7, 150, 171, 173, 176, 182–9, 243, 252–3, 279–80, 282, 304, 332, 340, 347, 348, 352, 357
shareholding society, world's first 165–6
Shaw, George Bernard 259
shekel, Sumerian 22, 27–8, 319
shilling, Kenyan 364
Sicily 96–8, 102–7
Silenus 33
Silk Roads 39, 137, 160
silver 164
British prohibit export of 218–19

Christianity and 56
Florentine economy and 118, 132
follaro and 97, 106
France/Law and 180, 181, 182, 183,
    190, 201, 207
German coins and 88–9, 91, 94–5,
    137–8, 150, 163
Greece and 47, 50, 53, 55, 163, 319
Lydians and 37, 83
New World and 155
Romans and 66, 70, 71, 73, 74, 75,
    76, 83, 84
silver dollar 219–20, 266, 273
Sumerian civilisation and 27–8, 32, 35
USA and 219–20, 222, 264–5, 266,
    268, 269, 273, 274, 275, 276,
    277–8, 320
Simon the Greek 120
sinking fund 53, 221–3
skilled labour 148
slavery 16, 27, 38, 44, 47, 49–50, 52, 62,
    66, 68, 96, 161, 168, 183, 185, 214,
    224, 247, 251–2, 253, 254, 258,
    271–2, 308
Smith, Adam 93, 237
Smolianoff, Salomon 'Sally' 307–8, 310, 311
Snow White and the Seven Dwarfs 277
social media 126–7, 291, 319, 359, 363–4
social mobility 37, 55, 114, 169, 223–4
social technologies 7, 20–1, 88, 126
Società di Minerva library 284
Socrates 49, 52
soft power 122
soft thinking 45–6
Solon, King 50, 52–3
Song dynasty 163–4
South Sea Bubble (1720) 188, 189, 191,
    193, 234, 352
SPACs (special purpose acquisition
    companies) 188–9
Spanish dollar 211, 218, 220
Spanish Flu pandemic (1920) 276, 294
speculative borrower 343, 345
speculator 69–70, 174, 185, 187–8, 190,
    204, 254, 267, 273, 302, 304, 305,
    318, 338
Spencer, 3rd Earl of Sunderland, Charles
    179, 188, 189, 191
spreadsheet 31
Spufford, Peter 90

St Petersburg 160
stable coins 358
standardisation 40, 232
status, social 42, 48, 55, 170, 309
sterling 3, 217, 311, 312–13, 324, 363
stock market 70–1, 159, 170, 179, 186,
    188, 234, 261, 280, 304–5
    Global Financial Crisis (2008) and *see*
        Global Financial Crisis (2008)
    New York crash (1929) 70–1, 277
    stockbroker 281–2
strength of weak ties 127
Stripe 291
Strongbow 103
Südbahn (Southern Railway) 283
Suez Canal 279–82
Sumer/Sumerians 22, 23, 25–6, 27,
    29–32, 34, 36, 40, 66, 109, 154, 155,
    319, 329
surnames, careers and 93
Swift, Jonathan 11, 351; *The Bubble* 352
Syracuse, Sicily 102, 105
Syria 62, 66, 71

Tacitus 70, 72
Talleyrand-Périgord, bishop Charles-
    Maurice de 11, 192–3, 197–204,
    206–8, 209–11, 222, 225, 298, 319
taxation 8, 17, 42, 254, 353
    balance sheets and 342
    central bank and 327
    centralised states and 28–9
    currency and 318
    farming and 138
    France and 183, 185, 186, 190, 191,
        194–6, 202
    Germany and 300, 306
    grain economies and 22
    Greeks and 52–3
    modern monetary theory and 361,
        362, 363
    Protestantism and 152
    Roman Empire and 63–8, 75–6, 105
    USA and 213, 216, 218, 220–1, 275
technocrats, age of 326–7
technological innovation. *See individual
    technology name*
Tell Harmal 28
Tenochtitlan 154
tetradrachm 46, 47

thaler 19
Tiberius, Emperor 69–75
tithes 36, 83, 85, 86, 141
Titus 64–5
Tláa, Shaaw 275–7
Tocqueville, Alexis de 218, 223
top-down economic system 36–7, 42, 54, 127, 169
Trente 198–9
Trieste 279–85, 287–93
Trump, Donald 350
Truss, Liz 363
trust 48, 49, 74, 76, 77, 118, 126, 130, 131, 132, 163, 168, 169, 178, 205, 220, 318–19, 329, 347, 350, 352, 354
Tulipmania (Tulpenwoerde) 173–6, 339, 340
Tyre 62, 71, 121

ullamaliztli 247
unemployment 273–4, 325, 342
Universal Company of the Suez Canal 280–1
universal value 9, 22, 37
urbanisation 87, 92–3
USA
    American Revolution and creation of 10, 191, 196, 205–6, 208, 209–22, 230, 231, 232
    Civil War (1861–5) 50, 220, 266, 268, 270–3
    Coinage Act, US (1792) 211–12, 230
    Continental currency 205, 211, 213, 220, 319
    decimalisation and 230–1, 232
    dollar and see dollar
    Federal Reserve 72, 182, 320–1, 331, 332–5, 338, 347, 349–50
    Founding Fathers 210, 212, 214, 217
    Global Financial Crisis (2008) and 71, 267–8, 337–9, 348–9
    Gold Standard and 263–78, 320–1
    Jim Crow laws 271–2
    lender of last resort 298
    presidential election (1896) 264–5, 269, 275
    Securities and Exchange Commission 360
    Wall Street 189, 272, 337, 353, 354, 358, 359, 360, 363–4, 365

War of Independence (1775–83) 211, 213, 216, 222
use value 48
'users' of money 41
usury 108–9, 123–4, 132–3, 137

Van Kerckhoven, Guillaume 246
Vanderbilt, Cornelius 272
VAT 300, 342
Vatican 114–15, 123, 127, 150
Veblen, Thorstein: The Theory of the Leisure Class 272
Venice 98, 118, 126, 131, 283
Verdi, Giuseppe: Aida 279, 284, 293
Vespasian, Emperor 11, 62–6
Vesuvius, eruption of (79 AD) 58
Vienna 193, 229, 283, 286, 293
Vietnam War (1955–75) 320
Villani, Giovanni 114, 121–2
Villiers, Betty 177, 178
Vinci, Leonardo da 98, 110, 112, 133
Virgil 98, 120
Vlad the Impaler 144

wages 74, 94, 146, 147, 204, 233, 238, 243, 264, 267–8, 295, 308, 321, 350
Ward, Herbert 256
Washington, George 210, 212, 214, 216, 224, 319
weights 26–8, 39–40, 97, 129, 231, 232
Weimar Republic 1, 205, 294–307
whiskey distilleries 215–16
white-collar workers 243–4, 306
William of Malmesbury 98
William of Orange, King 175
Wilson, Edmund 177–80, 188
windhandel trading ('trading on fresh air') 171, 173, 174
Wisselbank 164–5, 176, 182
Wizard of Oz, The (film) 263–4, 269, 277
World Bank 328

Xenophon 11, 44–6, 48–9

Yeats, W. B. 284

zero, concept of 97, 99–101, 104, 111, 233
Zeus 11, 16, 23
zombie companies 343